Al and Judy

My education about
independent filmmaking
started with John Sayles and
has now been updated by
Paul, my mentor from Hollywood
I hope you'll enjoy the book.
All the best,
Gerry

JOHN SAYLES

JOHN SAYLES

An Unauthorized Biography of
the Pioneering Indie Filmmaker

Gerard Molyneaux

BOOKS

Library of Congress Catalog Card Number: 00-101885
ISBN: 1-58063-125-8

10 9 8 7 6 5 4 3 2 1

Design by Susan Shankin

Published by Renaissance Books
Distributed by St. Martin's Press
Manufactured in the United States of America
First Edition

Dedicated to my brothers and sisters:
Jack, Marianne (Simpson), Dick (d.), Bea,
Kath (Coyle), Jim, Joe, and Peg (Taggart).
Thanks for taking me to the movies.

CONTENTS

Acknowledgments IX

1. The Independent Filmmaker and His Production Model 11

2. The Making of *Return of the Secaucus Seven:* The Script 17

3. The Making of *Return of the Secaucus Seven:* The Production 31

4. The Sayles Family of Schenectady, New York 39

5. Number 80, John Sayles, 1967 All-County Football 49

6. The Odd Duck of the Green Room 59

7. The Real World and the Writer 71

8. Writer for Hire: The Roger Corman Years 79

9. Writer for Hire: Theater, Film, Television, and Print 89

10. *Lianna* and the Rise of Maggie Renzi 103

11. *Baby It's You* and the Battle with Paramount 113

12. *The Brother from Another Planet:* Back to Guerrilla Filmmaking 125

13. What's a Genius to Do? 137

14. *Matewan:* The Sayles Production Company and Its First Celebrities 145

15. *Eight Men Out:* The Players and Their Pastime   165

16. *Shannon's Deal, Los Gusanos,* and *City of Hope:*   181
     The Sayles Disciples and Community Issues

17. *Passion Fish:* Some Critical Conversions   197

18. *The Secret of Roan Inish:* A Gift to Maggie Renzi   209

19. *Lone Star:* A Big Score, a Second Start   219

20. *Men with Guns:* Financing the Sayles Film   235

21. *Limbo* and the New Deal   249

    Appendix A: Filmography   261

    Appendix B: Videography   275

    Appendix C: Acting Credits   277

    Source Notes   281

    Bibliography   299

    Index   315

ACKNOWLEDGMENTS

IN THE "INTERVIEW" SECTION of this book are listed the names of those people who generously contributed to the content of *John Sayles: An Unauthorized Biography of the Pioneering Indie Filmmaker*. Here I want to acknowledge those individuals and institutions that have supported the research and writing in other ways. The reasons for inclusion are too manifold to list; the contributions, however, are deeply appreciated.

Academy of Motion Picture Arts and Sciences Library (Linda Harris Mehr, director); Archive and Research Center of the University of California at Los Angeles (Robert Rosen, director, and Laura Kaiser, research coordinator); Archive Film Productions, Inc. (Stock Footage Library, Larry Schwartz, director); Baltimore District of the Brothers of the Christian Schools (Benedict Oliver, F.S.C., visitor); Big Deal Productions, Inc. (John Carpenter, director); Joseph F. Burke, F.S.C.; California District of the Brothers of the Christian School (Bro. David Brennan, visitor); John Carpenter's Cathedral High School (Los Angeles, California, Bro. James Meegan, director); Christian Brothers Academy (Albany, New York, Bro. Henry Betz, director); Communication Department of La Salle University (Philadelphia, Pennsylvania, Lynne Texter, chair); Connelly Library of La Salle University (John Baky, director); Dr. Joseph Flubacher; Jody Gillen; Andy Gwiazda, Charles Hilkin, F.S.C.; Joseph Alemany Community; La Salle University (Bro. Michael McGinniss, president); Eric Leong (research); Louis B. Mayer Library (American Film Institute, Los Angeles, California, Caroline Sisneros, librarian); Michael McDonald; John McErlan, F.S.C.; Gail McKenna; Sid MacLeod; Thomas McPhillips, F.S.C.; Martha Heaseley Cox Center for Steinbeck Studies (San Jose State University, San Jose, California, Susan G. Shillinglaw, director); Shena Molyneaux; Museum of Television and Radio (Jonathan Rosenthal, research); NBC Television (New York, James DeMarco, research); Brian Newman (South Carolina arts commission); Paradigm Talent and Literary Agency (Stu Robinson, agent for John Sayles); James Robert Parish, editor; Penn Photography (Michael Penn); Jo Proctor; Ralph and Helen Renzi; Saint Mary's College of California (Craig Franz, F.S.C., president); Don and Mary Sayles; Doug Sayles; Schenectady County (New York) Historical Society; Bro. Clarence Schenk; School of Arts and Sciences of La Salle University (Dr. Richard Nigro, provost, Dr. Barbara Millard, dean); School District of Schenectady (Dr. Ray Coluciello, superintendent); Joe Simon; South Carolina Arts Commission (Brian Newman, assistant coordinator); Allan Taylor; Theater Collection, Philadelphia Free Library (Geraldine Duclow, director); Elaine West, photographer; Vernon White; Kevin Wildes; Williams College Archives (Lynne Fonteneau-McCann, archivist); Williams College Public Relations (James G. Kolesar, director); Williamstown Theatre; Writers Guild Foundation (Jody Gillen, public relations).

1

The Independent Filmmaker
and His Production Model

If you don't put those innermost thoughts on the screen,
then you are looking down not only at your audience,
but at the people you work with.

FILMMAKER JOHN CASSAVETES, 1994

FILM MAJORS, GRADUATE STUDENTS, and novice directors, among others, describe him as "my hero," "the guy," and "my role model." In their young eyes, John Sayles, in his quest to make movies his way, stands as the Don Quixote of the American independent film movement. In his uncompromising choice of matter over money and his constant assault on the windmills of the Hollywood system, Sayles continues to realize his "impossible dream" of creating literate films for an adult audience.

Now nearing fifty years of age and with twenty years of experience in the film industry behind him, Sayles has shown little inclination to change his aesthetic philosophy and creative disposition. Yet his idealistic independence is counterbalanced by a rugged pragmatism that, often against staggering odds, results in films of almost epic proportions and sees them to completion, on budget and on time. Therein lies the paradox of this guru of

11

American independent film: to pursue his goal of producing quality movies for his audience and, at the same time, to do this with the savvy of the stingiest of the Hollywood moguls of old. Having no film school training, Sayles learned how to stretch a production dime from Roger Corman, the exemplar of the low-budget filmmaker. From the outset of his movie career, Sayles was shooting for the stars while grubbing in the back alleys of the movie production world looking for financing.

The paradox of an iconoclastic film artist, coupled with a mastery of moviemaking skills, sometimes escapes the notice of those who would follow in Sayles's footsteps. Some see only his professional integrity, a vision that is never tested by the hands-on business of taking ideas from brain to paper to screen.

Others of more practical bent have followed Sayles's lead and found ways of producing their films independent of the traditional Hollywood studios. Many of these erstwhile disciples, however, have fallen by the wayside. After a successful picture or two, some have been seduced by getting more production money for bigger films. And then, once in the system, they capitulated to the demands for more "bankable" stories and stars and more easily marketable movies. Others have been sidetracked by the prestige or the perks that big studios offered in exchange for a few creative compromises: changes in their stories and stars for their movies, whether fitting or not. Still other successful independent filmmakers cave in because it's far easier to make a movie within the establishment system.

Francis Doel, a former script supervisor at Roger Corman's New World Pictures and Sayles's first scriptwriting coach, described the impasse faced by the Sayles wanna-be's. "John Sayles is the hero of independent filmmaking, but people who feel that they want to make films as John does don't understand the kind of or degree of integrity it takes to do that—and the resourcefulness. Knowing what he wants to do, he takes for granted that he will find a way to do it."

This depiction of Sayles raises the questions first pondered by the fledgling filmmaker twenty years ago. What lies at the heart of Sayles's ongoing decision to turn down the bankrolling of the big studios and persist in the almost bargain-basement production of his own movies? How has he overcome the obstacles posed in the financing, production, distribution, and exhibition of his products? Without the staples of sex, violence, heroic stars, and contrived but happy endings that satisfy the typical moviegoing audience, how have his features found any box office? After two decades in the motion picture business, what are the lessons he now applies to his craft? Among the twelve movies he has written, directed, and edited to date is there a discernable thematic pattern and style at work that would aid those looking to him as an example? Is he the kind of filmmaker whose control of his vision identifies each of his films, creating a Sayles "oeuvre?"

None of the answers comes easily; both Sayles and the movie industry are too complicated for that. The questions, however, can serve as guidelines for the retrospective covered in this book. Each of his films addresses these queries while advancing an understanding of his take on independent filmmaking. Simply put, the umbrella question is this: Why does Sayles insist on making movies his way, and how does he get them produced and out to an audience?

Sayles's inspiration lies partly in himself and partly in film history. The insistence on creative control of his pictures places him squarely at the center of a long-standing filmmaker tradition: the right to exert independence from those who would make inroads on the artist's preserve. Two giants of American film stood squarely with the independents. Seeking creative freedom, D. W. Griffith (1875–1948) formed his own studio, as did Charlie Chaplin (1889–1977). The two later joined forces with Douglas Fairbanks (1883–1939) and Mary Pickford (1893–1979) as co-founders of United Artists Corporation, a production and distribution company created to protect the rights of filmmakers. Their leadership in the 1920s has spawned a legion of followers and created the category of independent filmmaker that today has dozens of permutations.

The "independent" label has become so pliable that it now includes moviemakers throughout the economic spectrum. Steven Spielberg, George Lucas, Martin Scorsese, and Robert Altman represent the mainstream directors who, while supported by the major studios, have repeatedly resisted corporate attempts at control, especially concerning extremely personal projects. Aligned with them, but from the ranks of the low-budget and more maverick moviemakers, are Steven Soderbergh (*sex, lies and videotape,* 1984), David

Lynch (*Blue Velvet*, 1986), Abel Ferrara (*The Funeral*, 1996), and, even farther removed from the Hollywood tradition, Jim Jarmusch (*Night on Earth*, 1991). Allison Anders adds a feminist perspective in films such as *Gas, Food, Lodging* (1992) and *Mi Vida Loca* (1993). Between these two groups fall directors who, like the high rollers, have arrangements with the studios but retain a large degree of control. This group includes Joel and Ethan Coen, Woody Allen, and Spike Lee.

The numbers in these ranks may rise or fall as younger filmmakers leave for the studios and veterans, often badly scarred by the studio experience, find their way back to artistic freedom. Swelling the membership are moviemakers such as Nancy Savoca (*True Love*, 1989), Kevin Smith (*Clerks*, 1994), and Edward Burns (*The Brothers McMullen*, 1995), who often get their jump-start from prizes won and contracts signed at Robert Redford's Sundance Film Festival.

As the list of directors suggests, *independent* does not always mean outside the system or low budget. The constant is creative freedom and control, often arrived at in lieu of money. More importantly, the independent filmmaker needs to deliver movies that say something important and involve stories the studios won't touch. As Sayles has often observed, there is no sense staying independent and making movies that the studios are already doing. In the November/December 1997 *Entertainment Weekly,* Lisa Schwarzbaum described independence: "On the one hand this means there's no Paramount or Warner Bros. safety net to catch a falling director. On the other, it ensures that no pinhead business school grad can reduce a director to nervous tics with a note about third act problems. Independent films are not only free of big publicity departments to help sell wares, but they're also free from the secondhand guessing and endemic messing around that so regularly makes the big budget movies so safely *boring.*" Unfettered by the constraints, the independent filmmaker can pioneer new approaches to old stories or adapt old methods to make movies with a new vision.

Over the course of independent filmmaker history, it was John Cassavetes (1929–89) who provided the model and inspiration for many of today's independents including John Sayles, as Sayles himself has freely acknowledged. In his book on the business side of independent filmmaking, *Spike, Mike, Slackers, &*

Dykes (1995), John Pierson wrote, "With his 1960 feature, *Shadows,* Cassavetes is often credited as the inventor of the American independent cinema." In the late 1960s and early 1970s, Cassavetes parlayed his mainstream acting talents into the directing arena. Performances in popular Hollywood entries like *The Dirty Dozen* (1967) and *Rosemary's Baby* (1968) provided the backing for his more esoteric and influential features, most notably *A Woman Under the Influence* (1974). He scripted and directed that movie, which starred his wife, actress Gena Rowlands. Like Charlie Chaplin, he took control a step farther and owned and distributed *Woman* as well as his subsequent features. For the more rebellious young people of the Vietnam War era, Cassavetes was not only "telling it like it is," he was, by resisting the dictates of the establishment, coaching his disciples for the future. He provided a model not just for making movies but for making personal pictures beyond the reach of Hollywood, and that is the path Sayles and some other directors are now following.

Pierson also noted, "Cassavetes' insistence on doing his own movies his own way with an ensemble group of actors was instructive." For Martin Scorsese, Cassavetes was the mentor who made thinking about moviemaking possible and who advised him to get out of the trap of the Roger Corman studio and make his own films. The result was Scorsese's *Mean Streets* (1973). Ten years later, heeding that same wisdom, Sayles moved from his status as a Roger Corman cohort to that of an independent filmmaker with the creation of *Return of the Secaucus Seven* (1980).

In making their first features, both Scorsese and Sayles followed the lead and the low-budget production pattern constructed and employed by Cassavetes. In describing the seven-step formula followed by today's mavericks, Pierson reiterates Cassavetes' working methods: (1) a script geared to the budget, (2) a compressed shooting schedule, (3) cheap or cost-free locations, (4) minimal deferred salaries for a small cast and crew, (5) low shooting ratio (usually in 16mm and, now, with digital video cameras), (6) good catering, and (7) postproduction done at home on a rented Steenbeck editor or, today, in downtime on an Avid video editing system.

With the recognition of the reduced production costs allowed by digital camera and editing equipment, this seven-step program accurately captures the typical low-budget process. Not surprisingly, however, independent film-making stubbornly resists cookie-cutter inscriptions and predictable results. Individual variations do occur anywhere in the different phases of the process. An overview of Sayles's movies clarifies his approach to the low-budget formula and helps place him among his peers on the American independent film scene.

Now starting his third decade of making movies, Sayles has made his name synonymous with quality in the American independent film movement. Without deviating from his ambition of making films about truly ordinary people, and without compromising the complexity of the subjects he tackles, he has compiled a remarkably diverse and powerful library of work. For his followers, his films are a needed response to the steady diet of slick and pandering pictures emanating from the studios. Sayles is now being called on as a leader for both the independent movement and for the industry as a whole. Respected by both groups, he may serve to bridge the chasm that separates independent from studio, giving low-budget films access to audiences and an opening for the studios in the for-adults market—generally the preserve of British and foreign filmmakers.

The Sayles model is still in the making. An examination of his movies and methods provides the signposts for the direction in which he will take his career and, by extension, the American movie. Without one of his pictures, there would be one landmark missing from film history. To revisit that film, *Return of the Secaucus Seven* (1980), is to expose the bedrock of the Sayles phenomenon and the spring from which his lengthy, productive, and intriguing career has flourished. As his friend and contemporary, director Joe Dante, told me, "I think we always tend to go back to what we did when we first started making movies. Whether it's an emphasis on script or on action, that experience shapes and colors the films that follow."

As a prologue to a survey of the life and works of John Sayles, the examination of the making of *Secaucus Seven* provides a three-dimensional portrait of the man and his methods. It turns the clock back to a twenty-seven-year-old budding genius with $40,000 in his pocket and a desire to make a movie. For the first time, Sayles asked himself, "How am I going to do this?"

2

The Making of *Return of the Secaucus Seven:* The Script

I'd say the most pragmatic of all my movies was Return of the
Secaucus Seven—*we had the budget before we had the movie.*
The difficulty is that it takes a while to think of a way
that you can get the same results for less money, time, whatever.
Some of your best ideas come out of that.

JOHN SAYLES, 1996

THE ROOTS OF JOHN SAYLES'S idealist-vs.-pragmatist paradox lie in his
initial forays into the film business. His experience as an aspiring filmmaker
lead him to Roger Corman, king of the Bs and champion of low-budget,
"never-lost-a-dime" genre pictures. With titles like *Naked Paradise* (1957), *The
Wild Angels* (1966), *Rock and Roll High* (1979), and *Stripped to Kill* (1987),
Corman's double bill–bound features entertained generations of the teenage
drive-in crowd. In the mid-1970s, Sayles's first job at Corman's New World
Pictures would educate the already award-winning novelist about film production realities and the gritty necessities of low budgets.

With the ambition of one day making his own features, Sayles and his life
partner, Maggie Renzi, left Boston in 1976 and moved to Santa Barbara,
California. Two hours north of Los Angeles, their new Ortega Street digs
were not exactly in Hollywood but sported a rent he could afford while

breaking into the movie business. His literary agency, Robinson, Weintraub, Gross and Associates, connected him with Frances Doel, script supervisor at New World. She was looking for a rewrite of the screenplay for *Piranha* (1978), one of the many *Jaws* (1975) spin-offs in the works at that time.

After completing a final draft plus some on-site revisions for director Joe Dante, Sayles wrote two additional scripts for the Corman cameras: *The Lady in Red* (1979), a *Bonnie and Clyde* (1967) send-up; and a science fiction thriller, *Battle Beyond the Stars* (1980), which was *Star Wars* (1977) minus the effects. *Piranha* was the best of that lot, all of which made money. Sayles showed he could turn out a script with blinding speed and could bend his writing to Corman's standards.

Prophetically, Sayles had enrolled in the premier preparatory school for anyone facing a career in low-budget filmmaking. With its offices on Sunset Boulevard, New World stood squarely on twin production principles: fast and cheap. Horror, rock, hot-rod, gangster, prison, and science fiction films poured out of the studio and on to awaiting screens. Corman knew the marketplace, and his most famous employees—both directors and actors (Martin Scorsese, Francis Ford Coppola, Ron Howard, Jack Nicholson, James Cameron, and Jonathan Demme)—soon adapted their talents to his ninety-minute genre productions. At New World, Sayles struck gold; he was now earning $2,000 a week! By 1978, after a single year in the studio stable, however, he was itching to direct his own movies. The money earned through writing had put directing within his grasp. He recalled that moment at a 1985 American Film Institute seminar in Los Angeles: "When am I going to have $40,000 at one place again in my life? I should make a movie and spend it all."

John had options. Writing his way into directing for the studios would take too long. Corman might let him direct, but New World action movies were not projects likely to get him directing assignments from the major studios, nor did he want to invest his time in such genre pictures. Like Martin Scorsese a decade earlier, Sayles wanted to tell a screen story, but not one about people getting eaten alive at fifteen-minute intervals. As his published fiction showed, he had a mind brimming with narratives about everyday Americans. John decided that he would fund the film himself.

For Sayles, ordinary and offbeat characters embodied the "innermost thoughts" that John Cassavetes was urging aspiring writers and directors to produce for the screen. In Robert Altman, Stanley Kubrick, Francis Ford Coppola, Brian De Palma, and Scorsese, Sayles found models for making the un-Hollywood motion pictures that blossomed briefly in the early 1970s. By the second half of that decade, however, the radical edge they gave the American movie was blunted by box-office "demands" for more splashy thrillers. According to *Entertainment Weekly,* one movie was to blame. "The Great Modern Era of independent movies begins with *Jaws,*" says Owen Gleiberman. "When Steven Spielberg's shark thriller conquered the world in 1975, Hollywood forgot about the artsy angles and downbeat endings it had explored in the late '60s and early '70s."

With studio filmmakers now taking the reins once again and gearing movies for mass appeal, the fringes of American cinema were once again left open. As one consumer publication (*Entertainment Weekly,* November/December 1997) has noted, "With the reappearance of the prepackaged demographically tested mainstream, the indie underground cranked up the alternative energy and flourished anew." Sayles was ready to seize that opportunity. In pursuit of creative freedom, he would fall into the company of such rebels as Spike Lee, Abel Ferrara, David Cronenberg, Jim Jarmusch, Susan Seidelman, David Lynch, and Steven Soderbergh. All of them were under thirty and eager for a chance to direct and rechannel American movies. Describing these young turf seekers, Lisa Schwarzbaum wrote in *Entertainment Weekly* (November/December 1997), "The American independents were pretty easy to spot: restless, experimental and marginalized, the preference of college film societies everywhere."

Faced with the studio system, Sayles found his alternative. He later told *Sight and Sound* (September 1993), "I went the Stanley Kubrick route and made my own f***ing movie with *Secaucus Seven.*" As John Cassavetes did with his income from acting, Sayles applied his scriptwriting revenues to fund his first picture. His idealism and stockpile of stories would seem a likely breeding ground for the production of a picture that he "always wanted to do." From the start, however, his practical nature ruled, and he looked not just to his literary imagination but to the film's box-office potential.

What ingredients could help him make a movie within a budget based on expected returns on investment? This first film probably would never play at the multiplexes or even at the art houses, but he believed it might catch on with PBS-TV for its *American Playhouse*. (At the time, this small-screen showcase was the chief financial backer of independent movies.) At worst, the project would serve as his directing demo. The artistic choices for the film had to wait on the answer to the economic question: What kind of film could he make for $40,000?

The answer lay in large part with his friends. In 1977 Sayles spent Christmas vacation in New York discussing his movie idea with Jeffrey Nelson, a former Williams College classmate who eventually would become the coproducer of *Return of the Secaucus Seven*. Back in 1974 the two had acted and directed together at the Eastern Slope Playhouse in North Conway, New Hampshire, where Nelson was now the manager. Sayles and Nelson recognized that they had the resources at hand to stretch the production dollars. The playhouse's acting company included several friends from Williams. As Sayles later told Steve Katz in *Cinematic Motion: Film Directing: A Workshop for Staging Scenes* (1992), "I figured, 'Well, I can't afford SAG [Screen Actors Guild] actors, so who do I know? I know all these really good actors. Why not have it be about people turning thirty?' So it evolved from practicalities."

In the fall of 1978, with the playhouse season ended, the actors would be available for the film, and so would the 300-seat playhouse itself. It would provide the site for one sequence. During the summer, the playhouse staff stayed at the nearby Winwood Ski Lodge, which, in September and early October, would be both empty and cheap to rent. With Nelson, Sayles started talking about the kind of money they could save by building a film around the lodge.

Always alert to budget, John's screenplay was now following the lead of available people and low-cost locales. As playhouse cast member David Strathairn told me, "The Winwood Lodge was right in Eastern Playhouse's backyard. After the Thursday and Friday night performances, all of us went to the Oakley Tavern, and on the weekends we'd go swimming at Crawford's Notch. All of those places became locations for the movie."

Sayles now realized that his story would focus on a group of thirty-year-old, former college classmates and campus activists reunited for a fall weekend at a friend's house in New England. Catching up with each other's lives, reviving old memories, and reopening old wounds, the characters' interaction would provide the narrative thrust. Referring to *Secaucus Seven* as this "ratty, raggedy" little movie, participant Maggie Renzi told the *Washington Post* (October 15, 1987) the basic plan: the film would "be shot in friends' living rooms with contemporary characters who liked to talk." It was that simple.

Arriving in Boston from the West Coast for the summer stock season of 1978, Sayles and Renzi were acting at the Eastern Playhouse even as they were planning the shooting of *Secaucus*. They also were rejoining many of their friends from Williams College. Among these, Jeffrey Nelson, David Strathairn, Gordon Clapp, and Adam LeFevre all had been "theater jocks" at Williams in the early 1970s. The clan would gather at the lodge for a Sayles-cooked Mexican or Italian dinner and discuss the forthcoming project.

"The film was a lark," Strathairn recalls. "None of us had any aspirations about acting in Hollywood. We were just extending the summer season a little and doing John a favor helping him crash the party in L.A." The Williams alumni recruited still more friends to join the cast. In *Sayles on Sayles* (1998), the director recalls his feelings about the group: "Because they were playing regular people our age, I figured, 'Okay, well, how big a stretch is it going to be? This is all recognizable human behavior.'" To assist the players, Sayles gave them brief biographies of their characters, a predirecting device he continues to employ today. Their "ratty little movie" would be released three years before Lawrence Kasdan's better known *The Big Chill* (1983), a film that, according to Leonard Maltin in his annual *Movie & Video Guide*, "bears more than a passing resemblance to John Sayles's *Return of the Secaucus Seven.*"

Prior to writing the script, Sayles made two key production decisions that distanced the movie farther from the studio system. First, the hero of the film would be the entire ensemble of characters who comprised the Secaucus Seven. (Secaucus is the New Jersey town where the seven characters were arrested while traveling to an antiwar rally.) Second, he would shoot the movie in 16mm, which, in the pre–digital video camera days, was the cheapest way to make a professional film.

While based on the practicalities of available cast and cash, the two choices nevertheless exemplified the spirit of independence. The ensemble idea bucked Hollywood traditions twice over. First, most filmmaker manuals argue that new directors should deal with just two or three characters and develop them carefully. In indie films like *David and Lisa* (1962) or even *Easy Rider* (1969), two clearly identified, fully drawn principals unify the action around them. Second, American movies and moviegoers needed onscreen heroes played by handsome stars. As the plot unravels, the heroes unify the action and anchor the attention and sympathies of the audience. The antiensemble factor provided novice filmmakers with the most basic ingredient of the Hollywood formula: seamless continuity. The resultant movie might be dull, but it was easy for the viewer to follow. However practical this rule of thumb, in Sayles's eyes it did not serve the occasion.

With his literary publications and his experience writing for Roger Corman, John was no typical movie newcomer. His fiction had already shown the bias his films would continue: the community, not the individual, was the hero. In his novel *Union Dues* (1977), Sayles had established his ability to preserve continuity while elaborating on several characters and various stories. Using the ensemble cast, *Secaucus* would continue the focus on community as protagonist. According to New World's Frances Doel, the ensemble is precisely what distinguishes John Sayles as a filmmaker: "He's interested in people in groups, not just in a hero or heroine."

However radical the approach to centering his screenplay was, Sayles's use of 16mm was standard practice among independents. The resultant image and sound suffice for classroom, film society, and first-film contest screenings, and if the movie catches on, it can always be blown up to 35mm for theater screens. Documentary moviemakers like the compact portability of the equipment and have used it to award-winning advantage with entries like *Hearts and Minds* (1974) and *Roger and Me* (1989). Likewise, Spike Lee's *She's Gotta Have It* (1986), Richard Linklater's *Slacker* (1991), and Kevin Smith's *Clerks* (1994) are among the many low-budget entries that started out in 16mm, then went to

35mm for theatrical release. With 16mm's cheaper camera rental and film stock, John could shoot his first feature. Satisfied with his choice, Sayles turned to face the first test of his creative integrity.

Back in Hollywood, when Frances Doel learned about Sayles's production plans, she spoke with her boss, Roger Corman. The studio head had come to admire John professionally, and Sayles showed his appreciation by readily adapting his writing to the studio's needs. The movie mogul knew the limitations of 16mm. "Tell John," he told Doel, "that it would be much better to shoot in 35. He'll have a better chance of getting a release." As Doel recalls, Corman then added an uncommonly generous offer. "Tell him that if he shoots it in 35, I'll kick in a little money to make up the difference. I could even loan him some equipment."

Doel remembers Sayles's response. "I was excited and I called John up and told him the offer. He thought for half a minute, if that, and quickly said, 'Tell Roger thank you very much, and I really appreciate his offer, but I don't think I can accept it. It's my belief that when someone gives you money, they expect something back. I'm concerned that Roger might want me to put something in the script or take something out or do something with it. I just wouldn't want to do that. I just want to do the movie as I've written it.'"

According to Doel, Corman was not likely to have interfered and Sayles probably knew that. In effect, Sayles's statement may have been a declaration he needed to make out loud to himself. It clearly established his integrity in Doel's mind. "I never met anybody with a first shot at directing who thought that way."

With Corman's tempting offer now declined, Sayles revisited his budget. Because his actors were not members of SAG, they would not get even the guild's minimum. Instead, they would receive the same salary they had earned for summer stock: $80 a week plus room and board. Like everybody else on the project, they would receive deferred payment, that is, part of the profits *if* the film eventually made money. With that, the above-the-line expenses of script, producer/director, and cast were now in place.

■   ■   ■

Sayles next turned to the below-the-line needs of the film. For the early fall, he could lease the Winwood Ski Lodge for an off-season pittance, about $800 for the five-week shoot. The lodge would provide headquarters for the production, rooms for the cast and crew, and settings for the movie. At a dollar a day per bed, the lease also eliminated travel expenses to and from the set. Most of the movie's other locations, like the Oakley Tavern, the swimming hole, and the basketball court, were within a few miles of the lodge. Ida, a live-in friend of actor Adam LeFevre, would provide catering. Typical of all Sayles's movies, the bulk of this first budget, $29,000, was being spent for what would show up on-screen.

Sayles now devised a screen story. In 1968, when these same actors were just entering college, *Time* magazine had designated the American youth of that decade as its Man of the Year. They were the baby boomers whose long hair and pot smoking were testing the patience of parents and whose political activism and peace marches drove President Lyndon Johnson from the White House and infuriated his successor, Richard Nixon. Now this war-protesting, free-love-touting, rock-music-loving generation was leaving behind its association with events in Chicago, Berkeley, and Woodstock. As *Time* magazine teased, the boomers were "turning thirty, jogging toward the compromises of middle age."

The John Sayles of 1978 disagreed with this facile conclusion. He told the *New York Times* (March 16, 1981) that he objected to the myth perpetuated in the media that his peers "had sold out and gone to work for banks and corporations . . . [that] just wasn't part of my experience." As such, the novice filmmaker began weaving his narrative out of his own view of the 1960s and 1970s.

Return of the Secaucus Seven revolves around a three-day weekend at which seven college friends are reunited, each of them with a need to be satisfied. More than plot, character development was the spine of Sayles's emerging script. In writing the screenplay, John kept fiscal economy first in mind. In his book on moviemaking, *Thinking in Pictures* (1987), he said, "I had to back up a bit and start thinking in budget." From the start, he knew this was not going to be an action movie. During an interview for *Cinematic Motion* (1992), he recalled thinking, "We won't be able to have a lot of crane shots, dolly shots, and all that equipment we won't be able to rent. So how do I have movement?"

He found his answer in two sources. First, experience (and awards) had showed him that what he could do best was write. Consequently, contrasting characters would create a sense of onscreen pacing, with each speaking fresh, relaxed, spontaneous dialogue. Second, the ensemble would work to his advantage, as it had done in Robert Altman's highly successful *Nashville* (1975). By cutting away to the different characters during the scenes, John could vary tone and intensity and offset the static camera. The characters and subplots would provide the motives for the cuts. The rare scenes with physical movement (the basketball game and the running and diving at the swimming hole) would help change the pace of the movie and establish his ability to capture broad physical action on film.

He was also writing dialogue to make the picture cost effective and dramatically workable. As he has often said, "Sometimes a line of dialogue can save you a lot of shots that look great but don't tell you much." Economy-minded scripting in his hands could stimulate creativity. "It's true," he told *Film Comment* (May 1981), "a lot of the specifics of *Secaucus Seven* arose out of financial constraint. But when you start writing with those givens, it's like a poem as opposed to blank verse." *Secaucus Seven* centers on the community of seven people, on their individual and collective histories, and on their attempts to chart their future. What it omits by way of violent on-camera action it makes up for in the human victories of reconciliation and small but heroic steps toward self-realization and human fulfillment.

As a writer, Sayles had been mulling over *Secaucus Seven* ideas for a year and was even tailoring parts of the film to suit certain actors, notably David Strathairn and Gordon Clapp. At New World Pictures, he showed Roger Corman that he was an exceptionally quick and efficient writer. In shooting film, however, the new director had only secondhand knowledge from watching Joe Dante on *Piranha*. Nevertheless, John turned his technical inexperience and lack of resources into virtues. As he said at the American Film Institute in 1985, "I didn't want technically to distract from the characters because the stress is on the actors. . . . So the crew had to light faster or give up a camera move so the actors would have more time to concentrate." The cast, with only its theater experience, was worried about being too low-keyed. "Trust me," Sayles told them.

Unexpectedly, the opening scenes of *Secaucus Seven* announce the themes of ordinary life in its most mundane manifestations. To a film title that suggests cowboys and criminals, the movie then adds credits with quick black-and-white head shots of the characters and, with a nod to *Bonnie and Clyde,* has their onscreen names turn red. Meanwhile, composer Mason Daring's flamenco guitar is linking these faces to the outlaws' "Wanted" posters of the 1860s. The phrase *Secaucus Seven* recalls the war protestors arrested in the 1960s, even as the film's score hints at *The Magnificent Seven* (1960). The expectations of political activism and Hollywood heroics alluded to in the title are abruptly dashed by the first image of the movie: a toilet plunger doing its thing. Welcome to the world of John Sayles!

Rather than a movie with hombres riding into town or flags burning at the Pentagon, *Secaucus Seven* has a vacationing couple straining under the pressures of hosting five old college classmates plus a friend. The excitement here lies in looking for blankets and worrying about who sleeps where and with whom. While Mike (Bruce MacDonald) fixes the commode, Kate (Maggie Renzi) makes the beds, and the couple banter back and forth. In conveying the communal bonds among the guests, the dialogue captures the couple's 1960s offhandedness about sex. In the course of the give-and-take, they introduce the other characters and allude to the group's bygone days in college and in a Boston commune. Jokes are tossed about, but there's concern as well for each friend and how the outsider will impact the group. In *Ordinary People: The Cinema of John Sayles* (1994), author Jack Ryan notes, "By splicing conversational topics and establishing crosscurrents, Sayles cleverly renders what is at the heart of *Return of the Secaucus Seven:* how individuals intertwine to form community."

In the manner of Sayles's short-story collection, *The Anarchists' Convention* (1979), the 106-minute film effectively uses the characters to vary the picture's tone and pace. The old friends arrive singly and in pairs, and their catching-up conversations further individualize them. While the characters may represent a generation, they are not baby-boomer stereotypes, nor are they hippies turned yuppies.

With the pals now reunited, the movie begins a thematic investigation into the lives of each one of the septet plus one. Alternating scenes of the whole group with others that focus on their individual lives, careers, and interpersonal histories, Sayles shapes his study of the constituents of this reunited community. There is folk singer J. T. (Adam LeFevre), who still clings to his college dream of making it in show business. In contrast, liberal-minded Irene (Jean Passanante) and conservative Chip (Gordon Clapp), the interloper, have grown accustomed to their jobs in Washington.

Like Chip and Irene, hosts Mike and Kate are settled into their teaching careers, but their long-term living together is being tested by their rough passage from late adolescence to adulthood. Kate harbors a lingering grudge about Mike's one-time dalliance with Stacey (Jessica MacDonald), a mutual friend, and Mike worries about trading his freedom for the confines of marriage. Thus, Mike scrutinizes his basketball-playing buddy, the now married Howie (John Sayles).

As the professional of the group, Frances (Maggie Cousineau-Arndt) is still smarting from a bad medical internship. The personal price tag of getting to be an M.D. is suggested by her arriving alone but with a diaphragm in her suitcase. Her fling with Ron (David Strathairn), the local car mechanic, points to a disparity between Frances the career woman and Frances the still experimenting college dormie.

While Frances is facing her responsibilities, Jeff (Mark Arnott), a drug counselor, and his ex-wife, Maura (Karen Trott), who directs inner-city children's theater, seem to be ducking theirs. When the whole group gets arrested for killing a deer and the sheriff recites Jeff's history of arrests (mainly for drugs), Maura's continued dependency on Jeff is measured by her "me too" role in their relationship. As her sleeping with J. T. may indicate, Maura could finally be starting her own life.

On all levels, Jeff still commits himself to nothing. On the ritual departing of the group, Jeff separates himself, leaving a childishly guilt-inducing message: "I'm sorry." Within the film, Jeff is farthest from maturity because he will not face the consequences that even the juvenile J. T. has.

For the glue of this diffuse story, Sayles uses Chip. From Chip's perspective as newcomer—like the audience's—he wants to understand these seven individuals. Gradually, his inquisitiveness elicits information from each one about the others. Chip recognizes the challenge he faces as the outsider whose credentials will be tested against the standards of the Secaucus Seven.

The revelations to the group and to the viewer about the real Chip provide comic moments for a Sayles screenplay. On arrival, Chip looks and acts like the establishment. As events unfold, however, he is revealed to actually be a pliant and personable human being, less uptight and more self-assured than any of the insiders. Chip continually challenges their preconceptions and prejudices. Athletically inept, he still jumps into the basketball game and does well. His status is further enhanced at the swimming hole, where the clothed women rate the naked men, and it's the wimpy-looking Chip who catches their fancy. Finally, it is Chip who brings with him the once indispensable re-creation of the alienated generation: dope. By testing the Seven's tolerance and reversing their expectations, he gauges their abilities to respond to the complicating subtleties of their future.

Chip's exit provides one of the two framing devices for the film. He finishes the weekend having successfully integrated himself into the group. Meanwhile, Kate worries about the community that has once again disbanded. With their farewells completed, each of the Secaucus Seven faces a continuous challenge to respond to his or her own needs for a community in which to survive.

■   ■   ■

The script's lack of classic closure pays tribute to the complexity of the characters and their dilemmas. One of the actors, Adam LeFevre, spoke to Steve Lawson (*New York Times,* April 17, 1983) about a director who would neither create phony characters nor tack on an emotionally charged ending to appease the audience. "John has a clear eye that sees all the pimples. There are foibles but no heroes, no villains. John does not have an imagination that romanticizes things."

While Sayles has denied that the film is autobiographical, *Secaucus Seven* does employ people and imagery from his past. In the opening sequence, for example, the film cuts to J. T., the guitar-playing drifter, standing on a country road. Recalling his own cross-country trips, Sayles often uses hitchhiking as a metaphor for the search for film financing and prudent tenacity: sticking out your thumb and hoping for the best, but knowing when to get in or not to get in the car. The "Hitchhiker's Lament" scene captures many of the disappointments of life (and film production). As each car approaches J. T., the music comes up, then abruptly stops when the car roars by.

The swings of the narrative are paralleled by the demands Sayles would face in putting his ideas on film and getting his movie out to the marketplace. That he accomplished both those feats on such a low budget was a triumph that undercut the industry's attempt to drown the independent movement in a tide of big action pictures. The *Secaucus Seven* phenomenon also raised the question: How does he do it? Friends, careful planning, and budget-conscious scripting were some of the means used to produce the film. In the history of production and distribution of *Return of the Secaucus Seven* lies the other answer to that question and, more importantly, the roadmap to the future of Sayles and his movies.

3

The Making of *Return of the Secaucus Seven:* The Production

At the end of the day, the maxim of his movies is
"Spend the money on what's on screen. If you have an extra dollar,
it goes to production values, not to hotel rooms."

DOUG SAYLES (BROTHER OF JOHN), 1998

"I'D SAY THE MOST PRAGMATIC of all my movies was *Return of the Secaucus Seven,*" John Sayles told Meagan Ratner (*Filmmaker,* Summer 1996). "We had the budget before we had the movie." For Sayles's first feature, the consequence of considering dollars first resulted in a realism that suffused both his screenplay and his production choices. In his script, he created characters who seemed like low-profile neighbors rather than big-screen celebrities. Through the use of unfamiliar, inexperienced film actors who looked like they were wearing their own clothes, the film had a natural air. The onscreen settings were far from the usual Hollywood veneer. Sayles had scouted several neighborhoods to find them but refused to decorate or dress them up for glamour; consequently, in the kitchen or at the swimming hole, his characters looked equally at home. From this "artless" style and from the resistance to topical issues and cinematic fads emerged a movie that then, as now, seems without artifice. The story and the shooting picked up the realism that evolved out of economic necessity and made it the hallmark of *Secaucus Seven*.

The camerawork continues the down-to-earth theme as it captures the movie's human interactions in a minimalist, almost documentary style. The unfamiliar faces, ordinary settings, and lack of action embellish the feeling of people caught unawares by the camera (a theme prevalent in many of Sayles's later films). John attributes much of the home-movie look to his practical inexperience. He had been on sets but had never looked through a camera. As he explained to *Film Comment* (May 1981), "It's the first movie I shot, so I didn't even know how to cover things. I made some pretty basic mistakes, but I salvaged most of them o.k." Consciously or not, the influence of director John Cassavetes was at work. In the *New York Times* (May 12, 1991), Sayles wrote about the Cassavetes model: "His early movies were on the job training . . . but they managed to hit notes that slicker movies couldn't approach. . . . It was raw cinema, no place to hide a performance in a tricky cut or camera move."

The choice of cinematographer for *Secaucus Seven* also contributed to a sense of cinema verité, a style John would utilize in his later films. Shooting the color movie was a joint project of Aydelott Associates of Brookline, Massachusetts, and Film Associates of Boston, two companies specializing in documentary pictures. The project's thirty-day shooting schedule left the director and his crew little time for filming anything beyond the most essential needs of the story. Even if there had been time, the crew was using only the most rudimentary camera and lighting gear. As would other early Sayles movies, *Secaucus* called for improvisational, guerrilla filmmaking with lots of technical improvisation and jerry-rigging. The bar scene illustrates the crew's ability to work fast with only basic tools.

By shooting for thirteen straight hours (with a nonunion crew), the producers worked around the Oakley Tavern's regular business day. For what was supposed to be a crowded tavern sequence, ample extras were hired but could stay for only twenty minutes. The crowd shots were done, then the two-shots (just a few people in the frame) were filmed in an empty bar room. Crowd noise, recorded at Ken's Pub in Boston, was added later.

In May 1999, while working on the transfer of *Limbo* from film to video, Sayles told Sony colorist John Persichetti of another bit of ingenuity used in shooting that tavern scene for *Secaucus Seven*. With time running out and his film supply shrinking, Sayles still had to capture a woman's song. Adapting a television approach, John employed two cameras, one for the long shot, one for the close-ups of her face. Using his hand and a long stick, he edited as he shot, alternately tapping the cameramen on the shoulders, once to shoot, twice to stop. The "big stick method" saved time and film. It was another example of the stringent budgeting that forced Sayles to be extremely resourceful.

The lighting for the bar scene and throughout the film is flat, with the shadows left unfilled and the image tending toward the white side of the spectrum. With the 16mm film later blown up to 35mm, the images have a grainy newsreel look that at the time bothered purists but worked in a film that documents rather than romanticizes personal relationships.

Even the exhausting all-night shooting schedule for the bar scene finally aided the film. As actor Jean Passanante, who played Irene, recalls, "Since the next scene required everyone to be drunk and wiped out, it worked perfectly." In the end, the unknown actors and technical limitations made the lives of the Secaucus Seven look less contrived.

Serendipity, sweat, and invention also would mark the picture's music and editing phases. Hired as the film's lawyer, Mason Daring emerged as composer, then musical director for *Secaucus* and all but one of Sayles's later movies. Daring's original job was to devise a compensation deal for actors and investors in the film. "About a year after the film wrapped, John called," Daring told me. "He asked if I would like to do the music—with a $700 budget—with my composer's fee included. I said, 'Heck yes.'" Familiar with the recording studio and the Boston music scene, Daring rounded up three friends who did six or seven cues. He then added audio touches such as the grunting sounds under the basketball scene. The workable 1960s score would win plaudits for its gentle whimsy. While Daring was synching the music, Sayles was learning how to edit the film.

Poverty again was a player, this time shaping the postproduction. John needed money to edit the movie. For that purpose, in the spring of 1979,

Sayles and Maggie Renzi returned to Santa Barbara, California, where he resumed his bread-and-butter job—writing movies for others. The *Secaucus Seven* project faced a long road to completion. As Sayles related to Eliot Asinof for *DGA Magazine* (December 1997/January 1998), "It wasn't until we got back to Los Angeles for postproduction work that all our mistakes became evident. Years would pass, 1978, 1979, 1980, and the $40,000 became $60,000." To pay for the editing equipment, John scripted for a television special, *A Perfect Match* (1980), and for Roger Corman's *Battle Beyond the Stars* (1980).

Over coffee one morning in May 1998, Sayles's brother, Doug, recalled his visit to the Sayles/Renzi house on Ortega Street, now the "editing suite." "John and Maggie were sitting in the living room with this big Steenbeck editing machine. They had a manual next to them and were learning as they went." Since the company was charging $500 dollars a month for the machine, twice the rent of their house, they used it round-the-clock. In the *New York Times* (October 25, 1983), Aljean Harmetz described the routine: "He wrote during the day and edited at night. . . . Maggie edited during the day and worked at a salad bar at night." Because Sayles believed the film would never play in theaters, he had shot it in the square TV format. Now, looking to show it on the big screen, he was both cutting the footage and synching the music for the 16mm version while panning and scanning to convert the images to the widescreen theatrical-release format.

By 1979 a 16mm copy was ready for its debut screening at the 1980 Los Angeles Filmex Festival, where it found a receptive audience. "It was an instant success," critic Roger Ebert recalled in the *Evening Bulletin* (Philadelphia, February 28, 1981). "It sold out every performance. It got great trade reviews. At other festivals—Toronto, London—it was also well received." The standing ovations were followed by bids from film distributors, notably Specialty Film, United Artists Classics, and Libra Films. Sayles weighed the offers.

Later that year, now converted to 35mm, the movie opened in New York as part of the New Directors/New Film series sponsored by the Film Society at Lincoln Center and the Museum of Modern Art. Meanwhile, in Randy Finley, a Seattle, Washington, theater owner and West Coast film distributor,

Sayles had found a collaborator whose road-show approach and grassroots advertising stirred up interest and brought filmgoers to the box office.

It helped that the time was ripe for American independent movies. The art houses saw French and Italian films declining in popularity. Ingmar Bergman, Federico Fellini, and François Truffaut were fading out. Small films from the United States, Australia (directors Fred Schepisi, Peter Weir, Bruce Beresford, Gillian Armstrong), and New Zealand (director Jane Campion) picked up the slack.

In the distribution deal with Sayles, Finley had subcontracted Ben Barenholt's Libra Films (one of the original three bidders) to handle the New York opening and East Coast distribution. As with many releases, the marketing and exhibition efforts for Secaucus would vary in different markets and meet with unpredictable results. In Seattle (today a favorite site for testing Sayles's movies), Finley's campaign included radio promotion, press screenings, and the presence of novelty items in theaters, such as stickers on popcorn boxes and lobby posters. That blitz led to a hefty gross of $260,000. In San Francisco the same approach fizzled; in Washington, D.C., it worked like gangbusters. The difference probably can be attributed in part to the local critics, who exert enormous control over any film, especially low-budget indies.

With three hundred seats, the Orson Welles Theatre in Cambridge, Massachusetts, was the right kind of intimate setting for screening Secaucus Seven, and performances sold out night after night. "The place was rocking," Mason Daring remembers. "On Harvard Square, everybody got his jokes." In the wrong theater—the 620-seat Fifty-seventh Street Playhouse in Manhattan—the movie got a good start, then dropped off and closed after four weeks.

A year later, 1981, using the strong showings elsewhere and good press clippings from Seattle, Los Angeles, and Boston for hype, Libra Films reissued Secaucus Seven in New York as "the film everyone missed." The Village Voice reviewed it for the first time and the New York Times for the second. Thereafter, critical acclaim led to a twenty-two-week run at the cozy Quad Theatre in Greenwich Village. First citing Secaucus Seven as the "Return of the Most

Successful American Independent Film," the print ads then quoted the *Village Voice*'s "Rush to see" advice. The *New York Times* said, "It's a joy to watch." Enthusiasm seemed to be everywhere: "John Sayles has done wonders" *(Newsweek);* "An important American film" *(Los Angeles Times),* and "Wildly Entertaining" (Newhouse Newspapers).

The little-movie-that-could also earned critical and industry honors, being named to the Ten Best Films of 1980 list by the *Los Angeles Times,* the *New York Times, Boston Globe,* and *Time* magazine. The Screen Writers Guild nominated Sayles for its Best Screenplay Award. The picture also started a movie trend about the 1960s generation. Lawrence Kasdan's *The Big Chill* (1983) would be the most obvious follow-up on the theme of "where are the radicals of yesteryear?"

In contrasting these two similarly themed pictures for *Off-Hollywood Movies* (1989), author Richard Skorman acknowledged *Secaucus*'s technical problems in the tinny soundtrack, jerky editing, and amateurish camerawork, then opined, "But even with all its faults, the movie has far more substance than *The Big Chill.*" In *The Big Chill,* some critics see a *Secaucus Seven* rip-off, but in *Sayles on Sayles* (1998), John says, "Even though the form of the two movies and the plot in some ways are very close, they're really about very different people, which is why I never felt it was a rip-off."

In 1993 Great Britain's *Sight and Sound* critic Trevor Johnston described *Secaucus Seven* as the seminal reunion picture and as an indicator of things to come. "The film now stands as a fair record of the forms and questions its maker would continue to address." Over the years, critics continue to cite Sayles's debut feature as a landmark. *Filmmaker* magazine voted it one of the five most important independent films of all time. In 1997, in its special issue on independent production, *Entertainment Weekly* included *Secaucus* in the list of the Top Fifty Indie movies. "This is arguably the true birth of the independent movement," its writers said, "if only because of the way its end-of-the-1960s melancholy is counteracted by the movie's own giddiness. If the counterculture is gone, Sayles seems to be saying, at least its spirit can live on in filmmaking."

Sayles and *Return of the Secaucus Seven* started a wave of countercultural movies. The filmmaker had rightly estimated that an audience, perhaps small, might share his attraction to the kinds of films only foreigners had then been making. He told Eliot Asinof *(DGA Magazine),* "The Hollywood pictures I'd seen were a bunch of Rock Hudson–Doris Day romances, Dean Martin and Elvis [Presley] pictures. They had nothing to do with anyone." According to Asinof, Sayles's hunch and timing were exactly right. "There was a substantial new audience that hungered for something new, something different from what the Hollywood studios were offering, something more serious."

In the wings were Sayles and other writers and directors ready to oblige that neglected taste. In *Vogue* (September 1981), Peter Rainer cited "The Young and the Gifted: Six Directors Make a Splash during Hollywood's Low Ebb." Rainer named: Jonathan Demme *(Melvin and Howard,* 1980), David Lynch *(The Elephant Man,* 1980), screenwriter Steve Tesich *(Breaking Away,* 1979), Carroll Ballard *(The Black Stallion,* 1979), Joan Micklin Silver *(Hester Street,* 1975), and Sayles. A few years later, Rainer might have added Jim Jarmusch, Spike Lee, and Susan Seidelman to that list.

Back in 1981, when he accepted his award from the Los Angeles Film Critics Association for Best Screenplay for *Return of the Secaucus Seven,* John received an unexpected bonus at the event. He finally met actor Robert Stack, who had starred in the television series *The Untouchables* (1959–63). The winner confessed that many of his early boyhood "scripts" were imitations of that TV program. The highest honor that *Secaucus Seven* would receive came in 1998 when the Library of Congress added it to the National Film Registry for preservation as part of American film history.

Despite an initially checkered economic report, *Return of the Secaucus Seven* was finally an enormous popular success. In his book *Spike, Mike, Slackers, & Dykes,* John Pierson says the film "was also the first indie feature to make serious hay out of promoting the low, low budget—$60,000!" As estimated by *Off-Hollywood Movies,* the box-office grosses came to more than $2 million, with a percentage for the filmmakers estimated at $195,000. Today the *Secaucus Seven* actors who took "the points" or deferred payments over the

SAG wages are still reaping income from revenue earned through home video, pay cable, nontheatrical release, TV broadcasts, and foreign markets. Pending is a release of the film on digital video disc (DVD).

■   ■   ■

In 1981 John Sayles was at a career point where he had a critically acclaimed movie and a reputation as a Hollywood writer and director with unlimited possibilities for the future. As Tom Bernard, then a distributor with United Artists Classics, recently told me, "Everyone had an eye on John Sayles [in 1981]. He was hot." In subsequent months, the major studios would tempt him with offers of big budgets to make *their* movies while declining his counterproposal that they help him to make his. Seemingly his pictures did not fit their mold. John, however, now had the success of *Return of the Secaucus Seven* behind him to prove that he could make movies his way.

4

The Sayles Family of Schenectady, New York

The main way my parents were influential is that they encouraged
us to read a lot, and they didn't lay any big trips about
"This is what you're supposed to be or do." . . . *I wanted to be a*
pitcher for the Pittsburgh Pirates.

JOHN SAYLES, 1991

TO WALK THROUGH THE HALLS of Mont Pleasant Middle School in
Schenectady, New York, with Donald Sayles is akin to accompanying a former
admiral making rounds on a tour of his flagship. This was not just John Sayles's
father with whom I was walking. This was Donald Sayles, Ed.D, and the school
was Mont—not Mount—Pleasant. Like his son, Dr. Sayles is a sturdy looking
six feet tall. He's graying and bespectacled, but at seventy-plus years, he is fit
and ready for skiing or boating, his winter and summer hobbies. Eighteen
years have intervened since he last entered what was the old Mont Pleasant
High School, and he wonders aloud about the changes he'll find.

A graduate of the class of 1938, he returned to Mont Pleasant in 1954 as
assistant principal. Three years later he succeeded Dr. George W. Spaine, the
founding administrator. The building that once saw nearly two thousand
teenage students now serves a younger and smaller population as a junior high

school. In the early 1990s, faced by a shrinking number of students (from 13,000 to 8,000), the school board amalgamated its two high schools. The board members selected the tonier, more modern Linton as the new Schenectady Senior High School. Now, having just visited John's former middle school, Oneida, and found it worn down, the once principal walks toward his former domain not sure of its condition or his status.

Set in the inner part of Schenectady (a city about ten miles west of the state capital in Albany), Mont Pleasant has the solid look of the school buildings of the 1930s. The red brick Georgian architecture gives the structure a historic and academic image that rises three stories into the sky and extends for almost a block along Forest Avenue. Its massive shape points to serious business; the school seems like a centerpiece rising out of the neighborhood without dominating it. This is a structure with shape and form that were meant to last, and it has.

To Sayles's delight, the interior sparkles. The former principal climbs the familiar stairs, takes a peek into his old chemistry lab, and looks into the basketball court where he once watched his sons, Doug and John, start for the Raider five. At each turn, someone greets him as a former teacher or colleague.

With the tour completed, Dr. Sayles leaves Mont Pleasant reassured about its future. Like many of his neighbors, he finds in this revered building memories of the best characteristics of education and of a supportive city that he longs to see again but very likely won't. Economically, Schenectady is enduring hard times, and the crisis is far from over. In 1998 it was still trying to rebound from the economic slump that has been emptying its homes and schools.

■   ■   ■

During a visit to the lakeside lodge that he built himself in Northville, New York, on the shores of the Great Sacandara Lake in the rolling foothills of the Adirondack Mountains, thirty miles northwest of Schenectady, Sayles leads the way up the tightly spiraling metal staircase to his den and the Sayles family archives. The pine walls are covered with photos dating back to John's grandparents at the turn of the twentieth century alongside posters (one in Japanese) of his son's latest films. With commentary from Dr. Sayles, the gallery captures the background of a family that has been part of Schenectady's history since the 1800s.

Don's father, Henry, was born there in 1893 and grew up to volunteer for the peacetime army. From 1909 to 1916, before there was a National Park Service, he was a soldier in the horse cavalry protecting the vast Colorado forests from poachers. Mustered out of the army in 1916, Henry turned his military experience into a civilian job by joining the state police patrol. Pointing to panoramic pictures of the Mounties of Troop D, saddled up for their assignments, Sayles describes his father's living in the police barracks at Oneida and patrolling the northern counties of New York from 1917 to 1923. After apprehending culprits, the trooper would haul them before the nearest magistrate. With the war against Germany still raging, however, the young officer concluded that the name "Schlensker" might stir some unwanted antagonism toward him in the smaller local villages. Justice, he reasoned, would be better served if allegations came from a more neutral-sounding source. In short order, Henry Schlensker became Trooper Sayles.

In the late 1920s, Officer Matthew McGinnis was promoted to captain of the Schenectady Police Department, and a surge of anticrime sentiment allowed him to hire eight new police officers. One of them was his son-in-law, Henry Sayles. At the time troopers were required to live in state barracks, which separated Sayles from his family. Now, with this new position, he could rejoin his wife, Mae, and bring her and their three children, Burton, 7; Doris, 5; and Donald, 3, back to Schenectady.

Over the next several years, Hank would serve as a patrolman in the Mont Pleasant precinct. In the early 1930s, Fred Rousch, John Sayles's maternal grandfather, also applied for a policeman's job. As a young man, Don Sayles could see in the police ranks his maternal grandfather, father, three uncles, and future father-in-law.

Henry Sayles's children received their education in the Schenectady school system and their religious upbringing in the Lutheran Church. Once out of Mont Pleasant High School in 1934, older son Burton joined the

10,000 employees at the General Electric plant and worked there until his retirement. His sister, Doris, class of 1936, would also remain in the region, marrying Everett West and rearing her children in nearby Ballston Lake. Both are now deceased. In 1941, after a January graduation from Mont Pleasant followed by his own six-month stint at GE, Donald matriculated at New York State College for Teachers at Albany (since 1948 the State University of New York in Albany, or SUNY–Albany).

With the lingering effects of the Depression still determining the economy, 50 percent of the country's students did not finish high school. The needs of their families forced them into the workforce. Still, the demand for teachers justified the state's use of taxpayers' money to support teacher-training programs. For Sayles and all the other commuters, college was practically free. In January 1943, now in his sophomore year, Don Sayles, like most male college students, was drafted into the army. By August he was embarking for North Africa, and months later, just after the infantry had cleared the way, he landed in Naples, Italy, where he served for the duration of World War II.

■　　　■　　　■

In the next hour, Sayles gives me the tour of the house, the outdoor basketball court, and the sailboat—the latter two the favorites of Andrew, his eight-year-old grandson, Doug's boy. After lunch and the hour-long drive back to Schenectady, Don eases his "new" maroon 1994 Buick along the streets and shows me the four neighborhoods of his adult life. After his discharge from the service in December 1945, Sayles returned to SUNY and resumed his studies. At a bowling alley, an army buddy brought along his cousin Mary Rousch and introduced her to Don, now a junior. Mary was a 1945 Mont Pleasant graduate who was also enrolled in the education department at SUNY. At Easter 1948, Don and Mary were wed. She was twenty, he was twenty-four and about to receive his degree. Mary's would have to wait.

That afternoon, when Don visits the home of Mary Sayles on 1222 Sumner Avenue, the two of them recount for me the early years of their married life. Don's first teaching assignment required them to move about two hours north and east to Willsboro, New York, a small village just outside Plattsburg, twenty-two miles south of the Canadian border. For a time the housing shortage there sent them scrambling to find living quarters. Eventually, they moved into the rectory of St. Phillip's Roman Catholic Church. Mary Sayles was raised Catholic and wanted to bring up her children the same way. Don, a nonbeliever, was supportive. Over the next two years, Mary gave birth to Doug (January 4, 1949) and then John (September 28, 1950), at Schenectady's Ellis Hospital. In June 1950, the Schenectady School District offered Don a position in the science department at Nott Terrence High School. He snatched the job and headed back to his hometown, this time for good.

The transition was not easy. In the early 1950s, the United States faced a huge housing shortage brought on by lack of construction during the Depression and World War II. The need for homes was suddenly exacerbated by the return of the nearly eleven million veterans and by their subsequent marriages and the arrival of the baby-boom generation. For newly married vets of Schenectady, the country and state responded by offering affordable housing in the "GI barracks" on Dartmouth Street. For the next three years, the Sayles family made the barracks their home. Among the parents' memories of Dartmouth Street is the day Johnny literally tasted danger for the first time by drinking kerosene that had leaked from the space heater that warmed their quarters.

That near disaster prompted their father to pay even closer attention to the children's safety when the family moved again. In 1953 the Sayleses settled into a house on State Street owned by Mary's father and shared with her sister's family who lived upstairs. To protect his children from local traffic, Don quickly erected a fence separating the front lawn from the street. He then dumped a truckload of sand into the backyard sandbox.

The Sayles family soon began looking for their own home, but Don was facing economic reality. "When I was a classroom teacher," he told me, "I didn't think we'd have a home unless I built my own. That's when I began reading about building houses." For the time being, however, a professional promotion intervened and postponed the need for his construction efforts. In 1954, having just completed a Leadership Apprentice Year, Sayles was named assistant principal of Mont Pleasant High School. His salary increase and the GI Bill provided the financial wherewithal to buy, not build, a new house in suburban Charlton on the Schenectady border.

Just thirty-five years old, the new administrative appointee now sought to add to his academic credentials the hard way. Each Saturday morning, Don and three other teachers drove to Columbia University in New York City, attended classes, then drove back, a six-hour round trip. Six years of those Saturday courses and one summer in residence on campus eventually earned Sayles his doctoral degree from Columbia's prestigious Teachers College. Now, driving leisurely through the old neighborhood, Don Sayles stoically recounts the stamina needed to get that degree. He barely hints of the resourcefulness eventually called on when he finally did build his own house in Northville. Still, I hear in his history hints of the legacy of determination and calculated creativity found in his son John.

When they arrived on Korman Street in Charlton in 1954, Don and his family comprised one-half of the Sayles compound, with the family of Doris and Everett West, his sister and brother-in-law, inhabiting the house on an adjacent lot. For kindergarten, young Doug went to one of the state's last remaining one-room schoolhouses. A year later John followed, going on to attend Burnt Hills School through the sixth grade and then, finally, on to the Howe School back in Schenectady.

Before the move, Mary had resumed her college education, completing her senior year at SUNY and earning a bachelor's degree in secondary education in 1953. A critical need for elementary school teachers sent her immediately into a special training program in primary school education. In 1958, master's degree in hand, she commenced a twenty-three-year tenure in the Burnt Hills–Ballston Lake School District. Over the years Mary taught thousands of fourth graders and earned a salary that would help put her two sons through college. Now retired, still with the alert eyes of a schoolteacher, she showed me a well-cared-for clipping and photo file she keeps in a closet. While I perused the collection, Don mowed the lawn. As both parents agree, "We are very proud of what John has done."

At ages eight and six, respectively, Doug and John started showing the traits and tendencies that would distinguish and connect them through the years. Doug's being just one year ahead of John in school closed the age gap between the two. A little bigger, Doug soon was demonstrating the talent and prowess that would make him a natural athlete. In the early years, John was the "little brother."

The still athletic-looking Doug told me about growing up with John. "When we moved to Charlton, we hung out with guys who played sports. John was the little guy that got pulled along because he was my brother. He was always the last kid picked for baseball. He'd play catcher." Those humbling experiences would later provide fodder for John's fiction; at the time, he could occasionally escape Doug's shadow and enter imaginatively into the world of the Wild West. His great-aunt had given the two boys a model of a Western fortress complete with cowboy and Indian figures. Setting aside her glasses, Mary remembers, "John would set up the figures and play with them for a long time. But Doug would come around and want John to play catch, so he'd disrupt the drama and start moving the pieces around. John would get very upset."

John's interest in stories found plenty of other outlets and support. As he told the *New York Times* (April 17, 1983), "I zipped through all the stuff you were supposed to read from comic books to sports books to *Freddie the Pig*." On Saturdays their father would drive the boys to the main library, letting them check out a dozen books or so. Sundays saw the youngsters going off with their mother to church. As John recalled for the *New York Times* (September 6, 1981), "I liked listening to the gospel at Catholic mass. You didn't have to kneel while they told you a story. Christ's progress to the cross was what I had instead of Buck Rogers serials, and the parables made me aware of metaphors and allegory."

John also was adapting his narrative talents to the classroom. In *Writers Dreaming* (1994), a collection of articles on the impact of dreams on writers, Sayles says, "I liked writing stories for class assignments and was pretty good at it. It was like getting high grades for lying." His dreams were yet another source for his fantasies. A nun "grossed out" his Sunday school class by telling them that people's hair and fingernails kept growing after they died. Having dreamed of a friend "mowing hair" in the parish cemetery, young John wove that anecdote into a story.

In addition to testing his writing, he was adopting other permanent attitudes and habits, one of which was an utter disdain for confining clothes. In almost any photo of him today, John Sayles is likely to be wearing jogging shorts and a short-sleeved, open-necked shirt, if not a tank top. On the set of his film *Limbo* in Juneau, Alaska, Caroline (Hall) Otis, a college friend working as a production assistant, told me about "everyone else putting on two or three layers of Gore-Tex protective gear" while "John was walking around in nylon shorts and a shirt with the sleeves rolled up."

The Sayles family album includes a yearbook photo of the high school French Club showing its members decked out in dark suits, white shirts, and ties. Seventeen-year-old John was in the back row, wearing a brown blazer and sports shirt, collar wide open. Doug Sayles attests that this choice of clothes was in no way a protest against established style. "He just didn't care about that stuff and still doesn't." Indeed, over the past three decades, the Sayles family has seen John in a suit exactly twice, both times at weddings. Asked about its later disappearance, he told his dad that he "lost" the pants. For every ritual that put him off, however, there was a treat to turn him on. Stories in almost any shape or form were one, and movies were another.

Moviegoing in the pre–home video era was a family ritual. Each Friday night, drained by their hours in the classrooms, Don and Mary packed the boys into the Chevy station wagon and headed to the nearby Mohawk Drive-In. There young John saw the first film that "did it" for him. "It was a trailer for a horror movie that scared the shit out of me," he recalled in *Venice* (California) magazine (April 1998). "It was a giant locust movie or something." John began developing a knack for quickly detecting a picture's overall plot structure. As his father told me, "He could tell you early in a movie where it was going and what would happen—even then. We didn't realize what that meant, but in retrospect we know he had that kind of mind."

Today John ascribes some of that instinct for story analysis to the vivid and horrifying dreams he had in his youth. Perhaps those nightmares also help explain the insomnia that afflicted him from childhood through his college years and furthered his penchant for watching films on TV until the wee hours. One other consequence of the insomnia was a schedule of work, study, and relaxation that was at best unconventional. Surprisingly, the schoolteacher parents took a casual approach to the boys' sleeping schedule. Believing that their sons would get rest when they needed it, the parents imposed no lights-out policies. Consequently, for years Doug and John would be watching late-night television until "The Star-Spangled Banner" served as their taps.

In *Venice* magazine, John recalls his early film education: "I watched westerns because they were in color and had horses going through the water and people shooting each other, stuff like that. The black and white movie afterwards was almost always about the man in the gray flannel suit, and I didn't get it." His absolute favorite TV show was *The Untouchables,* which later inspired him to create send-ups in junior high English class as well as a college play script and production. Another Sayles favorite led critic Randy Sue Coburn (*Esquire,* November 1982) to see a moral awakening in Sayles: "Showing early signs of social conscience, he thought *Leave It to Beaver* [1957–63] was good because Wally's best friend Lumpy was a real loser."

In 1959, when John was in the fourth grade, he learned of two physical impairments that he would carry throughout his life. He had developed astigmatism in one eye. Ironically, his mother first noticed it when they went to the movies. "Looking at the screen, he would turn his head a certain way to compensate," she says. "John never did bother to get glasses, but to this day he has this way of slightly angling his head to get a better view." His father adds, "When he played basketball for Mont Pleasant, it was always interesting to watch him shoot foul shots."

The eye problem had no detrimental impact on John's reading or on his ability to hit a baseball. That same year, however, a physical examination in school uncovered a more serious malady. His mother remembers receiving a school referral and taking her son for a medical examination. After testing, the doctors concluded that John had a missing vertebra. Playing team sports throughout high school, John never complained about any discomfort in his back, but by the time he started college he was sleeping on the floor and, more importantly, receiving an exemption from military service.

As a consequence of his back problem, John today often writes while standing at a desk, and at one film premiere his dad remembers seeing him enter on crutches. Over the years he has visited specialists for treatment, but he has not allowed himself to indulge in self-pity nor let the problem constrict either his rigorous production choices or his participation in pickup basketball games.

Perhaps as challenging as any physical problem was the emotional need he faced as a boy who frequently had to adapt to new neighborhoods, new schools, and new friends. By 1961 his father had completed a four-year term as Mont Pleasant High School principal and now assumed the office of assistant superintendent of schools for the Schenectady School District. Not because it was required but because he felt that he should, Dr. Sayles left the suburbs. He moved his family back into the school district and enrolled his sons there, Doug in seventh grade and John in sixth. After some searching, Don and Mary found a house on Sumner Avenue, a tree-shaded section of the city that felt like their former Charlton neighborhood. Don immediately constructed a backyard basketball court. Always intense, always friendly, the hoop games played there would help measure the maturation of the Sayles sons from boys into young men.

5

Number 80, John Sayles, 1967 All-County Football

He was good, solid. You're a star on an undefeated
state championship team. You're a good football player.
That's it. Let the facts speak.

COACH LARRY MULVANEY, 1998

IN 1960, OPENING THE FRONT DOOR of his Sumner Avenue house, ten-year-old Phil Mara looked down the block to see a new family moving in with two boys about his age. He now had other kids to play with for the next eight years. The Sayles house at 1222 Sumner Avenue was bigger and more substantial than its Charlton counterpart. The white Cape Cod–style residence also had ample grounds out back that would serve as the playing field for John and Doug and many neighborhood youths.

Over the next decade, Phil spent a lot of his spare time in the Sayles back-yard. Today, he's fifty-year-old Dr. Philip Mara, and his offices are only a few blocks from the old neighborhood where his mother still lives. The soft-spoken physician recounts for me those boyhood days with John and Doug. "We struck up a friendship mainly through baseball and basketball. We would trade stories about the Charlton and Schenectady Little Leagues. At the time John was still playing for Charlton."

In Mara's eyes, the Sayles backyard remains a sports venue that any stadium owner would envy for its flexibility. It was an all-weather baseball park and basketball arena. "Mr. Sayles had put up the basketball pole with a cement foundation," the doctor says. "The court was compact dirt, and we used it all year round. We'd shovel snow off the court, and it didn't matter if it was muddy or icy. We'd put on gloves, sweater, and hats and be out there playing in subfreezing weather."

When spring came, the boys would break out the Wiffle ball and turn the yard into an imaginary baseball stadium. Usually the game pitted twelve-year-old Doug against both Phil and John. The other players were make-believe. If the sides sound uneven, they were not. Nearly two years older, Doug was twice the ballplayer that Phil and John were. In Phil's eyes, Doug was an athlete on his way to the top.

At age ten, John was still two inches shorter than his brother. By the time he was eighteen, though, John would surpass him in height (6'4" to Doug's 6') but never in physical dexterity or ease of performance. Dr. Mara recalls that what John lacked in natural ability, he compensated for with courage. His father and brother concur that from the start, John was fearless. He simply would not back away just because other kids were bigger. In playing ball and competing with his pals, he also was gathering material for fiction and film. His first novel, *Pride of the Bimbos* (1975), and the movies *Return of the Secaucus Seven* (1980) and *Eight Men Out* (1988) all would employ baseball settings and rituals. From those yard games, he also would take with him a favorite and enduring recreation: pickup basketball games, a.k.a. "hoops."

Mara was never in class with John, but all the kids at Oneida Junior High knew his reputation for being a "brain." Another classmate, John Marmros, would typically walk over from the next block and join Sayles and Mara on their way to school. The other boy was in the same classes with Sayles and used to talk about John's performance. "Marmros would say how great John was in English, writing, and math and just about anything they'd throw at him." John's habitual reading took him way beyond the required textbooks. As Sayles told the *New York Times* (April 17, 1983), "In junior high, I got into [Franz] Kafka, especially the story I called 'the one about the roaches.' At the same time I was taking a look at *The Caine Mutiny* [1951] and *Lord of the Flies* [1954]."

As Mara recalls, when John was thirteen he was also venturing into fiction writing. "His seventh-grade English teacher, Mrs. O'Conner, challenged the class to compose short stories, and John came up with one that was fantastic." Sayles titled the story "Earth Dead Ahead," and it appeared in the 1963 edition of the Oneida Junior High literary magazine, *Arrow*. A seventh grader's account of an astronaut flight and crash, the piece harks back to Sayles's early fascination with space and perhaps anticipates one of his first motion pictures, *The Brother from Another Planet* (1984).

Sayles's independent streak and unique perspective were now giving a special twist to his writing. Doug recalls John's response to the traditional junior high essay about the arrival of autumn. "Most kids responded with rapturous reports of New York foliage. John's essay was titled 'The Dirty Brown Leaves.' It was a dialogue among the leaves as they gathered in the gutter. Then John wrote an essay from the point of view of eggs in the refrigerator and how they were taken away one by one." Clearly, the now-published fledgling author had a different take on class assignments, and he would apply that offbeat point of view to school in general. Meanwhile, the proud father showed one composition to a colleague who concluded that the boy had a flair for writing. Perhaps too close to the action then, Dr. Sayles admits that he perceived his son "not as a writer but as a kid who just liked to write."

In 1964 Doug was finishing junior high. Although fourteen-year-old John was just entering the ninth grade, he was eligible for a new engineering-oriented technology program at Mont Pleasant. Don Sayles now faced a critical decision: Which high school should his sons attend? The choice was not casual, as the end result would affect their future lives.

The father cites three reasons behind his decision. First, in Schenectady, real estate agents promoted the idea that Linton High was the superior school. They then steered professional and even middle-class families to the more expensive homes on the Linton side of town. This was a bias that did not sit well with an alumnus and former principal of Mont Pleasant. Second, in a city that respected engineering, Don's alma mater had inaugurated a new high-tech program sponsored in part by General Electric. Although stirring interest in academic circles and attracting some bright students, the program was being short-circuited by its own ambition. After only a year or two, enrollment was declining because of the program's rigorous math courses and science labs. In response, the school administration decided to admit selected, highly qualified ninth graders, thus opening the door for John to join Doug.

The third reason for Dr. Sayles's choice of Mont Pleasant over Linton had nothing to do with academics and everything to do with his sons. While Linton High stood right around the corner and Mont Pleasant was a couple of miles away from their home, Don had raised a couple of MPHS Raiders fans. Year after year, he had taken the boys to the Mont Pleasant home sports events, and both were now schooled in that tradition. For these academic and athletic reasons, the father chose Mont Pleasant, but it was the school's diverse socioeconomic environment that had the most decisive impact on his younger son, who, along with Doug, quickly dropped out of the engineering program.

According to their father, in the fall of 1964 the two boys dutifully went off to the other side of town and never voiced complaints about the journey or the school. Yet Doug, president of his graduating class at Oneida Junior High, found the transition to Mont Pleasant fraught with obstacles, misunderstandings, and frustration, especially at the social level. "Going back to the city school was bizarre," he told me. "We were strange to the academic kids because we were athletes. Then, because we were academics, the athletes thought we were from the moon. Making new friends? It just never happened." Admittedly, Doug's perspective may have been skewed by the separation from his girlfriend who attended Linton. Nevertheless, several factors might have contributed to the discomfort felt by him and John.

John was not just a new student from a different neighborhood. He was the new guy who was a gangly 6'4" tall, a height even more remarkable back in the late 1960s. The physical difference was coupled to another "eccentricity": he was extremely bright. Further unwanted attention fell on him because every teacher and many students knew he was the son of the assistant superintendent of schools, who recently had fired the school's beloved athletic director. Back then, Doug was always more personable and outgoing. His classmates soon connected him to the pie-throwing star of TV's *The Soupy Sales Show,* and "Soupy" became his high school moniker. John, on the other hand, retreated into a shell.

While his neighbor and pal Phil Mara walked around the block to Linton, John was plunked down on planet Mont Pleasant High. His classmate Al Aldi remembers both the situation and John's attempts to acclimate himself. "A lot of us, Italians and Polish mainly, were coming from blue-collar families," he told me. "In the sixties, if you were from a family of educators, you were in a minority." The economic and education disparity bred antagonism to outsiders, perhaps best caught in the school's unofficial but deeply ingrained athletic motto, "Mont Pleasant Against the World." Aldi (now the assistant superintendent of schools in a neighboring district) feels that the Sayles brothers in the late 1960s helped break the barriers especially through their participation in sports and other activities. "It wasn't his coming from the other side of town. Ask anybody in my class. They liked John. But he was so quiet that a lot of people didn't know him."

The high school record of the Sayles brothers gives some credence to Aldi's view of "acceptance." Doug, for instance, made the varsity football and basketball teams as the lone tenth grader and went on to quarterback the football team and letter in basketball and baseball as well. Like John, he scored in the 1500s on the college boards and was clearly academic scholarship caliber, later completing his degree at Dartmouth. Unlike his younger brother, Doug graduated near the top of his class. The less gregarious John would fashion his own record of distinguished achievements in athletics and activities but finish farther down academically. According to Dr. Sayles, his sons never griped about their school. They simply may have been too busy with sports to bother.

■   ■   ■

In 1964, dictated by various sports schedules, the routine at the Sayles home clicked into place for the brothers' high school years. School was followed by practice or games, then supper, naps, and TV, then bed. To that late-night television regimen, John added snacks. Homework got token treatment; sleep was also randomized depending on the late-night movie. As his father concludes, "Growing up so fast, always being in one sport or another, and staying up and watching TV, John was always short on sleep." Indeed at Mont Pleasant, his catnapping was near legendary. He would nod off as he was leaning over his typewriter in Mrs. Moon's business class.

The description John himself provides interviewers about his high school years suggests that he was academically marginal and athletically inept. He says in *Sayles on Sayles* (1998): "I really didn't like school. I didn't care about getting A's. . . . There wasn't anything that interested me except sports. . . . I wasn't great at sports but I was okay at them." Both descriptions are misleading. Setting the record straight now, his brother asserts that although John was "always bright and still concerned about grades and being competitive, he was bored stiff. He fell asleep all the time in class, but he had things figured out." Although John may have been academically cutting corners, he was in Al Aldi's eyes an inspiring student. "At a very young age, he made me respect academics. Honestly, John's talents impressed me to the point that I wished I knew some of the words he was throwing out and could write the way he did."

Simply put, John's "figuring out things" led to a pragmatism that focused his attention on his writing and even led him, a college preparatory student, into a typing course that he knew would serve his purposes very well. While by no means radical or troublesome, he settled for scraping by in classes he didn't like. For English classes, however, he could dash off an essay or short story with an ease that simultaneously delighted and exasperated his peers.

As in junior high, the Sayles pieces started to appear in *Ebenwyck*, the Mont Pleasant High School literary magazine. Usually restricted to seniors, the 1967 edition included his junior-year poem "Family Life," about which his verse takes a grim view. For the 1968 *Ebenwyck*, Sayles wrote a lighter piece ("Stop the World—I Want to Go to the Men's Room") and a Kafkaesque short story ("The Mind's Eye"). For that entry, the author included ink sketches, one of a brain, the other of an eyeball. Taken up as a hobby, drawing later would allow him to do the storyboarding and design the production crew T-shirts for his movies.

■　　　■　　　■

At Mont Pleasant, few events rivaled the annual Senior Talent Show in importance. According to Aldi, it took this production to unmask the comic actor and class clown in Doug's younger brother. "A lot of kids thought John would just write the scripts, but he was in three skits. Five seniors on the basketball team did a 'tribute' to our coach. We were all dressed in diapers and called ourselves the Five Drips. On the back of each diaper was a letter of the coach's name. At the end of the skit, we sorta 'mooned' the audience. It was pretty raucous for 1968." With the football team, John also acted in a *Playboy* parody that saluted their coach. As Aldi concludes, "For the skits, he just came out of his introverted personality, as he must do now for interviews."

As his publications and skits make clear, John Sayles may have been a silent or even a sleeping observer in class, but he was in no way a recluse. Even as a ninth grader, the big kid from Sumner Avenue was settling into the Raider football scene on the junior varsity squad. Perhaps as with the talent show, football, as Aldi sees it, provided John with the chance to just "stick on a helmet, join the rest of the guys, and do his thing."

There can be no mistaking that sports was the primary focus of John's high school years. "That was what kept me coming every day," he says in *Sayles on Sayles*. "My attendance was very high, not because I wanted to go to school, but because I had to practice." Thus, sports came first. At seventeen, John still dreamed of becoming not a writer but a right fielder, like his hero Roberto Clemente of the Pittsburgh Pirates. Seasonally, he shifted the focus of his passion from baseball to basketball to football. In these three—especially football—one can see the intensity John brought to sports then and to moviemaking now.

Football at Mont Pleasant high school was big time and not just for the school kids. In Schenectady's industrial setting, winning mattered a great deal. Everybody knew there were two kinds of folks: the company people and the people who did the work for the company. Italian, Polish, and, increasingly,

African-American students came from working-class families, and they had an ax to grind. They were just as good as the sons of the managers and engineers, and they would prove it. On Friday under the stadium lights, the Raiders put the neighborhood's self-image, self-respect, and pride on the line.

Under the tutoring of coach Larry Mulvaney in the 1950s and 1960s, Mont Pleasant played an old-fashioned, "smashmouth" style of football that led the school to three undefeated seasons. By any standard, Mulvaney led a high-profile football program, but even in the context of that excellence, the 1967 squad was legendary. Not only undefeated, they ruled as New York State Champions.

What contribution did Sayles make to that championship season? Aldi, the team's spirited captain and later a scholarship athlete at Holy Cross College, recalls that "John was not a locker room leader or a rah-rah guy, but he never missed practice, never missed a minute of playing time . . . and he was always tuned in." What the ex-teammate suggests by "tuned in," Mulvaney would describe as "very coachable, always followed directions, and didn't miss his blocking assignments."

With the quicker, more elusive Aldi as wide receiver, Sayles settled into his role as the "other end," primarily as a blocker and not often in the limelight. Still, after the second game of the season, Mulvaney took John to the quarterback, introduced him, and reminded the passer that John was also eligible and able to catch the ball. His father, his coach, and his teammates describe him in one word: fearless. He was later selected All-County.

In November 1967, after the traditional Election Day game and the victory over arch-rival Linton High, John Sayles pulled off his pads, kicked off his cleats, and shoved the grimy number 80 jersey into his locker for the last time. Those things he left behind; what he took with him were attributes honored by his teammates. They saw in him the steadfastness, self-effacement, and loyalty that in time Sayles's casts and crews would come to respect and revere.

■   ■   ■

There seems little doubt that football helped train Sayles for the collaborative efforts needed in moviemaking. Still, if one word has become synonymous with Sayles the director, that word is *respect*. Therein lies the real payoff for Don's choice of Mont Pleasant High School: the education in treating each person as important. Aldi recalls, "I saw something like it in class in John's patience with lesser lights like me." Doug adds, "The poor kids back there came from sound lives, loving parents, two-parent families. They were GE working-class guys. I think John identifies more with that group than with his natural peers, kids who would end up on Wall Street." In Mont Pleasant lay the seeds for films like *Matewan* (1988). Later John would tell *W*'s David Lida (June 15–22, 1987), "Most people I grew up with were in unions. This gave me a consciousness about being a worker and how this affects you."

The classroom for John's "problems of democracy" course was the hardwood basketball court in the high school gym. It was a team he would rather forget, one that lost forty-eight straight games. Instead he focused on learning about different cultures. Regarding Mont Pleasant's advantageous diversity, Dr. Sayles notes, "John would never have learned about black kids if we had stayed in Burnt Hills suburban Schenectady." In retrospect, John remembers the democracy of the classroom and the basketball court. As he says in *Sayles on Sayles,* "There were a lot of f***ed up things about being a black in northern society, but if you could play, you could stay. A generation earlier that wasn't true."

In these still formative years, John was making friends among his African-American teammates. Practices, games, and hanging out opened the door to this other world. At that time John was one of the few students with a car, and rides home endeared him to teammates. Tired after practice and disheartened after yet another loss, the players would pile into John's creaking Camaro. Rolling through the streets of Schenectady, the car was ethnic, cultural, racial, diversity, and team unity on wheels. No single experience or season would close the social chasm between the haves and the have-nots, but an enduring and proactive compassion and sympathy were in the making. As Doug concludes, "He was brought up middle class, but he has the soul of lower class."

A search for a way to measure the success with which John tried to meet minority students and comprehend their hopes, struggles, and frustrations brings us back to the Senior Talent Show in the spring of 1968. Having already made appearances in the football and basketball team skits, John saved his most memorable contribution for the last part of the revue. He walked on stage as Tonto to his friend's The Masked Man. As his father recalls, "The Lone Ranger asked Tonto, 'Why are you always calling me "keemo sabe?" What's it mean?' Tonto answered, 'It means honky white man.' A lot of black kids in the audience thought it was great. I hadn't heard the word *honky* before."

Evidently, John had created enough good will and credibility among his black peers that he could show his appreciation for their point of view and in their language. The acceptance his classmates gave Sayles the high school senior would be continued by adult African Americans respecting his right to make a feature about a black alien in Harlem, *The Brother from Another Planet* (1984) and to film the movie in Harlem. Still later, after John graduated from Williams College, he would return there just once—to accept a special tribute from the Black Alumni Association of Williams College in recognition of his positive representation of the black community.

After his 1968 graduation, John Sayles never returned in person to Mont Pleasant High School. No reason is given except professional obligations and, of course, the closing of the school. Consciously and unconsciously, however, his revisits via his creative efforts have been frequent and profound. In various forums, he speaks of high school as the one remaining citadel of democracy, as the place where the future Wall Streeter and the floor waxer study math and participate in sports side by side. His lone autobiographical film, *Baby It's You* (1984), centers on high school and, not surprisingly, depicts the tension between a middle-class young woman and a young, blue-collar Italian male.

Of John's high school education and its impact, his father concludes, "He thrived in the mixed nature of Mont Pleasant High School's student body. He has a place in his heart for people who are struggling—the everyday guy." This high school experience in democratic living makes even more problematic his choice of higher education: Williams College in Williamstown, Massachusetts.

6

The Odd Duck of
the Green Room

I was in college for my purposes, not theirs.

JOHN SAYLES, 1981

WHEN SOMEONE AT WILLIAMS COLLEGE proposed not so long ago that
John Sayles come back to his alma mater and accept an honorary degree, he
declined, saying he already had one from Williams. Implied is the admission
that he did as little as possible to earn the real bachelor's degree he received in
1972. For four years he courted and got the gentleman's C for most of his
courses. As his high school career has shown, John was not keen on attending,
studying for, or staying awake during his classes. Higher education allowed
him to expand further those liberties he cultivated at the secondary level.
From matriculation to commencement, the collegiate experience symbolizes
the unique interaction of freedom and constraint that characterizes his formal
and informal education.

On the surface, for example, his was not the kind of high school profile to
send college recruiters scurrying to Schenectady, New York, looking for the

bright light of Mont Pleasant High. The late-night hours, the habitual sleeping in class, and knocking over a stop sign while driving comprise the kind of delinquency that usually lead to the principal's office as well as the police station—from which he was, in fact, freed on one occasion, thanks to his father's timely intervention. As brother Doug attests, however, the behavior of the Sayles boys was traditional for their era: no smoking, no drugs, no drinking. Two facets of their family life personify the demands and allowances that the Sayleses honored: church and college choice, and in John's case, the one helped govern the other.

In addition to being so well behaved that the other kids tended to exclude them from their raucous parties, Doug cites another complication. "We had the added factor of growing up Catholic. We went to church every Sunday of our lives. We were raised old-fashioned, not modern Catholics, wooden kneelers, the whole thing. John was an altar boy and loved it." The seeming religious orthodoxy, however, comes out of a theological dichotomy. Mary devoutly practices her faith, whereas Don is an atheist who nevertheless sees value in religious upbringing. As a young man, Don once considered entering the ministry and taught at Lutheran Sunday school. Strict church regulations chilled his piety, however, and he went his own way. "I tried to be supportive, not by setting a positive example but by not interfering with Mary's hopes for them in terms of religion. I felt it was good for them to have an all-out exposure to a religion and had confidence that in time each would work through it in his own way."

For John 1968 was that time, and selecting a college included a response to his churchgoing past. His parents helped him pick his school both passively and actively. During his decision process, they stepped aside almost entirely. The choice was his, the expense theirs. Even though John had won a scholarship that was good at any school in New York State, Don and Mary wanted him to go wherever he wished.

Initially reluctant to continue his education, but aware that he might be drafted for the Vietnam War, John sought guidance. His high school counselor told him to apply to Colgate University in Hamilton, New York, and to Williams College. Colgate was eliminated for two reasons: the school might want him to play serious football, and it had a religion course requirement for all students. John had already endured enough of both. Years later his mother would grow quietly upset when in *Sayles on Sayles* (1998), John, "with a little flippancy," described himself as a "Catholic atheist." In 1968, however, she respected her son's right to choose. John selected Williams.

■ ■ ■

Chartered in 1793 and situated amid the rolling hills of western Massachusetts, Williams College today looks like a picture-perfect campus, with its towering church steeple, grassy quads, and undergraduates garbed in Polo, Tommy Hilfiger, and Perry Ellis. After World War II, the college admitted its freshmen "with a new and significant degree of selectivity." Like many denominational schools, and with students like Sayles in mind, it also abandoned its compulsory religious exercises. All told, Williams College was a quiet, conservative campus, a preserve of classic liberal arts education.

The protests against the Vietnam War and racial discrimination that fomented riots on other campuses were few and relatively tame at Williams. In *The Progressive* (November 1991), Sayles said, "When the black students rallied and took over the administration building, the first thing the white president did was to make sure they had enough food." The wry humor of John's observation may stem from the contrast between his background and that of his peers. In his *Rolling Stone* essay (October 8, 1987), Samuel Freedman wrote, "Unlike many of his well-to-do Williams classmates, Sayles had childhood friends who had gone off to Vietnam willing and naïve. He spent less time with campus radicals 'who were locking up their physics professors' than with the Vista volunteers who lived in the community."

In many ways, however, this bucolic, all-male, high-achieving atmosphere suited the eighteen-year-old freshman just fine. "It was real pretty, and people seemed reasonably tolerant of each other," Sayles recalled in *American Film* (June 1991). "To me, it was like I never had food that good. Everybody was complaining, but I thought, 'Geez, it's like a country club.'" (The tolerance that Sayles observed has since led Williams to diversify its enrollment; today minorities comprise 25 percent of the student body.)

Sayles majored in psychology, but that choice was made by default. Williams had no drama department, and its English Department had a reading program that was too intense. Aside from a passing interest in case histories and films about the sex lives of animals, John saw psychology as the easiest way of ducking classes. Long before computers popularized it, Sayles dove into individualized learning, creating his own schedule and bypassing the curriculum wherever possible. He was, for example, still having bouts with insomnia that led to watching late-night movies on TV and missing any classes held before lunch. Today few professors at Williams remember Sayles the student. Dr. Andrew Criden is one who does. He taught psychology of personality in 1971 and possesses a still unclaimed Sayles course paper. Its C-plus grade reflects the author's cavalier attitude toward course requirements, as does Criden's recollection: "John was a good psychology student," he told me, "but needed to work at it." Sayles, then twenty-one years old and a senior, had other plans.

During John's four years in Williamstown (1968–72), he developed an abiding distaste for academia and ivory-towered academics. Literary criticism courses in particular incurred his ire. In the British *Monthly Film Bulletin* (January 1984), Sayles described his college literature courses as wasteful. "They had so little to do with people that they were exercises in semantics. They never talked about the characters and how they relate to you presently." Instead John chose to spend most of his class time in the ivy-covered Sawyer Library, where he rekindled his interest in reading. In alphabetical order by author, he began pulling books from the shelves, skipping a couple of letters so he could get to Mark Twain. Thus, while claiming that he majored in intramural sports and foreign films, Sayles actually was constructing his own "great books" program, sometimes reading twelve a week. Meanwhile, his grade point average remained just that, average.

Pragmatism ruled. In high school he had cultivated his skills as a test-taker and now regularly employed those tactics in last-minute cramming for his college exams. He offset the C grades with A's and B's in creative writing, where he submitted fiction by the pound. Fortunately, John sometimes found the right professor and the right course. Most notable were the film courses taught by Charles Thomas Samuels. This scholarly author opened Sayles's eyes to such internationally renowned directors as Akira Kurosawa, Federico Fellini, Ingmar Bergman, and François Truffaut, whose movies were making the campus circuit in classroom courses and at nightly film society screenings.

In the fall of 1970, when John was a junior, Williams for the first time admitted women to the student body. Among the thirty or so young adults breaking the gender barrier was Maggie Renzi, soon to become the professional associate and personal partner of John Sayles for life. This junior transfer from Barnard College certainly knew the campus well; her father, Ralph, had directed the Williams College News Bureau until 1968, when he opened Renzi's College Bookstore. As one of the founders of the Williamstown Theatre Festival, Ralph also helped introduce Maggie to the stage at the age of twelve when she played Helen Keller in the WTF's production of *The Miracle Worker*.

Now, back on this familiar turf, the diminutive Renzi met Caroline (Hall) Otis, also a transfer student, from Mills College in California. The two flaunted their "too cool for school" attitude and their disinterest in the preppies, the young men who heretofore had done their socializing on weekends at nearby women's colleges such as Smith and Mt. Holyoke. With the arrival of women at Williams, the campus males now had to face last night's date over morning coffee. This awkwardness would be captured in Sayles's third film, *Baby It's You* (1983). For the next two years, Maggie and Caroline would crew for and appear in the productions staged by the campus theater group, Cap and Bells.

■   ■   ■

In the programs from those Williams College plays of the early 1970s appear names that would soon become familiar to American theater and film audiences: Tony Award–winning playwright William Finn, television and film actors Gordon Clapp and David Strathairn, and a handful of others who later appeared in *Return of the Secaucus Seven*. Strathairn, who went on to star in several Sayles features, continually played leading roles in college. With just two months remaining in his senior year, though, he left Williams and never received his diploma. Backstage hearsay said David went to clown school in Florida, and it was true. Strathairn was not the only seeming eccentric that the observant Caroline and Maggie met lingering around the green room of the student theater.

Caroline (Hall) Otis spoke to me of the two of them singing and dancing in Bill Finn's campus musical *Rape* and of Maggie as "an actress with a lot of authority." Now a freelance writer, Otis was ambivalent about John Sayles. "Personally, he came across as an individualist, going his own way. He was like nobody else. Tall, lanky, he looked like he won what he was wearing, and he was always writing stuff down and had that penetrating gaze. He was such an odd duck." Despite his quirky behavior, Otis recognized that he was also a "great worker for the theater and an extraordinary actor."

As a junior, John played his first dramatic role as Candy, one of the elderly farmhands in an adaptation of John Steinbeck's novel *Of Mice and Men*. Sayles had, however, performed on other occasions. In family photos, John responds to the camera by pretending to be a skier in one shot and, in another, scowls back as a moody teenager who clearly does not want his introspection interrupted by a photo opportunity. Posturing was not John's only pre-college preparation for the stage. "Even as a child," his mother recalls for me, "he could imitate dialects, as he did when a waitress in Florida asked how he would like his eggs. Without a pause, John slipped into the dialect and said, "I'd like thim frad," and did not embarrass her.

The casting for the Cap and Bells production of *Of Mice and Men* fell to the show's director, Gordon Clapp, who cast John, launching a lengthy personal and professional relationship. Later Clapp preceded his friend in relocating to Hollywood and then encouraged him to follow. Starting in 1978, their roles would be reversed, with Sayles directing Clapp in the off-Broadway production of his own one-act play *New Hope for the Dead* (1981) and in two feature films, *Return of the Secaucus Seven* (1980) and *Eight Men Out* (1988). Television viewers would come to know the versatile Clapp in his role of Detective Gregory Medavoy on the weekly drama series *NYPD Blue* (1993–present).

When *Of Mice and Men* opened at the Williamstown Theatre in 1971, drama critic Ron Jacobs of the *Williams Record* applauded the staging, the leads, and the supporting actors. "John Sayles '72 and Paul Hannan '71 were excellent in their roles as Candy and Slim respectively. Sayles has mastered his Southern drawl; his passiveness and simplicity gave strength to his performance." John's stage debut was followed by appearances in *Steambath* and, as part of commencement week, a part in William Saroyan's *The Time of Your Life*. In the summers after college, he performed at the Eastern Playhouse in North Conway, New Hampshire, appearing, as he says, as "large brain-damaged people" in *Of Mice and Men* and *One Flew over the Cuckoo's Nest*.

Sayles's offhand summary of his Cap and Bells days as a "little acting and directing in my senior year" omits one other contribution, perhaps one he'd rather forget. In the fall of 1971, he wrote and directed the play for the annual Freshman Revue. A compendium of gangster pictures and the Roaring '20s, *My Piece of Pie* trotted out virtually every line Sayles learned via his nightly movie watching. In an unidentified newspaper clipping, one of the cast, Peter Metry, recalled, "John Sayles was known at school for his love of gangster type shows. He knew every corny gangster cliché from every bad movie. The play is a spoof on every George Raft, James Cagney, Humphrey Bogart movie ever made."

In the *Williams Record* (October 21, 1971), the college's theater critic (Charlie Riaben) found the show fun in spite of a script that was "inconsistent, self-indulgent and overlong." The critique worsened, "John Sayles script is dreadful. There is hardly an original line in it; it is derivative of cliché if that's possible." The only glimmer of hope for Sayles the writer lay in his lyrics, which were categorized as "clever and catchy, if a bit simplistic." On a copy of that column sent home to his mother, Sayles inscribed, "Rave review."

■   ■   ■

John typically spent his college summers back in Schenectady, and his arrival and early agenda paralleled those of thousands of students glad to be through with classes, yet not overjoyed at the prospect of returning home. With John's modulated sense of humor, Mary told me about greeting her son. "He'd call, and I'd pick him up at a restaurant nearby. He'd talk on the way home and that was about it." The brief recounting of the college year was followed, as his father says, "by a lot of sleeping."

For the first two summers, John lived at home and worked as an orderly at a nursing home. He spent weekends at the Sayles summer home. Built entirely by his father, the cozy two-story cabin sits in Northville, a New York resort community on Great Sacandara Lake, about an hour's drive northwest of Schenectady. From Easter to Thanksgiving weekend, it provided a haven for the parents and a recreation center for Doug and John and their friends. To the traditional basketball court, Don added a raft that each spring was anchored about twenty yards offshore, the perfect place for swimming and fishing. As John wrote *Writers Dreaming* (1993), the exercise sunk into his unconscious, only to surface later in his dreams and nightmares. He would see himself trapped underwater, struggling to free himself, as he had seen Tony Curtis do in *Houdini*, a 1953 movie about the famous escape artist.

In the daytime, John's summers allowed him to set aside the middle-class, college-boy milieu of Williamstown and get back to the blue-collar people he knew from high school and summer jobs. At seventeen, he had already met American workers face-to-face during one stint at a plastic factory in a job that was, according to his brother Doug, like slave labor. Despite having to dodge the flames and sparks flying from the furnace, John stayed on the job. That was part of his code. "If John started a job," his mother says, "he'd finish it." Still, the fact remains that he was doing dangerous work on a daily basis.

Although jobs and recreation might weave their way into Sayles's fiction and films, the most easily traceable allusions in his movies are to his vacation travels. In 1971, home after his junior year at Williams, he announced, "I'm going to see the country." A professor had told him that if he wanted to write, he had to see the world and learn by experience. John decided to take his advice to heart.

His parents were scared to death about his safety. At the same time, both realized that their younger son's decisions were sometimes nonnegotiable, and that in this case he was not about to change his mind. Sayles set out on an odyssey that took him first down the Atlantic coast, then westward to California and home again—all within a three-month period.

The unpredictable luck of hitchhiking would call on the resolute part of John's character. Hitting the highway, the twenty-one-year-old Sayles fashioned a flexible image of himself with something to please different drivers. As he told the *New York Times* (August 28, 1988), "My hair was kind of medium length, and I carried a huge duffel bag my father brought back from World War II. So I got a lot of rides from hippies and a lot of rides from servicemen." Whether in a VW bug or a Chevy or an eighteen-wheeler, Sayles was practicing art forms learned in theater. For the trip he adopted an axiom that he later employed in his picture *Lone Star* (1996): "You live in a place, you should know something about it."

While occupying space in the driver's world, John patiently listened to the stories told by his highway hosts. After getting a feel for their interest and attitudes, he would then recount an experience or create a story for his companion, slanting it and lacing it with whatever exaggerations might appeal to the listener's disposition. About that kind of improvisation he told *Sight and Sound* (September 1993), "It forces you to think about the point of view so when you write different characters, they don't talk in the same way or about the same things."

Several of those tales and dialects would eventually find their way into his short stories and movies. Some of the former, such as "Golden State," which appeared in *Atlantic Monthly* (June 1977), he wrote from memory. The story reads like an unfiltered recounting of experience. In "I-80 Nebraska, m.490-m.205," also published in *Atlantic Monthly* (May 1975), Sayles takes his experience of riding with truckers and heightens it into an almost gothic horror tale. While that story appeared in print within four years of his West Coast odyssey, other tales would take longer to be distilled by his imaginative powers. It was while riding through West Virginia, for example, that he first heard about the striking coal miners of the 1920s. Those events and their dramatic possibilities he stored in his mind, using them sparingly in his novel *Union Dues* (1977), and then developing them further as part of the plot for his fourth film, 1987's *Matewan*.

■　　　■　　　■

Back on campus for his senior year, John was soon spinning more fanciful stuff. The script for *My Piece of Pie* displayed his ability to parody forms, imitate dialects and serve up an evening entertainment on stage. For Williams College's literary magazine, J. T. Sayles wrote a short piece, "Casey on the Slopes," about a student struggling to complete a poetry assignment for his creative writing course.

The fun found in John's comic play and poetic parody captures a key change in disposition that transpired primarily during his college years. After a season of freshman football, he had shifted his recreation from sports to writing, with consequent rewards he never felt in playing sports. In "Making of a Writer," a 1981 article for the *New York Times*, Sayles would recall, "I was writing for recreation anyway, and I seemed to have some aptitude for it. I had been a jock all through junior and senior high but never a natural. The times when I would break through the center of a game and make things happen or surprise myself were few and far between. In writing, I got that kind of payoff more often.

One piece, "This Place," was composed as a tribute to his alma mater and is found on the last page of the 1972 Williams College yearbook. The wry quality of the lone paragraph reflects Sayles's view of the responsibility of the student in the reach for higher education and his own "odd duck" response to that opportunity.

> This Place. Often you would hear someone saying This Place is getting on my nerves or This Place sucks or I got to get out of This Place. The road was always there, the door always open; few left. Or you would hear them saying This Place does nothing for me or, This Place is giving nothing to me or They haven't taught me anything at This Place. There were always things available to be taken, the door was always open; few entered. This Place never locked anybody in or out once they got here; that is more than you can say about a lot of places. John Sayles '72.

After college graduation, however, John needed a job. Twenty-seven years after his own graduation, Doug told me about his postcollege experience:

"We were privileged kids; our parents paid cash to put John through Williams, me through Dartmouth simultaneously. Huge costs. We ended up at really expensive schools, then both of us ended up unprivileged on the street, hoping we wouldn't get drafted." After his own inauspicious start, Doug added a Master of Business Administration degree from SUNY–Albany and turned to systems analysis and environmental control, which he now helps regulate from his office in Tampa, Florida. Meanwhile, John, in moving from Williamstown to Albany, then to Atlanta and on to Boston, would start his creative adult life in a cold-water flat on Maverick Street.

7

The Real World
and the Writer

John Sayles does not just ask that disbelief be
willingly suspended, he wants it lynched.

TIME MAGAZINE REVIEW OF

PRIDE OF THE BIMBOS (1975)

IN ITS POSTCOMMENCEMENT DAYS, the class of 1972 faced the threat of the military draft for service in Vietnam as well as a workplace with twin sources of trouble. The United States was feeling the pinch of an economy drained by the cost of supporting an ever-escalating war while also funding the domestic programs of President Lyndon Johnson's War on Poverty campaign. For white male college graduates especially, the job market was tight. Under the new affirmative action and equal opportunity laws, they faced increasing competition for entry-level positions as industry and management hastened to open their doors to women and minorities. Many felt the squeeze, and Williams College alumni were no exception.

Surrounded by the war and recession climate, John Sayles gave the description "odd duck" another spin. Lifelong physical impairments to his back and a perforated eardrum spared him from military service in a war he opposed. A personal epiphany then directed him away from plunging into the same workplace that was proving so unreceptive to his classmates.

Sayles had spent the last two years of college writing scripts, comic pieces for the literary magazine, and even a novel, which he described as "more like a survey course." Through those creative experiences, it now occurred to him that writing could provide both pleasure and a paycheck. That pleasant realization also exempted him from the lines at the Williams career placement office. A corporate job commitment would pull him away from creative writing; a temporary job, on the other hand, would allow him to mix temp work with his chosen career in front of a typewriter.

With that agenda set, John returned to the Albany, New York, area in 1972 and to the positions he once held there. Recounting his postgraduate adjustment, Sayles told the *Progressive* (November 1991), "When I got out of college, it was a bad time to get a job. I ended up working in nursing homes and factories because that was something I had done before. . . . I worked as an orderly because it definitely wasn't a career decision." His employment at the University Heights Nursing Home in Albany satisfied his interest in people and his particular concern for the elderly and poor who comprised the majority of residents. Occasional assignments in the physical therapy department proved to be the most fulfilling task of all.

■ ■ ■

Albany, the capital of New York State, lies about fifty miles west of Williamstown and light years away from Williams College. Like Schenectady and Troy, its partners in the Tri-City region, Albany in the early 1970s was dealing with a full slate of social and economic problems. With outside help, the city emerged far healthier than its two neighbors. Under the aegis of Republican governor Nelson Rockefeller, the state played a leading role in the Albany renaissance, mainly by constructing the Empire State Plaza. Home to the state government, the sprawling complex would comprise a vast, two-block-long complex surrounded by multiple high-rise office buildings.

John Sayles came to Albany in the midst of this boom and settled right on the edge of the construction site. He was just in time to see the impact of these corporate changes on the marginal citizens. Suddenly uprooted from their homes, they sought low-cost housing where they could find it, and John rented right along with this mix of racial and ethnic minorities and the displaced elderly. After four years at Williams, he was back with the average citizens, the ones who would populate his short stories, novels, and films.

John also was resuming the research started in his hitchhiking days. Given his memory for dialog and acting skills, it is not hard to imagine the orderly/writer finding the nursing home hallways filled with the inspiration for the cantankerous voices of his story "The Anarchists Convention" (1979) and the testiness of the paraplegic in his later film *Passion Fish* (1992). Likewise Albany provided a model for city and state bureaucracies.

Sayles was poised to absorb and transcribe the social and political events around him that were building—literally—dynasties of money and power on top of burned-out housing projects. Even though his nursing home job paid little, his financial needs were modest. As he said a short time later, "I can certainly live on $2,500 a year or even two years." To a blue-collar guy who didn't party, saw cars strictly as transportation, and continued to wear the clothes "he had won," the life and salary of an orderly suited him. This was not a job he took home; therefore, the nonworkaholic but always-writing author had the time for creating and stockpiling the stories that would soon go on sale.

In light of the effective balance he established between the hospital job and his writing, his sudden move from Albany to Atlanta, Georgia, in 1973 seems hard to understand, especially since his new job as day laborer provided less security and pay. Perhaps the relocation was a response to his hitchhiking wanderlust and the lure of warmer weather. While college might have kept him in the north, John Sayles has had a long-term aversion to warm, heavy clothing. A review of his films shows that aside from a few glaciers in *Limbo* (1999), the settings of his movies, though often brutally harsh, are never cold. With another winter approaching in Albany, maybe he felt he could escape to sunnier Georgia.

Meanwhile, the former Cap and Bells players were regrouping in Boston as what Maggie Renzi calls the Haines Street Bunch. By 1974 Sayles was out of Atlanta and back in their midst. The most significant person in this reunion was Maggie Renzi. Whatever her motive for moving to East Boston, it was not John Sayles. The two had barely known each other in college. As Maggie says, "We didn't have scenes together, but we had curtain calls together, and then we had mutual friends."

Maggie's father told me about the start of her relationship with Sayles. "At Williams, I knew John off and on between 1968 and '72, but Maggie and he weren't a number until '73. They went to Boston for a year and lived in a commune. We didn't approve of their going off unmarried, but time has proved them right. It's nice to have a 'son-in-love,' and let's keep that straight. Not son-in-law, son-in-love." Evidently, Maggie and John connected through mutual friends from college. One of them, Caroline (Hall) Otis, a companion of Maggie's, remembers the impact of that Sayles-Renzi romance: "However that happened, when they connected, it was fast and hard, and they never looked back."

In the Boston commune, Sayles continued his writing and was now randomly submitting his short stories to magazines and journals. Eventually he would devise a hierarchy of potential publishers to which he sent his manuscripts. He would start at the top of the list and work his way down. While waiting for acceptances, he was lugging around slabs of salami and making sausages at his job in an Italian sausage factory. He had joined the Amalgamated Butcher Workers and Meat Packers of North America and was paid the union's minimum wage. The hourly pay seems paltry today, but back then $4.40 was the best salary he'd ever earned.

The money and the working conditions also were educating him about the power of unions in controlling foremen and restricting hours. He would return to the union theme in *Matewan* (1987) and *City of Hope* (1991). Maggie was finding film fodder teaching hygiene to the wayward girls of East Boston. Together, the couple's wages paid for the apartment they moved to on Maverick Street. Just off the runways of Logan International Airport, the flat provided its own kind of melodrama. Furious at the landlord, one renter in the building spitefully turned on the water and stomped out of the house, leaving the open faucets to flood her place and, soon thereafter, Sayles and Renzi's apartment downstairs. On the way out the door, the disgruntled tenant impulsively snatched an envelope from Sayles's mailbox. In it was Don Sayles's annual Christmas present to his son, a check for $100.

■   ■   ■

Having graduated from Dartmouth in 1971, John's brother, Doug, had gone through his own period of postcollege drifting. By 1975, however, he had settled into a career as a financial analyst in Albany. He paid a visit to Boston to remind his brother about the future. "I remember telling him, 'Isn't it time to start thinking about something? You have an academic background. You have the advantage.' He wasn't having any of that get-a-career stuff." As Doug told me at an Albany coffee shop in 1998, "If a few breaks had not happened for John, he was so close to the edge. He would have written and lived that type of existence his whole life."

Shortly after Doug's departure, his brother's short story "I-80 Nebraska, m.490-m.205" won the 1975 O. Henry Award for Best Short Story. That honor, however, was not the fulcrum that lifted Sayles out of his writer's quagmire. Prior to submitting the story, two crucial breaks came his way. Because he could not make an idea he had into a film, he had turned it into a story, leaving open the possibility of lensing it later. He mailed his story "Men" to *Atlantic* magazine, where it found its way to the desk of Peggy Yntema at Atlantic Monthly Press. An editor whose track record would chill any novice writer, she had accepted only one "first story" in three years. In *Sayles on Sayles,* John said, "I got a call from Atlantic Press, and they said, "We have your novella, we're really interested, and we'd like you to meet an editor." Atlantic wanted to publish the work as a novella, and he quickly agreed.

Then came Sayles's second break. The sausage factory fired him. The layoff took a huge bite out of his income, reducing it from $176 a week to the $32 that, for seven months, he received as unemployment compensation. Perforce a professional writer, he now went at the "Men" revision without interruption, save for the conferences with Yntema. With a call for a stronger plot and a few clarifying questions about character or flow, she guided Sayles from amateur to the ranks of professional writer and turned the "short book" into *Pride of the Bimbos.*

With the novella now ready for publication, Atlantic Monthly Press gave the author his first check, a $2,500 advance on royalties. In the eyes of his father, that first publication in 1975 was the defining moment in John's career. Of the experience of opening the carton with ten copies of *Pride of the Bimbos* inside, Sayles wrote in the *New York Times* (September 6, 1981), "I think I felt like Samuel Colt must have when he saw all those .45s coming out of the factory. Something I'd made was being mass-produced, and if that isn't the American dream, I don't know what is."

Told from the point of view of Denzel Ray, the son of a washed-up minor leaguer, the novel follows the Brooklyn Bimbos on their barnstorming tour of the South. The baseball team's comic antics in drag on the diamond make them all the more compulsive about proving their masculinity everywhere else. Their travels from town to town allow the introduction of a large cast of characters and parallel actions, a narrative pattern that Sayles subsequently would give more unity than he did here.

Critics applauded *Bimbos.* The *Washington Post* (August 24, 1975) said the book was written with "wit, style, irony and thematic depth." In the *New York Times* (April 17, 1983), Steve Lawson cited another critic: "Henry Crews, a writer well versed in American grotesque [who] hailed *Bimbo* as 'a strong, sad, funny book which marks the beginning of what will surely be a remarkable career.' "

John's stories were now being solicited by the same magazines that earlier had spurned them. *The Atlantic Monthly* was running a series called "*Atlantic First,*" highlighting novice short-story writers. Between 1975 and 1979, they published "I-80 Nebraska, m.490-m.205"—a study of bored truck drivers talking on their c-bands to stay awake—and followed it with four more stories, some of them later republished in various anthologies.

In *The Nation,* Alexander Stille wrote that Sayles had "a good ear for the resourcefulness of people who make difficult situations tolerable by whistling in the dark, or making wisecracks." At twenty-five years of age, Sayles was being compared to some of the country's best writers, including John Dos Passos, Ernest Hemingway, John Steinbeck, and William Faulkner. Sayles admits the influence of this pantheon, but credits Nelson Algren and his novel *Somebody in Boots* (1935) for inspiring his writing about ordinary people. John had come across that novel when he was thirteen years old. As he told the *New York Times* (August 5, 1991), "Algren wrote from neck-deep in the trash of American culture [which was] the only place I was likely to be."

Again published by his previous publisher, now Atlantic–Little, Brown, Sayles's first full-length novel, *Union Dues* (1977), dramatizes the conflicts between the two generations. Hunter McNabb, a West Virginia miner, joins his fellow workers in fending off both management and union and fighting for the wages that will support him and his family. Meanwhile, his son Hobie runs off to a Boston commune trying to track down his older brother, Dar, a Vietnam War veteran and apparent victim of post-traumatic stress syndrome. The tension between generations and the 1930s-type struggle among management, unions, and workers are played out as Hunter pursues his son and Hobie witnesses the futile rallies and actions of the pseudorevolutionaries of the commune. Like the Algren stories and the proletariat novels of the 1930s, *Union Dues* ends on a grim note.

Critics almost unanimously praised the sprawling 385-page novel for its depiction of working-class life in the American landscape of the 1960s. *The Nation* saw the book's real strength as its "portrayal of the working class," and *Union Dues* as "the best book of its kind since Harvey Swados's *On the Line* [1957]." Even Sayles's excessive use of dialects and overly protracted scenes, as in the commune, were seen by the *New York Times* (August 4, 1977) as "problems that spring from a surfeit of talent which . . . is distinguished by wit, inventiveness, and profound involvement with character."

Prophetically, as it would turn out, *Esquire* was labeling Sayles "the literary equivalent of Bruce Springsteen, inventing lives circumscribed by hard choices." (Sayles and Springsteen would later team for various projects.) In 1977, *Union Dues* was the only novel nominated for both the National Book Award and the National Book Critics Circle Award. It won neither, but it did earn the author $10,000.

Sayles was now eager to try scriptwriting and moviemaking. Even within *Union Dues,* which he saw as a potential script, he had included ingredients that would be found in his fourth film, *Matewan.* John Sterling had negotiated his contract with Atlantic–Little, Brown and continued representing his literary works. Sayles looked for another agent, one with film industry connections. He eventually found Maggie Fields in Los Angeles. The twenty-seven-year-old Sayles gave her two tasks: represent *Union Dues* as a movie property, and represent him as a screenwriter.

8

Writer for Hire:
The Roger Corman Years

Sir, it's the piranha. They're eating the guests.

PIRANHA (1978)

BY 1977 JOHN SAYLES HAD his agents in place, one handling the sale of his literary materials, the other pushing his two novels as potential movies and their author as a new scriptwriter. Sayles himself was pursuing his own agenda. Even before he and Maggie left Boston for the West Coast in 1977, John was bending his efforts toward making his own film based on his own ideas. Before he had written a script or been on a sound stage, he was starting to give shape to what would become *Return of the Secaucus Seven*.

The pre-California era had found John often representing himself. As Maggie told the *San Francisco Chronicle* (March 8, 1998), "My job was to keep making cups of tea so that John and the people he was talking to about the great idea he had for a movie would keep on talking. . . . When we left for California, I started making lists [of film production needs] on punched paper because nobody knew anything about making movies. This was before

Sundance—before it was chic to make an independent film." Without labeling her job, Maggie was already handling some of the production chores. On their way to Santa Barbara, the two stopped in Minneapolis, to visit Maggie's now-married college friend Caroline (Hall) Otis. In the midst of recalling the old days on stage together, Maggie and John asked her to join them as part of the cast for a movie they wanted to make. Because of her two small children, Otis declined the offer.

For John the move to California had a double motivation: to become a screenwriter and to earn money to fund the making of his first movie. Therein lay the practical economy of Sayles's early movie career. As a novelist, he had earned enough to get by in East Boston, and the $10,000 he made on *Union Dues* was more than he ever hoped to make from writing fiction. Now what he needed was a bigger bankroll to support a film production, and more money could be acquired faster by writing scripts. About leaving books and going into the entertainment business, Sayles told *The Progressive* (November 1991), "I was not interested in getting a big house. All I was interested in was, 'I think it would be really great to make a movie.' "

Through his literary agents, Sayles had tried to spark interest in his writing for the big screen. The Hollywood agency Robinson, Weintraub, Gross and Associates first wanted to see a sample. In a little over two months, Sayles created a script based on Eliot Asinof's book *Eight Men Out* (1963) and sent it off. Because the rights to Asinof's baseball history book were unavailable, the script was rejected out of hand, but the agency agreed to represent Sayles provided he move to Los Angeles. To that end, he first looked at San Luis Obispo (150 miles north of L.A.), but soon he and Maggie found better housing in an unfashionable part of Santa Barbara, still eighty miles from the Hollywood studios where he soon would be working.

■   ■   ■

Two months after Sayles's arrival, his agent told him that Roger Corman, head of New World Pictures, needed a writer to redo the script for *Piranha*. From his penthouse overlooking Sunset Boulevard, the bright, sober Corman had been carving out a highly profitable film production niche: low-budget exploitation movies. For these nonunion, New World genre films, he had all but perfected the art of attracting cheap but gifted talent.

This movie company without a studio couldn't afford the overhead of keeping a stable of stars, writers, or directors under contract. Instead, New World relied on a cost-effective series of young talent, caught by Corman before they made their industry mark. Martin Scorsese, Robert Towne, Francis Ford Coppola, James Cameron, Gale Anne Hurd, Jonathan Demme, Barbara Boyle, Jack Nicholson, Dennis Hopper, Peter Fonda, and Ron Howard all cut their teeth producing, writing, directing, and editing at New World.

Talent like theirs was turned loose with neither the time nor the money to make good pictures, yet somehow they did. Their ability to innovate despite budget limitations helped account for the phenomenal success of this schlock film company that, six years later in 1983, Corman would sell for more than $16.5 million.

In recruiting for the *Piranha* script revision, Corman set down one typical stipulation: no Writers Guild members need apply. Sayles fit the bill— nonguild, talented, and hungry for experience. For Sayles, the $10,000 for five weeks of work opened the door to screenwriting and to making his own movie.

The initial contract between the frugal studio and the new writer put both sides on course for three scripted films and prepped Sayles for a lifelong "bread" job as screenwriter and script doctor. His fame had preceded him, thanks to Frances Doel. The first reader and script supervisor for New World, she was a graduate of England's Oxford University. Doel had already been reading Sayles's published work and saw his potential for screenplay writing. As she told me, "It wasn't that I thought that any one story or novel would make a great movie. It was, 'If only I could get characters as convincing, believable, and interesting as these into the films we're making.'" She had then convinced Corman that Sayles was right for revising the *Piranha* script. In a subsequent phone call, Corman related to me how signing Sayles for *Piranha* blessed both parties. "I was getting talent for less money than an established writer would want. And it was good for him because he was learning the job and becoming established."

From the start, the *Piranha* script sessions included Corman, Doel, producer Jon Davison, director Joe Dante, and Sayles. To this day John the writer still sees those meetings as exemplary for shaping a screenplay. In contrast to drafting screenplays for the major studios, where projects frequently stalled and fell apart, writing for New World meant that the script actually would get shot.

The first New World story conferences lasted barely twenty minutes, and basic agreements were few. As would be the case for the trio of films that Sayles worked on, the initial story idea belonged to Corman. For *Piranha,* he wanted a picture with a killer fish escaping into North American waters, followed by scary action in the manner of *Jaws* (1975). Once the tone was set and the monsters in place, the writer could take the story line in almost any direction. In *The New Hollywood* (1992), Sayles described the objectives. "You can come up with any story, any location, so long as you fulfill what was agreed upon: keep the fish in the country and keep it fun." One key to keeping the movie fun was to learn the difference between production value and cost, or simply how much bang you could get for the fewest dollars (or, at New World, dimes). Corman kept the production rules simple: "Don't shoot a day or a dollar over budget. Shoot it under and I'll be happier."

By policy, the studio also invited its writers to take liberties with the genre at hand, adding lighter touches and social commentary—even to the horror films. John responded by weaving film parodies and political satire into the thriller fabric. With the rewrite in progress, the subsequent script sessions turned on very specific notes from Corman and Doel, devoted mostly to pacing. As Sayles told a 1985 American Film Institute seminar in Los Angeles, "It would be like, 'On page 58 we feel that this is too early to have another piranha attack. Can you delay it five pages? We feel the audience needs a rest period.'" At New World, the writer was responding to one voice—Corman's—as opposed to the many diverging voices and demands found at the major studios. The clarity of direction from the top eased Sayles's anxiety, as did his awareness that these schlock entries probably would never be reviewed nor the screenwriter much noted by anyone, including the major studios.

The year with Corman taught Sayles how to structure a script to fit the needs of the genre (horror, gangster, and science fiction) and how to scare, relieve, and scare the audience again. Especially critical for the future independent filmmaker would be the lessons in the economics of movie production. Letting a line of dialogue stand in for the action, cutting an extraneous scene, and adapting to last-minute budget cuts were filmmaking realities first learned at New World.

For his part, Sayles found several ways to keep his mentor happy. First, he could write almost anywhere and with incredible speed. According to John, "They'd say, OK, we want a movie about piranhas. People get eaten, and either the piranhas get away or they kill them all. I'm just lucky I can write anywhere. I wrote my first novels in bus stations and on people's floors." Second, there was no writer's block. To the contrary, John could barely keep track of his ideas and would interrupt his typing to jot down notes for future scenes. Third, what he submitted went beyond all of Doel's expectations. Instead of standard film treatments and outlines, Sayles turned in full-blown drafts. According to Doel, "He didn't mind that we treated the draft like a treatment and objected to it and threw out half of it."

The Corman-Sayles story sessions coincided with the changing audience demographics and films fads. By the 1970s almost half the population was between twelve and thirty years old, and that group accounted for 75 percent of the box office. To satisfy the demands of that audience, mainstream Hollywood went back to its future, resurrecting the genre film of the 1950s that Corman had never left. Some of those producers took New World's low road, hoping to duplicate the youth cult phenomenon of *Easy Rider* (1969), a $400,000 project that Dennis Hopper and Peter Fonda, two Corman disciples, had turned into a $40 million movie miracle.

By the mid-1970s, Steven Spielberg and George Lucas charted the high-budget approach with summertime action epics: *Jaws* and *Star Wars* (1977). As Corman told me: "The plot of *Jaws* was very similar to the plot of the first film I ever made, *Monster from the Ocean Floor* [1954], and they were spending more and more, and making the movies that were bigger and, frankly I admit, better.

I thought they were putting a nail in my coffin. We couldn't afford the production values and special effects they had." The impact of those big-budget
movies spread across the industry, raising the typical cost of production five to
ten times what it was in the 1960s.

New World's budgets started to creep upward. Where once Corman
might have spent between $125,000 and $200,000 on a film like *Piranha,* he
now anticipated a cost of about three times that figure. With the majors now
stealing his ideas and invading his marketplace, Corman responded by investing in more production values and in upmarket stars for his films. For that reason, New World teamed with one of the major studios, United Artists, which
put up half the budget for *Piranha* in exchange for overseas distribution rights.
The new money would help make the movie marketable for the o-zones
(drive-ins) and acceptable for television, which also was demanding enhanced
production values. Likewise, the *Piranha* cast went upscale, including names
familiar to horror film and television audiences: Kevin McCarthy, Bradford
Dillman, Barbara Steele, Keenan Wynn, and Heather Menzies.

None of these early lessons about film financing was lost on Sayles. As a
writer, he also was refining his sense of tone, structure, audience, and pacing.
In the early drafts of the *Piranha* script, John was letting his anti-Vietnam politics override the scary, fun movie that Corman wanted. "Roger was not happy
with the tone," Doel says. Corman reminded the writer about including a little comedy in even the darkest script. It was a lesson that the earnest author
heeded at the time but seemed to forget over the years when serious themes
made for sometimes brooding films.

Throughout 1978, Sayles was proving himself to be a coachable and reli-
able writer. As Doel recalls, "He never objected. He listened to what we
wanted and then found the best way to deliver it." What Sayles learned to
deliver included well-paced shocks. Initially, Corman supplied the *Piranha* plot
with two key aquatic ideas and images: the voracious fish and the crowded
beach. Then he wanted a piranha attack every fifteen minutes, a few laughs, a
little nudity, and some liberal-leaning social commentary.

Sayles plotted the script around three central images: a river, a dam, and a
beach, drawings of which hung on his office wall. The constant was the deadly

piranhas, the result of scientific experimentation conducted to make them more monstrous so they could be released into enemy waters in Vietnam. With the war over, the fish were being contained at a supposedly secured army base pool while vacationers frolicked on the nearby beach. Sayles's script needed to get both groups into the river and the fish down to a dam, then to the beach. Just after the film opens, the scientist who helped create the killer fish learns of their escape, and a reporter pursuing that story remembers that his daughter and hundreds of other innocent people are at the beach. The chase is on and doesn't end until scores of people, including children, get chewed up. At last the piranha are driven off for good—or so the scientists say, but with two of the fish swimming off into the ocean, a sequel seems (and unfortunately was) inevitable.

■   ■   ■

Sayles looks at the monster genre as a machine that had to be fed and on the audience as people wanting a roller-coaster ride "taken up really high before you bring them down." In meeting these needs, John says that his drafts included specific directions for the shots. He elaborated for *The Journal* (July 1996): "Because the director had not been picked, I wrote it so a robot could direct it. Basically every shot of the movie was there." Those details, Sayles believed, also would ensure that anybody could act in the movie. In short, he had made the script director- and actor-proof. Joe Dante, however, told me he was hired to direct *before* Sayles wrote the script, and he has no memory of such directing and editing details in the script. In actuality, while Corman, Sayles, and Dante each stake a claim for having had creative control, *Piranha,* like most films, evolved out of compromises and collaboration, in which they all played active roles.

Joe Dante (b. 1946) came out of Corman's movie trailer–editing depart-ment, and he was eager to take on the directing and editing of features. He told me, "After making $50 a week, $8,000 was manna." With Allan Arkush, he had just co-directed *Hollywood Boulevard* (1976), but *Piranha* was his first solo job. Having developed various mechanical piranhas realistic enough to satisfy Corman's standards, Dante then faced the daunting challenge of shooting the picture in twenty-two days.

The director took extra insurance with him on location to San Marcos, Texas. He designated Sayles for a cameo role in the film—at no extra cost. For the first time, John would do final rewrites on location, a habit he soon adopted for his own productions. As Dante recalls, much of the rewriting focused on the climactic amusement park sequence. Shot at San Marcos's Aquamarina Springs Water Park, the scenes highlighted the promotional speech—a.k.a. lies—of the park's owner (Dick Miller) and another cameo, this one by *Piranha*'s porcine star, Ralph the Swimming Pig. These were the preamble to the gory attack scenes. John also had the on-site advantage of writing the characters for talented actors. In particular, he revised and embellished the drunken reporter/father role played by veteran Bradford Dillman.

In working with the actors and elaborating certain scenes, the fledgling movie writer was endearing himself to the director and to the creative forces at New World. Doel's evaluation explains why the studio was anxious to rehire him. "You knew that John would return again and again to work with actors on a project. He did create a real feeling of communal enjoyment, effort, and participation. That was a great experience." As Dante recalls, what Sayles learned from the *Piranha* set were lessons in "how not to make a movie."

After the shoot ended, Dante lived in the editing room trying to cobble the film pieces into a coherent feature. He now says, "I thought the picture would never work, but I did show John a rough cut. What he expected to see was his script on screen; what he saw was an editing juggling act that left him horrified and dazed. He looked appalled at the way things had been moved around, but he just didn't say anything." Later Sayles would acknowledge his innocence and learn to live with the fate that awaits a script at the hands of the director and editor. Both he and Dante had earned their stripes in *Piranha*. Like so many apprentices of Corman, they were now ripe for plucking by other Hollywood producers.

■   ■   ■

As evidenced by the score of imitations it spawned, *Jaws* had an enormous impact on the film industry, and *Piranha* made no effort to conceal its debt to that picture. It also effectively spoofed *Jaws* as well as the whole monster/horror genre. Young and irreverent, the writer and director tailored the film to an audience that was hip and self-aware. *Variety* (August 9, 1978) also saw a departure from traditional Hollywood sentimentality. "Not only is the requisite slew of cameo performers dispatched quickly (Keenan Wynn, Kevin McCarthy, Bruce Gordon), but an entire camp of school children and a holiday crowd at a lakeside resort get chomped. This is one film where the fish win."

Released in late 1978, the R-rated *Piranha* made its own mark at the box office. Produced for $600,000, it proved enormously popular in this country and abroad. United Artists ran an all-out promotional campaign that helped the thriller earn nearly $14 million worldwide. In some countries where the voracious fish are found, the movie even outgrossed *Jaws*.

In 1981 James Cameron would make his directorial debut with *Piranha II: The Spawning*, a "sequel." Leonard Maltin, in his annual *Movie & Video Guide*, describes it as a "silly horror film set in a Club Med-type resort where human mating rituals are interrupted by the spawning ritual of mutated flying fish (grunions) which are oversized deadly killers." In 1995 Corman himself produced a remake of the 1978 original for the Showtime cable network. Also titled *Piranha*, it featured piranha that could fly! However, lacking the tongue-in-cheek humor and the able cast of the first feature, this latest entry faltered.

Twenty years after the original, a remake of *Piranha* was in the works for Fox Family Films. By way of preview, producer Bo Zenga told the *Hollywood Reporter* (December 7, 1997), "We took the kids from *Scream*, we put them in *The River Wild*, and we surrounded them with piranha." The film has not yet been released.

With his movie successfully launched at the end of 1978, Dante left New World to pursue a directing career. In the not-very-distant future, he and Sayles would reunite to create more terror for their youthful audience. For now, John signed on for two more features at New World.

9

Writer for Hire: Theater, Film, Television, and Print

If the test audience doesn't like the way the Civil War came out,
maybe the studio will release another version for Alabama.

JOHN SAYLES, 1995

BETWEEN 1977 AND 1982, John Sayles created a body of writing that is staggering in its range, diversity, and volume. The works vary from a collection of short stories to two off-off-Broadway plays, more than a dozen film and television scripts (produced and not), and a magazine article about the 1980 Republican National Convention.

At New World, in addition to learning screenwriting on the job, Sayles was studying the opportunities then available for making his own movies. He recognized that writing low-budget genre movies was not one of the roads leading to his goal of directing. (Although Roger Corman would eventually offer John a job directing a horror film, Sayles had no interest in the investment of his talents for a genre piece.) Eliminating those other options, he deposited the $10,000 check for the *Piranha* script. For him that "easy" money pointed the way to filmmaking. He was determined to keep writing for dollars. His next two scripts for New World provided the bulk of the $40,000 for shooting *Return of the Secaucus Seven;* writing other film and television scripts plus a new book would support the editing and distribution phases of that film.

In retrospect, Sayles now takes a casual, fairly flippant view toward the staggering workload of this period. For interviews, he neatly segments his jobs into writing scripts at the studio while completing personal screenplays and other projects at home in Santa Barbara. In practice, the projects were constantly overlapping each other. In 1980, for example, he was simultaneously developing two scripts (1980's *Alligator* and 1981's *The Howling*), not at the studio or at home but in a seedy Hollywood motel on Santa Monica Boulevard. In addition to changing venues and shifting between the two screenplays, Sayles was finalizing a short-story collection and exploring other writing formats, stage and television plays and journalism among them.

■   ■   ■

With *Piranha* in the can and a raise in salary, Sayles set to work on the script for New World's *The Lady in Red* (1979). It was a film first test-marketed as *Dillinger's Mistress* and later retitled *Guns, Sins and Bathtub Gin.* The film originated as a continuation of the studio's gangster-biography cycle, with this installment focusing on the famed woman who betrayed Chicago gangster John Dillinger to the police. Sayles convinced Roger Corman to let him take the story line beyond genre boundaries. His screenplay would describe a woman who falls out of the mainstream and into the crime community of the 1930s. In a 1993 *Drama-Logue* interview, John recalled that change in emphasis. "It became a very personal movie to the point where I think I seduced New World Pictures into making a movie that was much classier than they really needed to make or wanted to make."

To avoid past script formula treatment, Sayles turned to the Chicago Historical Society records, especially to its documents about the working people. He emerged with a screenplay supported with sociological insights into the Roaring Twenties and the Depression era. On-screen telling details appear, especially in the rendering of the dressmaking factory where women are abused by the boss, his goons, and sometimes by each other. Tracing the downfall of the hero, Polly Franklin (Pamela Sue Martin), and her relationship with Dillinger (Robert Conrad), the plot leads to a tour of Prohibition/Depression institutions and locales, from dance hall to bordello to prison. Laced with an array of authentic details, each setting provides a variation on the theme of women being economically, physically, and emotionally exploited.

With the screenplay in place and the film ready to roll, Corman suddenly reverted to the studio's old shoestring methodology and a taut shooting schedule. Budget cuts just prior to production were standard operating procedure at New World. The sudden cuts to *The Lady in Red,* however, left first-time director Lewis Teague with a huge fiscal problem, and he turned to Sayles as the source of and solution for his predicament.

As Sayles recalled for *Sight and Sound* (September 1993), Teague screamed, "'I've got $800,000 to shoot this movie in Los Angeles. You've written a period epic, 130 pages long. It's set in 1933, we've got sixty-eight speaking parts, and we start shooting in two weeks. Do you know anything about the movie business? You're killing me.'" Sayles quickly acquiesced, but rather than simply deleting script pages, he undertook a wholesale rewrite. Teague gratefully accepted the revisions, and the two collaborated throughout the shooting.

Looking at the film's potential for television broadcast, producer Julie Corman, Roger's wife, recruited a cast from the ranks of TV stars. She capitalized on their fame and paved the way for the entry's small-screen showings. Pamela Sue Martin, former star of *The Nancy Drew Mysteries* (1977–78), took on the title role and stepped out of her clothes on camera for Corman's compulsory nude scenes. Robert Conrad also had impressive television credentials, mostly from good-guy roles: *Hawaiian Eye* (1959–63), *The Wild, Wild West* (1965–70), and *The D.A.* (1971–72). Here he played the notorious bank robber John Dillinger.

A few years later, Sayles expressed a high regard for *The Lady in Red,* describing it as "my favorite of that bunch. It had scenes of character development and it had action." The formula worked for *Variety*'s critic, who said, "Momentum is not as frantic as the many former New World productions and focus on character instead of mayhem is refreshing."

The Sayles screenplay that Martin recalls was much better than the picture the audiences saw. As she told me in a letter, "The script for *Lady in Red* was far and beyond the usual B movie fare. It had all sorts of political innuendoes and things about unions, all of which were butchered out of the movie in the process of filming." Now distanced from the budget constraints that prompted the cuts back in 1978, Corman told me he regrets he could not spend more money on that particular entry.

■   ■   ■

The idea of a New World send-up of Akira Kurosawa's film classic *Seven Samurai* (1952) belonged to Roger Corman, as did the relocating of the action from sixteenth-century Japan to futuristic outer space. For *Battle Beyond the Stars* (1980), the producer also broke from his usual stingy budgetary restraints, perhaps because the movie, while imitating *Star Wars* (1977), also would be competing with George Lucas's *The Empire Strikes Back* (1980). That epic was, according to *Variety*, "beginning to show signs of first-run fatigue" just as the New World entry started its late summer 1980 run.

Corman told me, "Now in *Battle Beyond the Stars,* we actually had quite a large budget, so we were able to afford slightly bigger name actors than for the other two pictures." The $2 million budget is reflected both in talent and in special effects. Two of the cast were top TV stars: Richard Thomas (*The Waltons,* 1972–81) and Robert Vaughn (*The Man from U.N.C.L.E.,* 1964–68). Ironically, Vaughn also had appeared in the Hollywood version of *Seven Samurai,* John Sturges's Western *The Magnificent Seven* (1960).

The other actors were for the most part well regarded: George Peppard, John Saxon, Sam Jaffe, Jeff Corey, and the latest Berlin bombshell, Sybil Danning. She provided the sex factor as a Valkyriesque warrior who helps the pacifist planet fend off the alien invaders but also tries to seduce Thomas's squeaky-clean rocket-ship pilot. Setting aside the sobering themes of Kurosawa's original, the revamped picture favored the sagebrush kind of characters and clashes of *The Magnificent Seven*.

Critics at the time were quick to cite the production values of *Battle Beyond the Stars. Variety* saw "an obviously lavish outing by New World standards." Today the movie stands near the top as a 1980s moneymaker for Corman's film factory. In addition to its box-office earnings, the project proved cost-efficient by subsequently providing sets and stock footage for scores of Corman science-fiction films that followed. Initially *Battle* won a Dog of the Week award from Gene Siskel and Roger Ebert, but most of the Internet critics now give Corman's feature two or three stars. It also has *Titanic* (1997) connections: for *Battle,* Corman teamed *Titanic*'s composer, James Horner, and director, James Cameron, for the first time.

Based on the *Battle* production alone, Sayles would no doubt agree with how Cameron felt about learning filmmaking technique at New World. As Cameron told *Omni* magazine (June 1987), "It was the best possible place for me. . . . You only got one or two takes and no rehearsals. The threadbare nature of the coverage and what we had to work with made it interesting." Sayles also took delight in creating a movie that bore traces of the wit of a "wiseacre Lewis Carroll." Having professed his love of short names, John indulged himself in *Battle Beyond the Stars* with characters like Zel, Mok, Feh, Lux, and so on. Then, tongue in cheek, he introduced the onscreen aliens to the edible American icon: the hot dog. (Years later, in the late 1990s, Sayles would team with Cameron on a film project, *Brother Termite,* as yet unproduced.)

Now, thanks to New World Pictures, Sayles had proven his ability to write commercial screenplays, and in the process earned the $40,000 that would fund the making of his first feature. In the summer of 1978, the maverick packed his bags and headed from Hollywood to North Conway, New Hampshire, to start preproduction for *Return of the Secaucus Seven.* In the spring of 1979, he returned to California with that still unedited feature.

■   ■   ■

Once back at their Santa Barbara, California, home-office-studio, Sayles and Maggie Renzi faced two pressing financial needs: money to rent an editing machine and money to help fund the release of *Secaucus Seven*. To raise the cash, he resumed his scriptwriting for others and, as mentioned earlier, Maggie got her old job back at a local salad bar. Both of them rotated their paying jobs with the editing of the film and kept the rented Steenbeck going night and day.

Meanwhile, director Joe Dante was now at Avco Pictures, thus moving one notch closer to the major studios. According to Dante, in 1979 Sayles was simultaneously writing the scripts for Avco's *The Howling* (1981) and for Group One's *Alligator* (1980).

As director of *The Howling*, Dante would visit Sayles in his dingy Santa Monica Boulevard motel room. Dante told me, "I'd knock on the door, and he'd say 'Who is it?' Then you'd hear him pulling the *Alligator* script from the typewriter and putting in *The Howling* so we'd know he was working on our film. Then I'd go in, and we'd talk about it." Both movies were intended as shockers. Avco wanted to release its werewolf movie for Halloween 1980, and *Variety* was reviewing *Alligator* as early as November that same year. *The Howling* was held back for more special-effects work and wasn't released until the spring of 1981. *Alligator* got stalled for unknown reasons after its initial showing in the late fall of 1980 and did not get a general release until the spring of 1981. Subsequent to their solo screenings, the two films often played as a double bill.

The late 1970s and early 1980s witnessed the emergence of a grotesque film subgenre featuring the beast within bursting out of victims in big-screen entries like *Alien* (1979), *Altered States* (1980), and *An American Werewolf in London* (1981). Whatever the psychosociological reasons that prompted this trend; it was the new technology and special effects that were scaring and delighting the audiences. The creative effects team of Rob Bottin and Rick Baker were bent on giving the genre and its creatures a new look. As with New World, Avco created these effects cheaply. Bottin and Baker produced theirs in *The Howling* for $200,000, and their werewolf creations set the standard for years to come.

The original script for *The Howling*, however, was lagging behind the inventiveness of the effects department, and Dante turned to Sayles to set the tone right. Joe wanted a script that would send the film "over the top as a hip, modern, clever handling of the genre." A longtime lover of scary movies, Sayles was up to the task. For this refashioning, his first change was to move the territory of the werewolves from an abandoned ghost town to The Colony, an Esalen-style self-help center on the California coast. The rustic clinical setting, with its neurotic clients who turn into baying beasts nightly, is juxtaposed with the same predatory wolves lurking in the urban lairs of Los Angeles: porn palaces, back alleys, barrooms, and TV studios. Now the audience had to worry about attacks from rural bodysnatchers who looked human and anticipate still other assaults from the psychopathic werewolves lingering in the alleys or breathing into the phone.

As with their joint project for Corman, Sayles and Dante teased the audience with inside jokes. The characters in *The Howling* are named after Hollywood's most famous horror film directors: Paul Landres, Eric Kenton, Sam Newfield, George Waggner, and others. In one scene, a stray copy of Alan Ginsberg's *Howl and Other Poems* (1956) lies by the telephone. Later, Disney's animated short *The Three Little Pigs* (1933) and Universal's original *The Wolf Man* (1941) pop onto television screens within the movie, and a box of "Wolf" brand chili can be seen on a kitchen shelf. Horror comic book king Floyd J. Ackerman does a walk-on. Roger Corman has a cameo. His part calls for him to enter a phone booth and, in self-parody, stick his fingers into the coin-return slot searching for dimes. As with 1978's *Piranha,* Sayles himself has a comical minute on screen, this time appearing as a doltish morgue attendant in a scene shot in a real morgue. Kevin McCarthy, John Carradine, and Slim Pickens also step into the plotline at various times to jog the memories of the werewolf and horror film cognoscenti.

Critical reaction to *The Howling* reflected the balancing act it was attempting between comedy and special effects. The *Los Angeles Times* (April 15, 1981) found the film "pretty scary and revolting" but also "more of a joke." *New York* magazine's David Denby in his February 15, 1983 review reported that he was so captivated by the "beautiful" werewolves that he "forgot to get scared." For every critic thrown off by the many allusions to old movies, another was mesmerized by the werewolf transformation scenes. All in all, the film accomplished what Sayles and Dante hoped it would: it scared the audience, and they loved it. At one Manhattan theater, *The Howling* played on two screens, and Dante recalls going from one to the other and reveling as the audience's screams came right on cue.

After the creative stress of making *Return of the Secaucus Seven,* Sayles enjoyed the return to the liberty of this low-budget production. "It was the equivalent of working in a hospital," he told *The Progressive* (November 1991). "You didn't have to take it home. Nobody took themselves that seriously. They worked hard. Nobody fought about, 'What does this mean?' What you knew was that every ten pages you were going to have some animal attack, and it's meant to be fun."

The rough language, violence, and frontal nudity earned this entry an R rating, but that didn't stop it at the box office. Made for $1.5 million, *The Howling* grossed more than $18 million in the United States and Canada. It not only helped revive the beast-within genre, but it also spawned five popular screen sequels between 1985 and 1991, none of them involving Dante or Sayles.

■   ■   ■

For *Alligator,* the other half of the horror twosome scripted by the then twenty-eight-year-old Sayles, John used the *Piranha* formula by blending an environmental nightmare into the monster movie. Once again, a former New World director, Lewis Teague, brought Sayles on for a rewrite. With the film already supported by foreign distributors, Teague required only a snappy solution to the scripting problems.

For Sayles's, his late entry meant two big pluses. He knew the picture would be made and, under the time constraints, nobody would have the opportunity to alter his script once he delivered it. Now employed as a script "carpenter," John zeroed in on a key narrative problem. In the original screenplay, the alligator was supposed to live in the sewers of Milwaukee and grow exponentially from lapping up beer runoff from the breweries. Sayles asked why the citizens drinking the same beer wouldn't also be giants. "That made them think," Sayles told Jim Hillier (*The New Hollywood,* 1992), "and in the end they said, 'Keep the name *Alligator,* keep the idea of alligators in the sewers and do what you damn well like.'" He shifted the setting to Chicago.

In the Sayles rewrite, Ramon, the discarded baby alligator, feasted on lab animals treated with illegal growth hormones whose cadavers had been dumped into the sewer. To this early version of "'roid-rage," Sayles added a political twist by turning the monster back on the perverse scientists who tortured the animals and on the corrupt local politicians who were ignoring the sewer problems. The script provides the policeman hero with plenty of motives for catching and killing the renegade alligator. He is primarily haunted by the memory of having failed his partner in a St. Louis shootout and then losing a rookie policeman in a sewer search for Ramon. Of course nobody, least of all the other cops, believes his monster story, but he gets the chance to redeem himself, and with the support of a smart and attractive scientist, does so. As with *Piranha,* however, John craftily shapes the ending to allow for the projected sequel, in this case another baby alligator flopping into the sewer, anticipating *Alligator II:The Mutation* (1991), in which he would not be involved.

Weary of the weak and stupid character motivation in exploitation pictures, Sayles worked on a realistic response of the characters to the alligator stomping around the streets. In an interview for the *UCLA Daily Bruin,* John asked reporter Libby Molyneaux, "How would people really react if that happened? Some . . . wouldn't believe it or they'd think it was funny or they'd cash in on it. I try to put the outrageous situations into context and have people react the way they would." With the realism in place, it is the greedy capitalists peddling the toy alligators that link the horror and comic tones of the movie. Veteran actors Dean Jagger, Henry Silva, and Jack Carter camped it up for the camera, and *Jaws*-referenced graffiti added to the fun. Sayles provided four endings. The best one was rejected because the studio refused to blow up their most expensive prop, Ramon the alligator.

Aside from the mechanical monster, the movie's special effects were marginal and the music by Craig Hundley no challenge to Pino Donaggio's score for *The Howling.* Still, most reviewers cited the movie's passion and enthusiasm, and the *New York Post* (June 6, 1981) endorsed *Alligator* as "a crock of wit." Nevertheless, both *Time* and the *Christian Science Monitor* (June 25, 1981) chided the award-winning writer about these scripts. *Time* called *The Howling* a "Sayles slip," and the *Monitor*'s David Sterrett opined, "Sayles will have to come up with something more substantial if he wants to fulfill his early promise." Behind the scenes, John was actually responding to the call for substance: earning the writing money to complete *Return of the Secaucus Seven,* extending his scriptwriting to the stage, and testing his journalistic writing as well.

According to *Film Comment*'s David Chute (May/June 1981), Sayles in this three-year period (1978–80) had written seven original screenplays and "had deals in the works to write and direct three modestly budgeted films for major studios." From the schlock movies alone, John garnered most of the money to pay for the editing of *Secaucus Seven.* As Randy Sue Coburn noted in *Esquire* (November 1982), however, it was the $5,000 advance on the publication of Sayles's short-story collection, *The Anarchists' Convention* (1979), that finally helped get *Secaucus Seven* into theaters. His fiction also put John back into the graces of the literati. As the *New York Times*'s Steve Lawson remarked (April 17, 1983), "Critics likened Sayles to the country's best short story writers—John Updike, Isaac Bashevis Singer, Stanley Elkin."

Had it not been for the need to release *Secaucus,* the stories might have stayed in his desk drawer. Once published, however, they revealed Sayles's ability to create fascinating, three-dimensional characters out of the most unlikely subjects. As Joe Dante told me recently, Corman's action-oriented movies tended to stifle Sayles's talents for characterization and dialogue. Nevertheless, as the short-story anthology showed, his talents for creating realistic characters and writing dialogue the way real people speak were still waiting to be tapped for his screenplays. In Sayles's short stories, ordinary folk again found a place in American fiction. Elderly Jews, old Leftists, truck drivers, bowling alley operators, Boston working girls, California vagrants, renegade kids, Vietnamese refugees, and Chicano dishwashers comprised an American panorama in John's anthology and previewed the populace of his future films. His empathy for them and ear for their speech seemed, to critics, unerring.

■　　　■　　　■

In two years in the film industry, Sayles developed a degree of immunity against the hurt of his scripted scenes being cut and reshuffled before the reassembled feature reached the screen. More aggravating was the realization that some of his screenplays would never be shot. Two early 1980s scripts, *Night Skies* and *The Terror of Loch Ness,* the latter written for MGM, suffered that same fate.

Night Skies represented filmmaker Steven Spielberg's first foray into celluloid science fiction, but Sayles's script delivered malevolent space creatures when Spielberg wanted benign aliens. John's screenplay offered only one such gentle character. "The last page," Sayles told *Premiere* (September 1991), "is kind of like the first page of *E.T.* [1982]—in my script, there's one neat E.T. who can communicate with a kid, and in the end he's left behind." Today Sayles makes no claims on *E.T.* and credits Spielberg for the movie, which was based on the director's research for *Close Encounters of the Third Kind* (1977). After initially agreeing to produce the film with Spielberg, Columbia Pictures finally backed off *Night Skies* in 1981 because, as Sayles wryly told a 1985 AFI seminar, "They thought the film to be too expensive and because they believed that sci-fi was all washed up."

While Sayles spent no time revising the rejected *Night Skies* script, he did dedicate years to redrafting *Blood of the Lamb.* Like Spielberg's project, this Ladd Company effort had a $4 million budget, with John as writer and intended director. The story centered on an attempt by two con artists to infiltrate a fundamentalist religious cult. Alan Ladd Jr. finally turned down the production. By 1983 Warner Bros. had picked up the option on the script and was still willing to let Sayles direct with complete artistic control. After seven revisions, however, *Blood of the Lamb* still failed to satisfy that studio and the project was again dropped. Still another film got canceled at this time. TriStar Pictures owned a Sayles script about one of his favorite topics, the 1930s Spanish civil war. It proved to be too big on politics and too slight on romance, and the untitled script stayed on the studio's shelf.

With the collapse of these deals between 1978 and 1982, Sayles was left financially richer from all the draft writing but professionally dismayed. Working for the major studios, he told *American Film* (October 1982), "is sort of like getting drafted by the Red Sox and sent to Pittsfield. . . . But they have the money to just look at drafts." The experience led him to construct one writer's axiom found in *Sayles on Sayles* (1998): "Basically, the more you get paid, the more you're working with big studios, the less likely it is to get made. . . . I've turned a job down because I could tell, 'You guys don't really want to make this.'" For example, in John's mind, neither Ladd nor Warner Bros. really wanted to make *Blood of the Lamb* but kept deluding themselves into thinking they might, and thus kept paying him for additional rewrites. Sayles told an AFI seminar that the latter is still a script he would love to buy back for his own eventual making.

Money aside, even the John Sayles scripts of that period that made it to the screen (big and small) offered him little of the fun or satisfaction found in working on the horror/monster movies, and they confined him even more to Hollywood genres and formulas. He wrote a TV movie-of-the-week, *A Perfect Match* (1980), a weepy feature starring Colleen Dewhurst as a woman in need of a transplant. Meanwhile, halfway around the world, director John Frankenheimer was in Japan launching a contemporary samurai film, *The Challenge* (1982), about a vendetta between two brothers and their families fighting over two Samurai swords, and brought Sayles on as co-writer.

The moviemaker had John fly to Japan. Once settled in a hotel, Sayles rotated marathon writing sessions with two-hour catnaps and eye-opening swims in the hotel pool. Five days later he emerged with the completed script. The story meetings foretold the revisions that would follow. As Sayles would recollect at a 1985 AFI seminar, "The director said, 'Well, I know they're Chinese in the script, but let's make them all Japanese because I can get Toshiro Mifune and who knows the difference anyway?'"

Later, in Japan, Sayles rewrote the script on one floor of the production headquarters while Frankenheimer was casting the film on another. The script was in constant revision as the writer accommodated new actors and the fluctuating Japanese production codes about what could and could not be shown on camera. Shot at the Kyoto International Convention Center, *The Challenge* emerged as a nearly two-hour action picture. As a modern twist on the theme of courtly honor, it was helped by Scott Glenn's performance, but with a domestic gross of only $3.6 million, the R-rated movie barely covered its production costs. For television, the picture was cut from 112 to 97 minutes and retitled *Sword of the Ninja*.

■   ■   ■

Like most of John Sayles's post–horror film scripts, those produced and not-produced screenplays eventually would help fund his forthcoming movies. He continued to stockpile ideas for future projects and took a stab at other forms of writing.

In July 1980 Sayles ventured into journalism as a "color" man for the *New Republic's* reporting on the Republican National Convention in Detroit. At the time the magazine, like John, leaned to the political left, and having read Sayles's *The Anarchists' Convention*, editor Mike Kinsley hired John and sent him to obtain offbeat coverage of the proceedings. John wrote six pages that captured both the sanitized, Ronald Reagan–scripted performance staged for the network camera and the seething paranoia of the far right, Jesse Helms–led pack that marked the milling on the floor. With a gift for total recall of conversations, Sayles caught the argot of both camps and what they were highlighting and hiding.

In the spring of 1981, *Return of the Secaucus Seven* enjoyed a "second opening" in New York City. This time the film received a cordial critical reception, and the East Coast distributor, Libra Films, used the reviews to stir up audience interest in the film. Meanwhile, John was testing his skills as a playwright with two one-acts, *Turnbuckle* and *New Hope for the Dead*, which that winter were performed in Manhattan without fanfare or critical reviews. By the summer, however, both plays found a stage as the showcase productions for the opening of the Boat Basin. Located on the Upper West Side of Manhattan, the venue turned a fountain shell into a stage and surrounded it with five hundred seats. The Boat Basin's theater-in-the-round structure seemed ideal for the two Sayles dramas, both of which employed sports arena settings.

In the midst of the *Secaucus Seven* triumph, the publicity capitalized on the audience interest in that movie's young cast, some members of which would now appear "live on stage." Gordon Clapp starred in the two-character *New Hope for the Dead,* playing an idiot savant who knows everything about ancient Egypt but passes his life stuffing popcorn boxes in the basement of Madison Square Garden. *Turnbuckle* featured Adam LeFevre and David Strathairn. In a play depicting marriage as a wrestling match, two sad sacks dream of being somebody and doing something that would last forever.

The critics directed their remarks as much toward the new theater as they did toward the two productions. Neither play lived up to the quality of *The Return of the Secaucus Seven,* they declared. At least one reviewer found both works flawed in that the characters were stereotypes. In the *New York Times* (July 8, 1981), Frank Rich cited "a heretofore secret fondness for clichés." What was most wanting, he concluded, was "Sayles's distinctive voice instead of his geriatric theater models."

Although the plays closed after a short run, they had given John a chance to showcase his work. The projects also may have been intended as a warm-up for a big theatrical production about frontiersman Davy Crockett that never materialized. In the summer of 1985, when Sayles next returned to the theater, it would be as an actor playing opposite Joanne Woodward.

While John was active in other media in 1981, audiences around the country were still lining up at the box office for *Secaucus Seven.* By now Sayles was pursuing backers for his next film, *Lianna.* In today's film business, a hit feature, especially one like *Secaucus Seven,* which was made for almost nothing and then grossed millions, would all but guarantee a surge of interest from Hollywood. Major studios line up with offers of film projects in the range of $10 million to $15 million. In the early 1980s, however, the industry was less venturesome and not inclined to take chances on young directors.

Neither *Secaucus Seven*'s critical acclaim nor its box-office success started a stampede of the major studios. Unlike many flashy young directors using first films as a springboard to the big time, the thirty-year-old Sayles posed conditions that chilled studio interest: he wanted to produce his own script, and he would direct the movie his way. The studios countered with offers for him to direct *their* pictures. The next two years would feature John Sayles doing *both* his films and theirs.

10

Lianna and the Rise
of Maggie Renzi

"John has no limits regarding his relationships with sex,
race, or language. His films steadily
survey the plight of men and women crossing borders."

ACTOR KEVIN TIGHE, 1998

AT THE CLOSE OF THE 1970S, as Suzanne Donahue notes in *American Film Distribution* (1987), expanding pay TV and growing videocassette sales were creating a need for more movie product. In light of that demand and of the box-office appeal of *Return of the Secaucus Seven*—which had grossed more than $2 million—thirty-year-old John Sayles seemed perfectly positioned to join the major studios as a moviemaker. All he had to do was decide what his next entry would be.

One choice was to return to New World Pictures, where Roger Corman had writing/directing assignments waiting for him. Sayles, however, declined the offer. Instead he opted to direct an autobiographical script by actor/writer/producer Amy Robinson (b. 1948) that focused on working-class high school kids in 1967. In 1979 Robinson had produced *Head over Heels* (a.k.a. *Chilly Scenes of Winter*). With Robinson and her husband, actor Griffin Dunne

(*After Hours,* 1985), as producers, Sayles considered their offer to direct their screenplay *Baby It's You* (1983) for Paramount Pictures.

The deal with Paramount held out the possibility of launching a career like that of Woody Allen, Paul Mazursky, Martin Scorsese, or Spike Lee. In this model, a gross of $100 million made by a major studio picture then allows the director to do a more personal film. The trade-off keeps the studio solvent and stocked with product and the directors financially secure even in their more adventurous moviemaking. The alternative to signing with the majors was to do what he did for *Secaucus Seven.* He could pick the project he wanted, keep the budget low, and eventually scrape together the necessary money from different sources: a studio, video pre-sales, and commercial broadcast. Between 1981 and 1983, Sayles would test both methods of filmmaking—the system's and the independent's. Having agreed to direct *Baby It's You,* he took his advance money and used it to finance the making of his second feature, *Lianna* (1983), which he had already scripted.

■   ■   ■

Back in 1978, Sayles had completed the screenplays for both *Matewan* (1987) and *Eight Men Out* (1988), but order of script completion did not dictate order of production. As he informed *Horizon* magazine (September 1987), "It's difficult to discern any pattern in what I do because it's not like I get to do what I want when it's written."

In pondering the script choice for his second personal project, he knew that the epic scope and period detail required for both *Matewan* and *Eight Men Out* called for a budget that would frighten away the big studios. As an alternative, the small cast, limited present-day settings, and structural simplicity of *Lianna* made it the practical economic choice. Now John faced the need for financing. In seeking that backing, he remained independent but was not alone.

Maggie Renzi was now officially stepping into the producer role she had performed without credit for *Secaucus Seven.* From this project forward (excepting *Baby It's You*), she became the chief financial negotiator for Sayles's movies. At age thirty, Renzi, the pert, 5'5" companion to the filmmaker, was already an established triple threat: producer, actress, and cordial location manager. She now faced the task of finding the needed $800,000 for *Lianna*. Jeffrey Nelson, the associate producer, would assist in that eighteen-month-long campaign. Sayles gave the fund-raising a running start. With money from his *Night Skies* scripts and with the advance from Paramount for *Baby It's You,* the director allocated $30,000 of his own money for the proposed 35mm color feature.

Sayles's profit from *Secaucus Seven* was another likely source for that *Lianna* money—or so it seemed. On the $2 million gross, he had earned about $200,000, but those profits quickly evaporated. He used the movie's first $60,000 to reimburse further the actors who had accepted the $80-per-week payments during the production. They now had their wages boosted to the Screen Actors Guild minimum. The *Secaucus Seven* investors among them also got a percentage of the profits.

On the remaining money, which he had earmarked to fund his next movie, the Internal Revenue Service made an unanticipated raid. IRS agents instructed the filmmaker about deducting film expenses: you cannot do that until the movie is released. In *American Film* (October 1982), David Osborne reports that Sayles was ignorant of that law when he filed his 1978 tax return and now reportedly had to pay $12,500 in back taxes and penalties. From that day forward, John would have an even steeper uphill fight to finance his pictures. He saw the tax structure as thwarting small independent productions. "There's no way I'm going to get far enough ahead to finance a film myself again," he told Osborne.

As an independent filmmaker, John saw little possibility of getting backing from the usual sources: bankers and real estate brokers. They knew little about the film business generally and virtually nothing about the small-budget movies in particular. As for the major studios, Sayles believed that in the early 1980s there was almost no chance for financing. In *Premiere* (October 1987) he recalled, "You didn't even bother going to the studios unless you had a commercial script. And even then, if you weren't connected through an agent or whatever, they wouldn't read it."

One of the "whatevers" who could open the studio doors was the potential star for the film, but actors had agents who served as gatekeepers. Predictably, they discarded low-budget scripts (which meant low profits and, more importantly, low agents' fees). Despite that, Sayles had two breakthroughs: Jane Fonda, the erstwhile radical, read the *Lianna* script about a lesbian coming out of the closet, then wanted to know "what else" the filmmaker was working on. Brooke Adams tentatively accepted the title role in *Lianna,* but as David Chute *(Film Comment)* learned, got cold feet about the material and backed out.

The actors were scared by the topical nature of the screenplay. Likewise, even had the studios or bankers read the script, its controversial, financially hazardous topic would have sent them running for cover, especially with the filmmaker insisting on full creative control. What capped their aversion to financing the film was the fact that the lesbian heroine not only was married, she had children.

Perhaps because Hollywood's male establishment could be perceived as suppressing a minority voice, it occurred to Renzi that the marginalized women's community might jump in with support. However, the response from women's groups had its own set of biases. In *Eye on the World* (1987), Renzi commented, "Lesbians weren't interested in helping a film written by a man. . . . Also the two women in *Lianna* don't end happily ever after. I think it was hard for women to put money into something that wasn't completely a positive story."

If bankers, studio, actors, and lesbians didn't want to invest in this movie, then who would? Well, for a time, a few high rollers made promises, one offering to finance the whole project. Nothing came of that hope except another lesson. "We learned," Renzi told the *New York Times* (April 17, 1983), "that you don't celebrate when someone promises you a check. . . . No, you call ten more people." The producer also revamps the project's size, schedule, and costs. In consultation with production manager Peggy Rajski, Renzi knocked $500,000 off the budget and continued to solicit financing. The now $300,000, 16mm film got a sudden boost. Two backers called with an assurance of $100,000. They had seen *Secaucus Seven* and decided that rather than make their own movie, they'd invest in one by Sayles.

With little hope for more big players, the film finally went public. Some thirty people, none having ever invested in a movie, signed on as limited part-ners. Their investments ranged from $1,500 to $50,000. For further assis-tance, the movie also became something of a family enterprise. Maggie got her parents, Ralph and Helen, on board, and Sayles tapped his mother and father. Don wrote a check for $1,000, and Mary, a stalwart Catholic who had no idea of the picture's content, added $10,000.

The Sayles-Renzi economic approach was to produce the film for about half a million dollars, then have it gross $3 million. With that goal realized, they theorized that the thirty people would be paid back in full. With a wistful smile, Mary Sayles told me, "I didn't make anything, but eventually I got back the money." One reassurance all of Renzi's "low rollers" shared was the knowl-edge that the director had put his own money on the line, which meant he cared about the project and also that he would not let it go over budget. Like them, Sayles would make money *if* the film made money.

As the little profit that Renzi and Sayles finally made on *Secaucus Seven* was poured into the *Lianna* production, they returned to their unpretentious house in Hoboken, New Jersey. She continued to drive a 1977 Rambler, and John, attired in jeans and T-shirt, commuted to Manhattan by bus. With the *Lianna* project now cut back to a thirty-six-day shooting schedule, the producer looked for novice crew members who would tolerate the deferred payments amounting to $40,000. As Renzi told *Monthly Film Bulletin* (January 1984), "We had to acquire new production assistants. They won't work for peanuts twice." She also was scouting for a low-priced cast of actors and extras, a task made easier by New York City's glut of acting talent and the dearth of available roles.

Family again stepped to the fore with Maggie's sister, Marta, lending her professional dance skills. She now agreed to choreograph and dance in *Lianna*. Her father also joined the cast and later recalled for me the direction he got for his cameo as a football coach. "John said, 'Put a whistle around your neck, put your arms on your hips, and concentrate on that building over there.' So I concentrated and he shot for about thirty seconds. That was it, my first role."

The shoot welcomed friends not only to the set but also onto the screen. In Sayles's low-budget films, every free extra or cameo saved the production at least $80 a day. There were still bigger savings to be made. With neither of them getting paid, Maggie played a supporting role, and John acted and picked up good reviews as Mike, a teacher first chasing Lianna, then, turning comically uncomfortable around her after finding out that she's a lesbian.

In addition, the new budget slashed the production values and later cut corners in the editing. Having aspired to make this a professional-looking movie, the director now reverted to some of the primitive shooting and other techniques employed in *Secaucus Seven*. Handheld camera shots and cheap film stock saved money and had the happy side effect of contributing to a look of flat directness and understated honesty.

Lianna is the realistic story of a mother (Linda Griffiths) who falls in love with a woman professor, Ruth (Jane Hallaren), then leaves her husband, Dick (John DeVries), also a professor, and her two children, Spencer (Jessie Solomon), twelve, and Theda (Jessica Wight MacDonald), eight. Lianna's affair with Ruth is cut short by the latter's reluctance to reveal her sexual preference—which would cause her to lose her teaching job—and by her attachment to another woman at her old school. Nevertheless, a fling with an army second lieutenant convinces Lianna that she is a lesbian, and she starts rearranging her own life. While not dwelled on in the script, the two children respond to the crisis: Spencer with cynicism and Theda with head-down, silent confusion. Better developed is the wavering relationship Lianna has with her straight friend, Sandy, who finally accepts Lianna as a soul sister. Sandy's husband, Bob, who has learned tolerance from the team's gay quarterback, also accepts the situation. Likewise, two straight women in Lianna's apartment house provide an oasis of companionship when Lianna's friends start acting like strangers.

Sayles based the script on three experiences he was witnessing among his contemporaries. As he explained to *American Film* (October 1982), "Couples were splitting up, and the pain worsened for those with children. There were gay women who were coming out, and there were divorced women who . . . had gotten married right out of school and hadn't done anything for themselves. . . ." These experiences were woven into the story of a woman who must make decisions regarding her sexuality and then live with the consequences of her choice. It would be a favorite theme throughout Sayles's works.

"You never get anything for free," he told *M* magazine (June 1983). "You pay for coming out of the closet, like Lianna, and like Ruth . . . you pay for staying in . . . why not pick which one you're going to pay?"

Because of budget, the drama had to be conveyed more in words than in time-consuming, money-draining visuals, and the editing had to cover for the pedestrian camerawork. As Sayles told various interviewers, "In *Lianna,* we worked on establishing a kind of cumulative mood and identification with character through a series of episodes, dramatic scenes once again using music and cutting to fill in for camera movement."

Drawn from the Broadway theater, the cast was a step up from the summer-stock company of *Secaucus Seven,* and the movie needed their professional experience. Linda Griffiths (Lianna) and Jane Hallaren (Ruth) faced some tough moments in shooting the film's several sex scenes. To alleviate their fears, John gave his usual precise directions about what they were to do. As Renzi said in *Eye on the World* (1987), "He didn't say, 'All right girls, go to it.' He'd tell them, 'move your hand here,' 'stroke her back.' He made it calm and quiet and as matter-of-fact as possible." Murmured endearments of almost subliminal voices added to the erotic feeling of the lesbian relationship and contrasted it with the more perfunctory coupling of Lianna and her husband, Dick.

As usual the picture was completed on schedule. With the movie now in the can, John and his producers turned to its distribution. His hot reputation and the state of the industry made the timing good. In the early 1980s, the film business witnessed a steady growth in the number of independent movies produced and exhibited. Setting the pace in the distribution of these products was United Artists Classics, led by Tom Bernard and Michael Barker.

As Bernard told me, "*Lianna* was technically a big improvement on *Secaucus,* and we wanted to distribute the picture." UA Classics knew they could provide some important advantages for the young filmmaker. "We were young guys ourselves who had gotten grassroots experience running college film series. So we knew about distribution, and we knew how to place the right movie in the right theater." The studio provided other advantages. "It was a safe haven because we were covered by a big company, and everybody got paid." Having convinced the filmmaker, Bernard and Barker picked up *Lianna* as UA Classics' second release for 1983 and sent Sayles on the road publicizing the film.

By the time John got to the marketplace, however, UA Classics had folded and Bernard and Barker had joined Orion Pictures. That left *Lianna* unprotected, with no one to push the distribution nor make the necessary contacts with the video companies. In *Sayles on Sayles,* the filmmaker bemoans the breakdown. "So we were left high and dry with *Lianna,* which got great reviews. It just wasn't well taken care of." In the 1990s, however, the same Bernard and Barker, in consort with co-president Marcie Bloom, would distribute Sayles's movies for Sony Pictures Classics.

Prior to making *Lianna,* Sayles had consulted with gay women in the film industry and concluded that each of them would script a different movie on the lesbian topic. He then produced, as he says, a film about a person—who is also a lesbian. While absolutely no sensationalism accompanied the promotion of the film, its exhibition stirred up predictable controversy in both the straight and gay communities in the United States and abroad. At a preview in Los Angeles, a large contingent of gay women came prepared for the worst. "In the first ten minutes," Sayles told *Drama-Logue* (June 9, 1993), "There was a lot of hissing [at] certain characters and lines, but by the middle of the movie, you could tell everybody had realized, 'This movie is on our side, there is nothing to be pissed off about.'"

As the promotional tour continued, he took reassurance from women in the audiences who in follow-up discussions cited the film's authentic characters. Many, but not all, were pleased at the picture's realism in depicting a lesbian affair that falls apart and leaves Lianna searching for a new kind of relationship. At the London Festival, however, John met a level of hostility not found in the United States. In *Monthly Film Bulletin* (January 1984), Maggie described the feminists' attitude and her reaction. "Men shouldn't write about women, let alone gay women. I was appalled by that."

Released in mid-January 1983, *Lianna* found a wide-ranging reception among the American newspaper and weekly film critics. What the *New York Post* (January 19, 1983) called "a sad, humorless depressing downer," *New York* magazine (January 31, 1983) saw as "a comedy with an earnest didactic side to it."

Time (March 6, 1983), Richard Corliss found both laughter and pathos as the movie "turned a problem drama into a social comedy." Noting the scenes of sensual passion and the heroine's disenchantment, the *Newsday* review (January 19, 1983) saw Lianna's redemption in her "unsullied friendship" for Sandy that "prevails and endures." The style of the film also provoked critical disagreement. While some commentators applauded the film's simplicity, the *Village Voice* (January 25, 1983) faulted the gap between script and film: "Sayles's tongue is quick but his camera is static." The *Christian Science Monitor* (May 12, 1983) attacked those critics, who seemed "snowed by the 'purity' of Sayles's forthrightly low budgets and artistic posturing."

The debate over the film's content took various turns, centering on the sex scenes as too little, too much, too tame, or too slack. The reviews in the gay-oriented magazines generally faulted *Lianna* for not restricting its focus to lesbian concerns. The *Off Our Backs* review (April 1983), for example, accused the film of depicting "how homosexuals aren't really that different." In *Film Comment* (March/April 1986), Marcia Pally agreed, calling it "the most popular of the welcome wagon films—those that try to persuade audiences it's okay to have lesbians on the block."

In his book *Celluloid Closet* (1987), Vito Russo saw *Lianna* as one of a flurry of films about gays released in the early 1980s. "About a dozen such films attempted to show gay and lesbian life as it really is. These films were like manna from heaven for a community of people who had never seen themselves depicted as real people." In 1991 the feminist journal *Camera Obscura* concurred, "What counts is the exhilaration and sense of solidarity women who love women feel."

Like *Secaucus Seven* and *Eight Men Out*, *Lianna* contributed to a trend, this time as one of the first films to treat lesbians positively. Ten years after the picture's release, James Robert Parish's *Gays and Lesbians in Mainstream Cinema* (1993) cited it as "the definite [*sic*] feature of lesbian love." Leonard Maltin in his annual *Movie & Video Guide* gives the picture three out of four stars, and users on the Internet Movie Database rate it 74 out of a possible 100. At the box office, *Lianna* grossed $1.5 million and returned a 1 percent profit to its investors. Later, cable and videocassette gave the film further exposure. The lack of playing dates at many regional theaters underscored the growing importance of home video for independent filmmakers.

Once again, through perseverance and austerity, John had gotten his vision from script to screen. While not as popular as *Secaucus Seven, Lianna* marked the arrival of two determining forces in Sayles's career. As producer, Maggie Renzi had risen to the challenge as fund-raiser and production coordinator, and Mason Daring had stepped up his role as composer. The overlooked *Lianna* score included a few remarkable tunes by Daring and Jeanie Stahl, with whom Daring had toured the folk circuit in the 1970s. Their rendition of "Nevertheless" reinforced the lesbian theme, and "I've Been Loving You Too Long" provided the music for the dance about breaking up.

The Sayles-Renzi-Daring alliance would continue over the next fifteen years. An interruption was at hand, however, as John turned to the directing of somebody else's movie for a major studio. For this single occasion, he was a feature director for hire.

11

Baby It's You
and the Battle with Paramount

The studio contract reads, "Paramount Studios, herein after known as
the Author . . . "So you're doomed in the contract.

JOHN SAYLES, 1997

THE CRITICAL AND COMMERCIAL SUCCESS of *Return of the Secaucus Seven* and later *Lianna* made John Sayles an obvious target for wooing by the major studios. Although new to the industry, he could craft successful movies while making them comply with the restrictions of budget and schedule. Co-president of United Artists Classics Tom Bernard told me that especially after *Lianna,* all the studio executives were competing to sign John to direct a film. Having witnessed the triumphs of the low-budget pictures, Sayles partisans wondered what kinds of movies he might make with a generous budget. Simultaneously, they worried that the money might corrupt the thirty-three-year-old filmmaker and turn him into just another studio player. Sayles's response to these speculations was his collaboration with Amy Robinson and their eventual contract with Paramount Pictures to make *Baby It's You* (1983).

In Robinson's story about high school in the mid-1960s, Sayles saw the possibility of a screenplay that would counterpoint teenagers and the twentysomethings, contrasting the years when everything seems possible with the times when barriers take shape. Both Robinson and Sayles knew the adolescent turf, she from the girl's locker room at Trenton High School in New Jersey, and he from the boys' counterpart at Mont Pleasant High School in Schenectady.

For their film, however, they planned to subordinate the teen years to the early adulthood stage that followed, when higher education and economic advantage would separate the movie's central characters. The complications arising from contrasting family backgrounds would sharpen the edge of this teen tale. Confessing that the movie is partly autobiographical, Sayles told the *New York Times* (April 17, 1983), "We wanted to take a good long look at certain kids as people." To his recollections of school plays, athletic teams, and cruising around Schenectady, John added the perspective of a young man who went from an urban public school to Williams College, an institution whose elegant setting and academically distinguished clientele paralleled those of the film's Sarah Lawrence College.

In searching for financial backing, Robinson and co-producer Griffin Dunne had their own credentials to add to Sayles's. The Griffin-Robinson team had already produced their first successful film, 1979's *Head over Heels* (a.k.a. *Chilly Scenes of Winter*). In pitching the teen-centered screenplay and Sayles as director as a package to the studios, they were getting mixed reactions from the mainstream-minded executives, ironically because in the early 1980s teen films were a hot genre.

Among the movies tapping the juvenile market at that time were *Porky's* (1981), *Fast Times at Ridgemont High* (1982), and *Valley Girl* (1983). Surrounding them were dozens of other entries recycling the themes and styles introduced by *American Graffiti* (1973). Now, by 1983, the studios wanted more "just-like-but-different" pictures about the 1960s, sentimental lampoons that were a little raunchy and had a lot of laughs, in short, another high school screen romp geared to fourteen-year-olds.

What separated Robinson's screenplay from pictures like *Porky's* was its emphasis on what happens after the teen years. As Kenneth Chanko noted in

Films in Review (February 1983), "It was Sayles's insistence on having the story explore the characters' lives after high school—a daring concept in a teen movie in Hollywood—that got the project in a bit of trouble." The basic difference in focus between the filmmakers and the studio would plague the effort from start to finish.

Initially, Twentieth Century-Fox had expressed interest in the screenplay with Sayles directing, but they decided they didn't want to use the college part of the story. Robinson and Griffin then turned to Paramount Pictures and worked out what the industry calls a negative pickup deal. Essentially, the contract gives the producers support from the studio: if they complete the production (the negative), the studio will distribute the film. The studio does not finance the film; nevertheless, its guarantee of the distribution will persuade banks and real estate corporations to invest in the venture. Consequently, as opposed to the $200,000 and $300,000 spent on *Secaucus Seven* and *Lianna,* respectively, the studio-endorsed *Baby It's You* would have a budget of more than $3 million. For the first time, John could begin directing the film with the assurance of its distribution, a comfort he soon would come to regret.

Having signed the agreement, Paramount then began voicing the same objections as had Twentieth Century-Fox, and tried to steer *Baby It's You* toward the adolescent audience. As Sayles told *American Film* (October 1983), "We had enough disagreements that it was clear that they had some movie in their head they couldn't express to me. . . . But it wasn't the one I wanted to make."

■   ■   ■

Given Sayles's oft-expressed admiration for high school as the "last bastion of American democracy," it's clear why he would be attracted to Robinson's script. Set in the mid-1960s, a few years before John's own high school graduation in 1968, the story concerns a blue-collar guy, Sheik Capadilupo (Vincent Spano), whose father is a trash collector, and Sheik's relationship with a physician's daughter, Jill Rosen (Rosanna Arquette), who is bound for the elite Sarah Lawrence College. In the high school section of the picture, Jill falls for the bad boy from the wrong side of the tracks who flaunts his disrespect for teachers and models himself after Frank Sinatra. For a brief time, he captivates Jill. The dividing of their paths begins when the school expels Sheik and denies him admission to the senior prom, hinting at the many barriers to follow.

Having fled the Hoboken-like city, Sheik washes dishes in a Miami nightclub and, with the manager's allowance, dresses up to mime songs for the patrons. On a weekend break from college, Jill flies to Miami for a visit. Sheik takes her to dinner at the Fontainbleau Hotel, but the dinner bores Jill. The romance continues to unravel when he takes her back to his colorless apartment.

His fumbling lovemaking further defuses the passion between them. Yet Sheik pursues Jill back to Sarah Lawrence. He storms onto the campus and into her dormitory. Finally recognizing that his future does not include Jill, Sheik nevertheless finds himself substituting for a college student who has stood Jill up and escorts her to the college dance. As Jill and Sheik dance to "Strangers in the Night," the camera slowly tracks away, leaving them together, but with the lyrics portending their separation.

Even in the casting stage, Paramount, without having yet invested a dime in the project, was making suggestions, especially concerning casting. They proposed John Travolta for the lead. He certainly had a convincing track record in similar parts, but at twenty-eight seemed too old to play a teenager. Finally, the studio offered Joey Travolta, John's brother, who at least had name recognition. Ignoring these ideas, Sayles settled on twenty-year-old Vincent Spano and teamed him with twenty-three-year-old Rosanna Arquette. The supporting cast included Matthew Modine in his first screen assignment and Robert Downey Jr. in his fourth feature film. Rather than spend time in rehearsals, Sayles told Spano to screen Frank Sinatra movies. The director then spent three days hanging out in Hoboken with Arquette and the actors playing her high school friends, never discussing the script but getting to know one another.

Shooting the film in sequence also put the young cast at ease. As Vincent Spano told the *New York Times,* "Moving right through the story in order reflected our growing familiarity as actors. That was smart of John. It really helped." Sayles also solicited ideas from the teenage extras about what their characters might see and care about in a scene. At a 1985 American Film

Institute seminar in Los Angeles, the iconoclast moviemaker said, "I ignore the Screen Actors Guild rules that a director should not talk to extras because they get upgraded or some bullshit like that. They're dying to have you talk to them."

If disregarding studio advice improved the casting, heeding it paid off in the music arena. For this film about young people in the 1960s, Sayles envisioned background music to capture the period and to comment on his screen characters. Reportedly, John wanted Bruce Springsteen to compose the whole music track but, at Paramount's "request," settled on something more eclectic and maybe more effective. He spent $300,000, 10 percent of his budget (and the full cost of *Lianna*), on the rights to some of the era's most popular tunes.

The high school half of the movie includes thirty familiar oldies, including "Venus in Furs," "Shout," "Chapel of Love," and the title song performed by the Shirelles. As the characters move away from the psychedelic 1960s, the picture introduces more contemporary themes, and the period rock-and-roll tunes are mixed with the antiromantic, gritty lyrics of Bruce Springsteen's four songs, including "It's Hard to Be a Saint in the City."

The opening minutes of *Baby It's You* indicate the kind of movie Sayles would make if given a decent production budget. The song "Wooly Bully" kicks in, classroom doors fly open, and scores of high school students pour into the hallway. With money to hire extras, Sayles loads the screen with students dressed by a professional costume department and filmed by a veteran cinematographer. The mid-1960s teens in their blue jeans, gold-letter jackets, and bright crimson skirts swirl in front of the camera, unleashing their youthful energy into this thirty-second explosion.

As the camera tracks back, Jill (Rosanna Arquette) walks into the foreground dressed in the baby blue skirt and red sweater that initiate one of the movie's color schemes. Gone are the faded colors of Sayles's first features that got washed out in the transfer from 16mm to 35mm. Instead, the gold-red-blue color scheme announced here remains vivid and varied throughout the movie, and the studio-supported film conveys that pattern and the action in clearly focused depth. As Sayles told the *New York Times* (April 17, 1983), "If you look closely at *Baby*—the performances, the crowd scenes, the driving and the use of music—it's a lot more kinetic than my first two movies."

In a film about teenagers, Sayles employed the visuals to convey what the characters could sense but not articulate about themselves. For example, in scene two, with the aid of sophisticated lighting, set design, and film stock, the camera arcs around Jill in a close-up as she auditions for a school play. With the technical care that money allows, the set design and camerawork gradually reveal the character and her ambition to perform.

Near the end of both the film and his romance with Jill, Sheik drives a stolen car through the city. The dark and empty streets are made even more desolate by the grime on the windshield, and in the background the Statue of Liberty comments ironically on the hero's potential lifetime prospects. Once the Romeo of the high school hallways and a Frank Sinatra wanna-be, Sheik has neither the pedigree nor the education to realize his dreams of stardom. What looms ahead is a life comprised of the same drudgery found in the lower-class home he fled.

Contributing greatly to the effectiveness was the $3 million, which allowed the hiring of expert technical talent, especially in the cinematography department. In 1983 Michael Ballhaus, director of photography, was in the midst of shooting films for the legendary German director Rainer Werner Fassbinder and for Martin Scorsese. Ballhaus was also en route to Oscar nominations for both *Broadcast News* (1987) and *The Fabulous Baker Boys* (1989). Operating the Steadicam for him on the Hoboken location was Garrett Brown, who invented and pioneered the use of that device and had scores of films to his credits. Later Sayles told *Films in Review* (February 1983), "I got a lot of good ideas from Michael Ballhaus, and eight out of ten of them I was able to use."

Like Ballhaus and Brown, the rest of the crew was teaching Sayles the art of cinematography. A self-educated film editor, John had the additional benefit of working with the knowledgeable Sonya Polonsky, who would stay with him for the next two films. Heretofore Sayles's crews were doing double and triple duty; now crew members filled the specialized positions found in a major production.

Even when unfettered from the constraints of low-budget shooting, John made a feature for $3 million that normally would have cost a studio two or three times that much. The film's sophistication made clear that the more money Sayles had available, the more that value would show up where he thought it belonged: on-screen.

■   ■   ■

Despite the stylistic improvements, *Baby It's You* emerged as a bastard and deformed child of the marriage between Sayles and Paramount. Thanks to Paramount, it does not appear on cable TV, and rental copies are scarce. Throughout production there was outright combat over the creative rights to the project, pitting the producers and director against the Paramount suits. With the submission of *Baby*'s first cut, the war between the producers and the studio began in earnest. Three pitched battles marked this one-time-only contretemps between Sayles and a major studio: the conflict focused first on the test marketing, then on the final cut, and finally on the distribution.

While Sayles argued for the integrity of his 140-minute version, Paramount mounted its own case for a 105-minute movie, basing it on demographics and audience polls. Two mall theaters, one in Chicago and one in Paramus, New Jersey, served as the proving grounds for the movie. With studio experts counting coughs, laughs, and people exiting the auditorium, Paramount's position hardened. According to the test cards collected at the theaters, the film got mixed reviews. According to John, *Baby* got every kind of opinion from excellent to poor, but scored particularly well with women ages twenty-five to thirty-five.

Faced with this stratified interpretation, the studio might have targeted the female audience. Paramount, however, was determined to gear its promotion for the masses. Seeking the common denominator, they ordered the director to recut the movie for the mass market and lop off thirty to forty minutes. When he resisted, Paramount's two studio heads, Michael Eisner and Jeffrey Katzenberg, called in their own editors to recut the film. As Harry Stein notes (*Premiere,* July 1999), "Only after the new version tested poorly did they go back to Sayles's original."

As Sayles sees it today, when released at 105 minutes, the film lost the complexity of his characters and the community orientation that typify his work.

In *Video Review* (November 1982), he cites a scene at a basketball court intended to reveal that however smooth Sheik was at dancing, athletically he was a fake. This telling footage was cut. Even less of the onscreen business developed for the peripheral characters got to the screen, and *Baby* became a Hollywood hero-centered movie rather than a typical Sayles community-focused movie.

When even the recut picture still did not satisfy Paramount, Sayles revolted and threatened to have his name removed from the project. At the time he told his brother, Doug, "I could only embarrass the colonial power, and I was willing to go all the way."

Sayles got his cut, but the studio got their revenge against a film and a director they now hated. As described by Sayles, the studio's distribution tactics seemed self-defeating in some instances and vengeful in others. For the Seattle, Washington, opening, Paramount produced a trailer filled with racing cars, screeching tires, and lots of action shots, creating the impression of a high school love epic and teen action flick. After a respectable $40,000 opening week, box-office receipts fell off because the audience didn't see what was in the trailer.

In New York City, Paramount picked the big theaters for *Baby*'s opening, where the houses usually grossed $25,000 a week, instead of at the smaller screens, where a $20,000 gross (which it earned) would have kept the film alive through word-of-mouth promotion. With only a bland newspaper ad campaign, the picture ran in Manhattan for four weeks at a slight loss, and the studio let the picture die. "They never even cleared the home video rights for the music," Sayles told David Rosen in *Off-Hollywood: The Making and Marketing of Independent Films* (1987).

In his 1985 AFI seminar, Sayles guessed that in the United States *Baby* "broke even or made a little money, but they're never going to tell me." According to the Internet's *All Media Guide*, the release grossed only $1.3 million at the box office. Among the publications ignoring the youth-oriented movie were two papers aimed at just that market, *Rolling Stone* and the *Village Voice*. Their indifference made *Variety*'s prediction even more ominous: "a dubious bet for more than specialized college area venues." Today the Internet's *Mr. Showbiz* site gives the film a 70 out of a 100. Leonard Maltin, citing the picture's loss of momentum after the high school scenes in his yearly *Movie & Video Guide,* gives it two and a half stars.

Paramount's foreign distribution for *Baby It's You* proved both erratic and insensitive. At a time when Sayles was vehemently opposing the South African government, that was the only foreign country (barring England) where the studio released the movie, and it was the only Sayles film shown in South Africa during the period of apartheid. In England's *Monthly Film Bulletin* (November 1984), Chris Auty carped about the release delay and sensed a problem. "Kept on the shelf for two years by UIP, *Baby It's You* joins *Over the Edge* [1979] as one of those films whose distribution seems genuinely inexplicable on commercial grounds." In her *New York Times* review, Janet Maslin also detected a problem of creative control over the film, which to her "felt more like two movies than one."

The animosity generated by the *Baby* production still lingers between the studio and the director. Rare is the video store that carries the film for rental, and the purchase price for it even now is a prohibitive $79.95. (At one leading mail-order outlet, Movies Unlimited, *Baby* is no longer available.) Likewise unavailable is the much admired soundtrack album.

In 1996, still pained by the experience, Sayles informed the *London Times,* "Being mad at Hollywood for being simplistic is like being mad at the ocean for being wet. It has its rules and those rules are about its survival not yours . . . it steps on anyone under its feet. What do you expect from an elephant when you're a cockroach?"

Maggie Renzi put those feelings in perspective. She told *Premiere* magazine (July 1999), "This is someone who'd always done exactly what he wanted— and never wanted anything more than that. And he was surprised, really and truly surprised when they took his movie away. . . . It made him more firmly anti-studio."

■   ■   ■

For Sayles the early 1980s seemed the best and worst of times. His two scripts for other productions both ran into problems. *Enormous Changes at the Last Minute* (1982) presented three Grace Paley stories of a trio of New York City women, all divorced, maintaining their independence and dignity. John admired the author's writing and, as a favor to producer Mirra Bank, worked with Susan Rice in adapting the stories for the screen. The project attracted actors Ellen Barkin, David Strathairn, and Kevin Bacon, as well as composer Mason Daring. With Sayles, they would help three young women (Mirra Bank, Ellen Hovde, and Muffie Meyer) start their careers as film directors.

Admirable in intention, the movie—shot over a few years—faltered badly at the box office and with the critics who found it "ambitious but uneven." In the *New York Times,* Janet Maslin saw a "haziness extending well beyond its indistinct cinematography and slightly muffled sound." *Ms.* magazine said the film's effective moments were "better than the parts, and the parts better than the whole." More positive, *The Nation* called *Enormous* "a most contemporary, credible and conscientious work." Its PBS name and video title was *Trumps;* by any name it now earns two and a half stars from Leonard Maltin's annual *Movie & Video Guide.*

As opposed to the low-budget production problems that marred *Enormous Changes, The Clan of the Cave Bear* (1986) had creative crises generated by the indecisiveness of its producers, Jon Peters and Peter Guber. The movie was based on Jean Auel's popular 1980 novel of the same name about a Cro-Magnon orphan girl, Ayla, who is adopted by a Neanderthal tribe still clinging to its vestigial ways. In a plot combining Stone Age history and the dawning of civilization as measured by the status of women, the smart and feisty Ayla (Daryl Hannah) emerges as a warrior and, after a rape, mother. She demonstrates her skill with weaponry used only by the men, but the intelligence, talent, and physical attributes (tall and blond) underscore her difference. In the end, recognizing that she will always be "other" and called to a higher life, she leaves the tribe and her son.

For two years the producers haggled over the choice of language for the movie. Should the tribe's people grunt and use hand signals, should they speak English (as they do in the novel), or should they employ another language altogether? Asked to develop the script for a two-part TV movie (dropped in favor of a theatrical release), Sayles kept dialogue to a minimum by employing a combination of gestures and voice-over commentary to convey the drama. Curtis

Armstrong played a leading caveman (Goov) in *Clan* and remembers auditioning with the Sayles script, which he found similar to the book. Once on location in Canada, however, the producers decided to invent a language (Sayles called it "ugga, bugga bear") and add subtitles. "After that," Armstrong says, "the movie was a mess. The director, Michael Chapman [the cinematographer for *Taxi Driver*, 1976], brought in his son Matt, a college student, who did a rewrite, and my acting partners, John Doolittle (Brun), Marty Doyle (Grod), and I wrote scenes that were used in the film. A lot of actors worked on improvising scenes."

Despite the many changes, Sayles's name remains in the credits, and more importantly, he was paid well. The credits made him feel queasy and the film disappointed him, but as John said, "It wasn't a terrible movie." Most critics disagreed. Parodying the film dialect, *Newsweek*'s Jack Kroll wrote: "*The Clan of the Cave Bear* is Dog . . . John Sayles good writer, why his screenplay so dull?" The *Village Voice* agreed and concluded that *Clan* "has just about nothing going for it." Both the *Los Angeles Times* and *New York* magazine cited another anthropological film, *Quest for Fire* (1981), as being far superior. Meanwhile, Jean Auel found the treatment of her novel so artistically damaging that she sued the producers. The distributor, Warner Bros., dropped plans to produce the next part of Auel's trilogy, *The Valley of Horses* (1982)—even after hiring Sayles to adapt it. By critical consensus, *The Clan of the Cave Bear* marks the low ebb of John Sayles as screenwriter.

■   ■   ■

While in the midst of battling with Paramount and scriptwriting for others, Sayles continued to push his own film projects. The writing and stockpiling of screenplays constituted insurance against the day when funding would dry up and he would have to finance his own movie. That crisis came in 1984. For years Maggie Renzi had pursued backers for the period drama *Matewan,* and she now had it ready for production in West Virginia. After its surprising cancellation, Renzi told *American Film* (September 1987), "We already had the phones installed in the Econo Lodge [in Thurmond], but one of the big investors dropped out." In the eyes of the major studios, the film had several red flags. The pro-union topic was too radical, and as opposed to other union films (*Norma Rae,* 1979, for example), *Matewan* had no stars, love story, or happy ending. That project was set aside until 1987.

To fill the gap in his work schedule and to keep his name in the public mind, Sayles hastily drafted the script of *The Brother from Another Planet* (1984). He would tap his own resources for the funds, and thanks to a 1983 grant from an unexpected source, the money was there.

While in the throes of mixing the sound for *Baby It's You,* Sayles received a call from the MacArthur Foundation office informing him that he'd won one of their annual awards. He laughs as he remembers his response. "I mumbled, 'Gee, great, I have to get back to work now,'" he told the *New York Times* (April 17, 1983). "I was so tired it didn't register. . . . I acted like my car was ready at the muffler shop. The only problem is that you have to sit still while Jane Pauley calls you a genius."

Nobody applies for a MacArthur grant, and nobody knows it's coming. A nominating committee of the Chicago-based James MacArthur Foundation combs the country looking for the most creative talents it can find and then sends a team of investigators to learn about them and their work. The foundation selects just twenty people annually, usually artists and scholars, then endows them with money that will reward the winners' past efforts, ensure the continuance of their work, and support a cause of their choosing.

In Sayles's case, the "Genius Grant," as it is known, gave him $32,000 a year tax free for the next five years. The fact that he won the honor at age thirty-two brought him more distinction but fewer dollars. "It's based on your age," he says in *Sayles on Sayles*. "If you're sixty-five years or older, you get $65,000 [a year] for the rest of your life."

While he kidded other older and younger winners about the timing, John gratefully accepted the grant and knew exactly how he would employ it. For a few years, he could ease off the scriptwriting for other people and attend to his own moviemaking. "The work I do," Sayles said to the *New York Times* (July 17, 1988), "is like walking a tightrope. With the MacArthur, it's a tightrope with a safety net under you." Together with the money earned from the earlier scripts, it was the Genius Grant that helped launch *The Brother from Another Planet*.

12

The Brother from Another Planet:
Back to Guerrilla Filmmaking

This was my salvation. I was ready to get a cab driver's license when Peggy Rajski called. So, yes, there was a lot of work to be gotten done quickly, but this was a real break for me to be making a professional film and with a hero of the NYU grad students, because he did things his own way.

DIRECTOR ERNEST DICKERSON, 1998

IN JULY OF 1982, while producers Jon Peters and Peter Guber were reviewing Sayles's drafts for *The Clan of the Cave Bear*, John had a week available for writing another script. With its cast and location in place, the pending production of *Matewan* suddenly lost its financial backers and was scrubbed. Coincidentally, the filmmaker had been working under enormous duress while completing the editing and scoring of *Baby It's You* (1983). That pressure, John said in *Writers Dreaming* (1993), induced three recurring dreams, from which emerged *The Brother from Another Planet* (1984). John admits that for him, exercise—especially swimming—sometimes brings about a kind of trance during which good film ideas occur, and dreams as well can inspire a scenario.

The first dream sprung from an old joke from director pal Joe Dante about making a B-movie called *Assholes from Outer Space*, a 1950s-type paranoia picture in which the alien assholes land and start working for the American government. In the second reverie, John is directing *Bigfoot in the City*, a film noir set in Seattle, Washington, with the plot and style of the British classic *Odd Man Out* (1947). As in the original, which starred James Mason, the hero races through dark, slick streets pursued by cops who believe he's a criminal. They trap him in an alley, shine a flashlight in his face and say "Book him."

Dream No. 3 would provide the heart of the forthcoming *Brother* script. In *Writers Dreaming,* the dreamer/director describes the key idea. Sayles finds himself in Harlem and spots a lost, frightened man wandering the streets. "Then I realized . . . that he's from another planet. No wonder he feels lost. He can't talk. How alienating, literally, that must be. How lonely he must be."

Fueled by his unconscious, Sayles spent just seven days developing the script. It presents the account of an alien who escapes slavery on his own planet and is pursued by its interplanetary cops all the way to present-day Harlem. Unable to speak but gifted with the power to fix everything from wires to wounds, the alien is like Charlie Chaplin's classic Tramp character. He is a mute who wanders about the city and whose innocent investigation measures the quality of life on Earth. In addition to appreciating the blend of comedy, science fiction, and social comment that the dreams had provided his script, Sayles, the eternal pragmatist, liked all the advantages of its location in Harlem. New York City was overflowing with talented African-American actors and good local film crews. There was no need to pay for lodging or dinners, no studio overhead, and great, free, and low-cost settings at every turn.

Ernest Dickerson, hired as director of photography, told me about another economic plus for this 1984 release: "In Manhattan, nobody shoots above 110th Street [as few films were being made about African Americans], so that left all the Teamsters downtown. There were no hassles." In 1983, with the script in place, Sayles started goading producers Maggie Renzi and Peggy Rajski to launch the film project while the favorable August–September weather was on their side. Restricted by the budget, the producers gave themselves four weeks to prepare the production and four more to shoot it.

Approaching his fourth feature, John was adamant about three matters. First, he would *not* take the project to the Hollywood studios. His post-Paramount antipathy toward the majors led him to insist, "I can finance this myself." He also knew that the film must cost no more than $350,000; that's all the money he had. Consequently, he could not follow the Directors Guild of America rules for employing a first and second assistant director and a production manager and paying them guild salaries. (This led the filmmaker, for the time being, to drop his DGA membership.) His third decision was that this would be another nonunion project. Crew salaries and professional memberships were, however, not his only concerns.

As problematic as *Lianna* (1983) may have been with a male making a movie about lesbians, *Brother* posed even thornier internal and external issues. In 1985, Sayles told the audience at an American Film Institute seminar: "From the day we decided to make a film about black people, we lost an enormous [potential] audience—all over the world." According to the filmmaker, the decisions that made the picture hard to sell ironically became the reasons for the film's success at the box office.

In shooting *Brother,* Sayles also faced the prospect of resentment toward a white moviemaker about to depict African-American life and about to do his production on the quintessential black urban turf: Harlem. The black community would be understandably wary of a filmmaker who professes to know about their culture and, as a result, would be watchful of his production style and treatment of them while filming. As location manager Paul Marcus told *Film Comment* (March/April 1984): "Particularly for a low budget production, befriending the locals is crucial for visitors. . . . We need to have them want us here. . . . But I think it makes a difference what we're doing; people like the project. This is a first time experience for many of us making a film in Harlem. Hell, BEING in Harlem."

As a gesture of his good faith, Sayles needed to be at his politically correct, sensitive best. For starters, he could rely somewhat on his own background and reputation. As he explained to the *New York Times* (August 23, 1987): "I've lived on the fringe, in and around black neighborhoods, and I played ball with black people and been around minorities, so I wanted to show what that was like to other people." He had also worked side by side with blacks as an orderly in Albany, New York, and on road construction crews in Atlanta, Georgia.

As Haskell Wexler, a three-time cinematographer for Sayles, told me, "John is one of the very few American directors who has done a day's work. He knows what that's like." Sayles's image also helped. There were no Polo shirts and Gucci shoes in his wardrobe. In his daily commutes from Hoboken, New Jersey, to Harlem, the Coors baseball hat, sneakers, shorts, and tank top was standard attire. He also preferred meeting reporters at the Gaiety Coffee Shop near Times Square rather than at the typical fancy hotel or in the back of a long limousine. His plain-folks style would be a positive sign to the Harlem neighborhood, as would his willingness to learn the six or seven degrees of black talk. Eventually, the community and crew helped teach him the varying cadences and styles with which blacks spoke in offices, homes, and bars and how homeless people kept a fire going in a barrel with newspaper and not wood. Still, initial practical measures were needed to make the African-American community comfortable with his project from the start.

The script established the groundwork. For one thing, *Brother* had a positive central figure. As an ensemble piece, the movie would include a wide range of African-American characters (ensuring against stereotyping) and therefore would involve several professional black actors, providing them with rare and welcome opportunities in a feature film. As always, Sayles expected to find his onscreen extras within the community. Having worked with him earlier, his co-producer and casting director, Barbara Shapiro, knew the kinds of talent he required. The New York stage was the first place she looked, because theater-trained performers could handle the dialogue in a two-minute-long take.

For the star of the movie and other principals, John also stayed local. Joe Morton was the first brought on board for the shoot. Raised as an army brat in Germany, Morton was still a boy in the 1960s when, after his dad's death, his mother brought him back to her neighborhood on Sugar Hill in Harlem. Having experienced racial prejudice on the army base outside Berlin, he found American youngsters put off by his German accent and studious looks. He completed his education at a military school in Newburgh, New York, then added two years at Hofstra University in Hempstead, New York, before turning to the theater and a role in the 1968 musical *Hair*.

To star in *Brother,* Morton took a double pay cut. His regular job at the time was on the NBC-TV network soap opera *Another World,* in which he played Dr. Abel Marsh. Bored by the one role, Morton submitted a treatment to the daytime drama producers for another character, the doctor's rock-and-roller twin, Leo. For playing that added part, he received a bonus. In *The New Yorker* (January 2, 1984), he explained his attraction to Sayles's picture. "It's very much like what would happen if I had been born in Africa and was seeing Harlem for the first time."

Initially, Sayles thought Morton at age thirty-five was too young for the lead. Barbara Shapiro, however, convinced him to allow the actor to do a reading. John came to appreciate the "alien" experiences of Morton's boyhood that he could bring to the film. As the filmmaker observed later, "He knew about cultures where he didn't speak the language."

Today Sayles jokes that Morton was the only actor he ever allowed to ad-lib. John gave his star ample leeway in delineating the Brother's character. At the 1985 AFI seminar, John remembered saying to Morton, "I'm not going to have much time to work with you. You're going to have to come up with things yourself. And you're going to have to keep track of what you understand about the world because we're shooting in sequence. . . . How much of what they're saying do you understand? Do you know certain patterns? Do you know who runs the bar?"

Because of the alien's extrasensory perception, Morton also developed a scale of reactions to places haunted by sadness (Ellis Island) or by death (a stool favored by a bar patron who was killed). The Brother's use of gestures instead of speech was thematically provocative: each of the other characters perceived him differently, thus revealing part of themselves. Practically, his muteness also cut down the cost of production, allowing Sayles to shoot film without sound, including the unwanted noises of the city.

To support Morton's performance, Shapiro rounded up a veteran cast, all willing to work for scale. Caroline Aaron was between plays and took the role of Randy Sue Carter, giving it the "strong, tough, from-the-South quality" Sayles required. For the scenes inside Odell's Bar, where the Brother seeks refuge, he hired Leonard Jackson (TV's *The Jeffersons*), Darryl Edwards (*Fort*

Apache, The Bronx, 1981), and Bill Cobbs (*Greased Lightning,* 1977). As *Time* would judge of this screen threesome, they "turn street talk into an art." John cast himself as the bad guy, teaming himself with his Hoboken, neighbor David Strathairn as the outer space cops chasing the Brother. In one sequence, their pursuit would be thwarted by Maggie Renzi as a social worker and master of bureaucratic gobbledygook.

■   ■   ■

As with all Sayles's screen projects, the production team for the new movie would be young, equally divided between men and women, and marked by an unusually high number of female department heads. All crew members received about $80 a week with the hope that the picture would make enough money to deliver their deferred payments. Given his new film's content and topic, Sayles wanted a racially representative crew. "We knew we had to make it with the people of Harlem," he told *Film Comment* (March/April 1984), "and we knew we wanted to work with a largely black crew."

Among the crew's young, aspiring filmmakers was Gil Taylor, an African-American who quit his job as ad traffic manager at Lord and Taylor department store to work as a production assistant. For *Brother,* he worked crowd control. John had decided that to maintain good community relations in Harlem, production assistants were preferable to police. Larry Justice had saved money in Dallas, Texas, then moved to New York City to jump-start his movie career. For three weeks' work on an earlier film, he had earned a total of $100, but he was still eager to continue even at the entry level. Fronza Woods had helped make short subjects for the Women's International Center and now was working the boom microphone on *Brother.*

Fresh out of film school, Kurt Davis found the experience scary. In fact, he admitted to hoping he could report in sick and avoid a forbidding all-night shoot. In his fear, he was not alone. Most of these young people working for A Train Films, as this unit was known, were seeing Harlem for the first time. Instead of threats to their safety, however, some of the crew discovered decent and affordable housing in the community and later moved there. For the film's script supervisor, Marco Williams, author of *From Harlem to Harvard* (1981), *Brother* was a homecoming. He contributed to the film by devising the Brother's unique three-toed foot.

On any crew, the linchpin is the director of photography, and for *Brother*, this linchpin could "fib" just well enough to get the job. Now a respected movie director in his own right, Ernest Dickerson had just graduated from New York University's formal film school. His brief but promising résumé included shooting Spike Lee's much admired thesis movie, *Joe's Bed-Stuy Barbershop: We Cut Heads* (1980). "John saw the film and liked it," Dickerson says. "It fit the style of his own film and being a black DP was a plus."

At a meeting arranged by Peggy Rajski, Sayles told Dickerson the film's full plot and then asked if he had any experience with 35mm. "I lied, but I knew I could do it," Dickerson told me. "It was just bigger film stock, but the lighting, exposure, lens—they were all the same." Having heard horror stories about unpaid-deferred payments, Dickerson was cautious, but the DP job beat his current occupation of cab driver. Ready to put his graduate school degree to use, he signed on for the four six-day weeks of production.

With a budget just one-tenth that of *Baby It's You,* Sayles saw *Brother* as an antidote to the political hassles he had experienced at Paramount. Nevertheless, the budget would impact every stage of the project. Sayles's opening shot— the spacecraft (cost: $12) hurtling through cardboard outer space (the camera rocking side to side) and splashing down on earth—signaled the film's economic and comic parameters. The audience immediately knew this was not the elaborate *2001: A Space Odyssey* (1968) and that laughing was OK. The Brother's landing also added social overtones to the science fiction parodying. The alien arrives the way millions of immigrants had, entering the country under the gaze of the Statue of Liberty and onto Ellis Island.

Proximity to Manhattan played a large part in the choice of Ellis Island as a location, but two years prior to the decision to make *Brother,* Sayles and Maggie Renzi had visited the tourist attraction. As he told the AFI students, "It was a holy, haunted place, filled with confusion, misery, and fear, all in these strange languages. And the minute I started writing the film, I said, 'He'll have to crash there.'" In 1983 Ellis Island had yet to undergo its multimillion-dollar transformation into a worthy national shrine; it was then half torn down. The National Park Service granted the producers just twelve hours to complete their shooting, though they did allow them to set up lighting beforehand.

Once on location, the crew inserted a little platform just below water level, lit it, and then filmed the alien "landing" in the water. (The splash was inserted later.) Prior to the takes, the props department created a sling so star Joe Morton could get out of the water quickly and onto the Ellis Island pier. "John didn't want to waste any time," Dickerson says. The "magic hour," as Sayles calls these hurried takes, got cut to thirty minutes and was followed by a night of shooting the scenes in which the Brother investigates Ellis's reception hall, with "moonlight" streaking through the windows. Earlier an assistant editor had taped sounds of babies crying and older people speaking Russian, Yiddish, and other languages all around New York City. In the release print, underneath the Great Hall shots, that compilation track with its haunting muted voices can be heard.

To complete the alien arrival sequence, John wanted a shot of the sunrise over Manhattan. "We finished the interior shots at Ellis Island, then John and I ran outside," Dickerson recalls. "We were racing through weeds, and the rats were not far behind us." The crew then tried faking the alien's swimming to and climbing aboard a tugboat, but Renzi finally convinced the director that the staging looked, in her words, "like the tugboat wasn't moving and people were throwing water in the Brother's face." Finally, they just shot him on board the boat. Vastly understating the night's professional efficiency, Sayles told the seminar students, "Sometimes you gotta move awfully fast."

The speed and adaptation to circumstances typical of guerrilla filmmaking carried over to the Peacock Bar at the corner of 125th Street and Adam Clayton Powell Boulevard. At times the action on the pavement rivaled in intensity the fiction being shot inside. Three different "owners" of the bar's building approached Sayles demanding compensation for using "their" property. On another occasion, when the crew forgot the keys and accidentally locked the day's costumes inside their car, a Good Samaritan stopped to help pry open the trunk. While the volunteer was unlocking the car, someone else stole his carryall, whereupon Maggie Renzi spent the remainder of the day with the victim at the methadone clinic trying to reclaim his daily dosage. That same day the owner of a fruit stand where the crew was shooting became alarmed at his loss of business, withdrew his agreement, and ejected the crew.

Despite these real-life scenarios, the telescoped production remained remarkably free of major roadblocks, thanks largely to the measures taken to elicit the community's good will. The interracial composition of the crew, the use of production assistants for crowd control, and the notices to the neighbors about possible disruptions were efforts that won support for *Brother*.

As planned, the 104-minute *Brother* builds to a comic climax, with a kung fu–style battle between the alien and his two would-be captors. For that scene the crew had developed the kind of lighting and shooting they'd need to make the action convincing. What appears on screen, however, is just a quick flurry of shots, then the battle is over. The cause of the discrepancy between plan and result speaks to the realities of budget *and* time. Shooting that scene on their last day of location work at the Peacock Bar, the crew was drowning in a late summer storm. The crew and all the equipment now had to move back into the bar. The mirrors behind the bar, the extras, and the equipment all thwarted the careful preparation for the scene. As Dickerson says, "There simply was not enough time to do the setups and angles we needed to do the parody of the Hong Kong kung fu movies. We got what we could."

Earlier, Dickerson had successfully employed his guerrilla tactics to overcome economic limitations on the props. In a nightclub scene where the Brother is attracted to a singer (Dee Dee Bridgewater), John wanted to backlight her and add light steaming from behind. "That shot needed a halo of smoke, but we couldn't afford the machine," Dickerson says. "So I gave out cigarettes to gaffers, PAs [production assistants], and extras and had them puff smoke onto the scene. It worked pretty well."

Likewise, flickering lights were placed inside a stationary car in the Subway Museum in Brooklyn to help create the scene in which a kid dazzles the Brother with card tricks. The cost of shooting that scene was $750 for four hours, an enormous outlay for this project. One more scene was needed for the finale, but the money had run out. Expeditiously, Dickerson and an assistant used tote bags to smuggle a camera and a single light onto a train platform at 4 A.M. With the light on and camera rolling, the subway train pulled into the station. Joe Morton entered the last car, walked to the back window, and looked back at the station as the train pulled out. At the next station, a van was waiting to bring him back for take two. While a PA looked out for transit police, Dickerson repeated the shot in a take that was perfect—until another passenger walked with Morton to the back of the car. "Take three went off without a hitch," Dickerson says, "and that's how the film ends."

The skirmishes with authorities, the noise level, and crowd control exhausted even this tireless young crew. For their part, producers Renzi and Rajski resolved that they'd never again try to produce an urban-shot film that fast. Sayles looked at the bright side of the trade-off and saw the energizing force that Harlem provided. A year later he told AFI's students, "I wanted the neighborhood to be a character. I was trying to make a movie about the community."

In response to the obvious question about why the Brother would not turn to a social service agency for help, Sayles pointed out a documentary-style scene shot in a real food-stamp office on a Saturday morning. What would have been distraction in another film became an integral part of the mayhem. Phones ring, papers get shuffled, and the social workers speak a language foreign to all but them. A special screening in Harlem revealed how close that scene came to capturing the gap between service providers and receivers. As Sayles detailed to the *New York Post* (September 10, 1984), "The kids in the audience all cheered when they saw that scene. They knew what their parents had experienced in government offices."

That enthusiasm foreshadowed the positive reactions to the film from both the critics and the public. The *Christian Science Monitor* (October 1, 1984), which had deplored *Lianna* (1983), now applauded. "The portraits of black ghetto life are richly affectionate, the characters all ring true, and the camera explores the action instead of merely gaping at it." *New York* magazine (October 1, 1984) called Sayles "incredibly resourceful" and his film a "hysterical parody of science fiction and an elegy for a wounded community." In a mixed review, the *Los Angeles Times* (October 11, 1984) cited the "marvelous gallery of street wise characters," but identified Sayles as "a better scenarist than director." The *Village Voice* (September 18, 1984) liked the "splendid brief encounters," even if John "didn't know where to put the camera."

In a 1998 interview, actor James Earl Jones expressed his admiration for *The Brother from Another Planet* and its director. He told me, "John was able to take a subject of black reality and make something interesting out of it instead of a bunch of clichés that would embarrass black people and also white people who know what black people are all about." A few years after seeing the movie, Jones was approached by Maggie Renzi to appear in *Matewan*. Remembering his admiration for *Brother*, Jones said yes to a production he normally would have shunned. Later Sayles would continue to showcase black characters in films such as *City of Hope* (1991), *Passion Fish* (1992), and *Lone Star* (1996).

Having impressed the critics, the little $350,000 movie turned over $4 million at the box office, and that was no accident. After being burned by the cavalier distribution methods of Paramount on *Baby It's You,* Renzi, Rajski, and Sayles entered the distribution phase determined to exercise more control. As Rajski said to *American Film* (September 1987), "Once you've worked so hard to make a film, you don't want just anyone to distribute. We wanted an uncommonly full say in distribution strategy, how to position the film and where to put it."

Sayles told the *Wall Street Journal*'s John Salaman (May 11, 1984) that he did not "want to peddle it from Hollywood studio to Hollywood studio where executives can turn the movie off after ten minutes or talk on the telephone while they're watching." Instead, his producers looked in France for American distributors at the Cannes Film Festival. Before leaving the United States, Sayles did extensive promotion. The novelty of a young white filmmaker shooting his film in Harlem caught the media's attention, and extensive interviews appeared in the *New York Times, The New Yorker,* and *Film Comment.*

Cannes called for the same kind of energetic public relations campaign. Screenings at the festival fall into two main categories: the "invited" with about twenty films, and the "unselected" with about four hundred movies, now including *Brother,* vying for distributors' attention. To lure promoters, Renzi and Rajski hired Affinity Enterprises. The marketing firm then spent $30,000 on making *Brother* an "event" and "getting the buzz going" with a sweepstakes (two round-trip tickets to Harlem and a soul food picnic). Affinity succeeded in attracting three European distributors: Virgin Visions (London), The Movies (Holland), and Films du semaphore (France). They agreed to playdates in November (London), December (Holland), and January (Paris).

For the American distribution, Sayles chose Julie Beaton and Cinecom after a highly competitive bidding war among several companies. In addition to assuring that the filmmakers would be involved in marketing the picture and pointing to its willingness to experiment, Cinecom came up with a substantial financial commitment. For all parties the chief concern was to get *Brother* to an audience beyond the art houses.

In stage one, Cinecom planned to open the film in the commercial art houses, then add neighborhoods in the black community. Stage two would send the film south to the Washington, D.C., and Atlanta, Georgia, areas, especially to the chain theaters near army bases. The producers were developing print ads, television promos, and a movie trailer. They also were negotiating rights to the Mason Daring soundtrack album, to be released with the film. Cinecom also predicted a long video life for the movie they hoped would become a cult classic.

The campaign worked well enough to please Cinecom and A Train and to give Sayles a rolling start toward the financing of his next project. The filmmaker was also rewarding his gallant crew. "On the day of the New York City opening," Ernest Dickerson recalls, "as we were walking into the theater, Maggie and Peggy were in the back handing out envelopes. After the sale of the film, they immediately paid off the crew's deferments." After that late September 1984 opening, *The Brother from Another Planet* enjoyed a successful theater run well into the following year. Eventually the tape version played to audiences not even John could have anticipated.

Sayles now looked to the financing of the much postponed *Matewan*. Since Cinecom was not yet ready to tackle a production of that magnitude, the producers had to look elsewhere. That search for support left a time gap that was quickly filled by Sayles's other writing projects, a return to the stage, and a favor to a family friend.

13

What's a Genius
to Do?

Written by a Woody Allen with a social conscience,
starring a stunning actress, Unnatural Causes *[1986]*
should make you very angry.

CRITIC JOHN LEONARD, 1986

IN *THE BROTHER FROM ANOTHER PLANET,* audiences got a preview of the varied expertise Sayles would demonstrate throughout his career. As Jack Ryan noted in *John Sayles, Filmmaker* (1998), John now had added lyricist to his credentials. His two songs included "Homeboy," sung offscreen by the film's star, Joe Morton, and the movie's closing tune, "Promised Land," performed by the Laborers in the Vineyard All Community Choir. On screen with his Williams College sidekick David Strathairn, Sayles created a windup-toy effect to depict the two *Dragnet*-style slave hunters from outer space by having them walk backward and filming them upside down. *Films in Review* (January 1985) appreciated the "good humor and wit" of John's performance.

With the wrap of *Brother* in October 1983, Sayles had before him the need to edit and mix the film, distribute it, and do the needed promotion. Despite these demands, he found time for other projects as well. For John, the years immediately after *Brother* and before the start of his next film, *Matewan* (1987), would include (1) a critically acclaimed starring role in a production of Tennessee Williams's play *The Glass Menagerie* opposite Joanne Woodward, (2) the directing of three video recordings for hit songs by Bruce Springsteen, and (3) scriptwriting, this time for the acclaimed television production *Unnatural Causes*, directed by the legendary Lamont Johnson. The achievements in these separate artistic enterprises suggest that Sayles, had he chosen, would have distinguished himself in any of these creative fields.

While the reviews cited the good humor of his "Joe Friday as alien" role in *Brother*, John's performances in his first three movies were more for cost cutting than career enhancement. In the summer of 1985, he would erase any doubts about his acting abilities in a brief but memorable stay with the company of the Williamstown Theatre Festival in western Massachusetts.

Famed as one of the country's leading regional theaters, WTF got its start in the 1950s thanks to Ralph Renzi, Maggie's father. During the vacation season, WTF is a leader in the summer circuit of New York and New England mountain area playhouses, reviving classics and testing new stage productions. Today Ralph remains a patron of the playhouse and its festival. He told me that back in 1985, just days before the August opening of *The Glass Menagerie*, director Nikos Psacharopoulis learned that Richard Thomas of TV's *The Waltons* would be unavailable for the key role of Tom Wingfield. Dutifully, Ralph suggested Sayles for the part, and the timing was right. "These three weeks," Sayles told Ralph, "are about the only ones where I've been available in three years."

By opening night, Sayles the trouper not only had mastered his lines, but he also was rivaling Joanne Woodward's performance. An Oscar and Emmy winner, Woodward was the house draw as Amanda, the disillusioned southern mother trying to keep her household together. Sayles's physical appearance— 6'4", brawny, and athletic-looking—made him perfect for the role of Amanda's son, Tom, a sensitive but earthbound writer.

Local critic Thomas Hulse of the *Berkshire Eagle* (August 21, 1985) approached the performance with grave misgivings about all-star miscasting, thinking of the thirty-five-year-old Sayles as a writer/director appearing in a part requiring "immense subtlety and skill." The skeptic left the theater applauding Sayles for "his wonderful southern lilt as Tom." Another *Berkshire Eagle* review by Molly Cliff judged John to be marvelous. "As both the narrator of the play and a character in the scenes he remembers, Sayles makes a smooth transition from time present to past."

Local newspapers were not alone in heaping kudos on the show. *Time* magazine critic William A. Henry III was in the audience for the opening, and the subsequent headline captured his excitement: WILLIAMSTOWN CAPS SEASON WITH A SPLENDID *GLASS MENAGERIE*. The staging gave a new twist to Williams's play by allowing Sayles and his colleagues to explore the Tom character and find shadings that suggested relationships to mother and sister akin to those of Williams himself. Devoting most of the article to Sayles's performance, Henry concluded, "Sayles, a novice actor, proved himself enormously gifted. He, not Woodward, emerged as the star of the show." In 1987 Paul Newman, Woodward's husband, employed the entire cast except Sayles, and staged the production for film. Sayles's part was played by John Malkovich.

■　　　■　　　■

Thanks to Maggie Renzi's sister, Marta, John now embarked on a new phase of his career: directing music videos. A professional dancer and choreographer in Manhattan, Marta had created a dance video for PBS-TV based on Bruce Springsteen's song "You Little Wild Heart." In the spring of 1984, she took the singer to Hoboken for dinner with her sister and Sayles. The two artists, rock star and filmmaker, exactly the same age, immediately found significant common ground: They loved baseball and hated high school. They also shared an upbringing in industrial cities and a strong allegiance to their blue-collar roots. Because of his admiration for Sayles's movies, Springsteen had allowed him to use four songs in *Baby It's You*. After this first face-to-face meeting over dinner, months went by before the musician could ask the filmmaker to direct the video of "Born in the U.S.A.," the title song of an album that had already sold nearly ten million copies.

Perhaps in return for Springsteen's favor for *Baby It's You*, John broke with his own policy by agreeing to direct somebody else's story. In *Glory Days*

(1987), Springsteen biographer Dave Marsh observed that the two reasons for Sayles's accommodation were "because their work had such strong stylistic affinities and because Springsteen was one of America's great undeveloped moving picture possibilities." There was the novelty for Sayles of directing a short-format video with Springsteen's music. The agreement gave Sayles what was for him an extravagant budget for the three-minute offering.

The downside of the video project was that John would be working under severe schedule restrictions imposed by Springsteen's concert obligations and by the musician's concerns about his image. Having recently been exploited by Ronald Reagan's patriot-baiting presidential campaign, Springsteen wanted a product untainted by the slick commercialism associated with those political ads. The Boss also was unhappy with the Brian De Palma–directed video of "Dancing in the Dark" (1984), which the *Washington Post* described as offering "a self-conscious Springsteen and a lip-syncing one at that."

For the "Born in the U.S.A." video (1985), lip-syncing was out. Sayles found footage of the Asbury Park area (Springsteen's New Jersey hometown) to mix with the shots taken at his concert in Los Angeles. At the editing stage, John faced a deadline made more urgent as the song was fast climbing the charts. Also, the mixing job called for a subtle joining of the live soundtrack with Sayles's documentary footage from a Veterans of Foreign Wars hall. In the media critique *Vulgar Modernism* (1991), J. Hoberman assails the "Born in the U.S.A." video as "an affirmatively patriotic beer commercial montage." Biographer David Marsh blames the hodgepodge on Springsteen's demands: "The documentary effect was undercut by the lack of live sound, and any inherent artfulness was dispelled because the sound didn't match Bruce's lip movements."

In 1985, when Bossmania was sweeping the country, Springsteen again turned to Sayles to direct the video for "I'm on Fire," a single slotted as the fourth cut on the *Born in the U.S.A.* album. This time Sayles and the singer developed a story line for a concept video that would play against the song's lyrics. Taped between Springsteen's American tour and his departure for Japan, the video featured Bruce as an auto mechanic lured to the estate of a sexy-voiced woman (unseen except for her legs and wedding ring) angling to reel him in. Once at her door, however, and with his finger almost on the bell, Bruce wistfully walks away.

Again, Sayles would edit the video while racing against the chart life of the song. This time he emerged with a coherent piece that showcased Springsteen as an actor (with dialogue). *Time* magazine (April 15, 1985) was impressed by the singer's performance, citing his "friendly relationship with the camera," and found him "ready for a major movie." The $10,000 fee Sayles earned for this project was contributed to a fund to send ambulances to Nicaragua to aid those wounded in the war being waged there.

"Glory Days" (1985), the third and final video collaboration of Sayles and Springsteen to date, reflects the "luxury" of time they had to shoot and edit. The production was spread over a Memorial Day weekend, right before Bruce would leave for his European tour and just before Columbia Records would release the "Glory Days" single. In expanding on the song's theme of choosing to live in the present and not the past, the video employs four locations: a construction site, a broken-down baseball park, a family home, and Maxwell's, a Hoboken bar. While rather plotless, "Glory Days" peaks in theme and energy with the performance of Bruce and the E Street Band at Maxwell's.

Of the "Glory Days" video, Marsh wrote, "It isn't what a 'real' Bruce Springsteen song looks like onstage, but it's exactly what it feels like." After Springsteen left for Europe, fourteen years would elapse before his next creative teaming with Sayles, on 1999's *Limbo*.

■   ■   ■

Among film actors, as with critics, John's acting skills are well recognized. Actor Kevin Tighe has seen him work in three movies and wrote in a letter to me, "John acts in a few of his movies—he never 'performs.' The roles are close to his experience and are unfettered by anything outside that experience." Sayles himself sees acting as a muscle that needs to be exercised. In his own films, the performance workouts lead to four or five minutes on screen—at most—and his appearances in others' movies rarely last more than a minute or two. Between 1985 and 1986, he would have three such cameos, two in motion pictures and one for television, none directed by him.

In casting his $5 million, seven-week production *Hard Choices* (1986), a feature about a troubled teenager, producer/director Rick King first turned to Sayles for casting advice, then picked him for a part in the project. Playing what he calls a "gentleman marijuana farmer," John had his biggest and longest screen performance, about five minutes. *Hard Choices* opens like an action picture, works its way through teenage and social problems, then turns to drugs and justice. Roger Ebert of the *Chicago Sun-Times* (September 26, 1986) cited the Sayles character as one of the film's strengths. "One role is especially well-written: an intellectual, philosophical drug dealer, played by John Sayles, who does not remind us of any drug dealer we've seen in a movie before." The *Los Angeles Times* (August 1, 1986) admired the honing of the character. "Sayles . . . has the loose, wary mannerisms of this rich-boy outlaw Vanderbilt cocaine dealer down pat." Sayles admitted to the *New York Times* (May 30, 1986) that performing was not a profession he wished to pursue. "The acting part is fine," he acknowledged, "but trying to get work is terrible."

That same year Sayles appeared in a cameo as a motorcycle cop in Jonathan Demme's *Something Wild* (1986). John's unexpected presence, along with that of another director, John Waters (*Pink Flamingos,* 1972), adds further quirkiness to a narrative about a hero's (Jeff Daniels) journey into the bizarre world of drink, drugs, robberies, and sex, all reminiscent of Martin Scorsese's *After Hours* (1985).

■   ■   ■

In the fall of 1980, Sayles had seen his first television script, *A Perfect Match,* produced for CBS-TV. It dealt with a woman searching for an organ transplant that can be supplied only by the daughter she had once given up for adoption. The film starred Colleen Dewhurst and Charles Durning and drew little critical comment. In his second foray into TV, Sayles scripted one of the most admired productions of the 1986 fall season. He also appeared in it, in a small role.

NBC-TV's *Unnatural Causes* provides an intense two hours about Vietnam veteran Frank Coleman, who has contracted cancer, and a Veterans Administration counselor, Maude DeVictor, who battles an entrenched bureaucracy set on ignoring the effects of Agent Orange. Known primarily for his sitcom talents, John Ritter (*Three's Company,* 1977–84) gave a robust performance as the dying veteran. The DeVictor character was based on a real Chicago crusader for war veterans and was played by Emmy Award winner Alfre Woodard, later the costar of Sayles's *Passion Fish* (1992).

The TV program paired Sayles the actor/writer with one of the medium's most highly respected directors, Lamont Johnson. Johnson found the script exceptional and, after gaining casting control, signed on. Then NBC got cold feet about the subject matter and delayed the production for three months.

In the winter of 1986, Johnson met Sayles on the first day of the shoot, which used Toronto, Ontario, Canada, as a surrogate for Chicago. On a freezing day in a cemetery, Sayles did his cameo as a Vietnam vet talking with the hero about their deceased comrades. Johnson remembers the shoot well. "[John] came to the scene prepared from the inside out and intuitively did the right thing. It was a sensitive, unaffected performance."

With the acting out of the way, Sayles settled down to work with Johnson on further script revisions. Johnson told this book's author, "As a writer/director, he could see the problems from a director's perspective, and he very pleasantly agreed to do the revisions on the spot." When the shooting finished and after in-house screenings had received positive reactions, the network again balked. NBC held a private screening for Dow Chemical, the manufacturer of Agent Orange, then started sending Johnson notes concerning the associating of genetic damage with the chemical—and Dow. As Johnson battled with the producers, he called Sayles and left messages, but never reached him.

Inevitably, cuts and changes were made to the telefilm. According to Johnson, *Variety* ran a headline at the time suggesting creative cowardliness: NBC EXECUTIVES: PAID TO BE AFRAID. Today Johnson takes a less passionate, more philosophical stance. "There was enough that did get across, so it was a case of swallowing a lot of shit to get the good stuff out there." NBC held a premiere screening at the Kennedy Center in Washington, D.C., and invited congressmen. "Representative John Conyers of Michigan loved it," Johnson says. "The Veterans Administration didn't."

Following its telecast on November 10, 1986, the eve of Veterans Day, the program drew unanimous critical praise for its tough-mindedness and sensitivity. *USA Today* (November 11, 1986) opined, "Unabashedly crusading, the film written by the immensely talented John Sayles details yet another Vietnam nightmare. . . . Agent Orange rained death not only on vegetation but on unsuspecting soldiers." *Washington Post* TV critic Tom Shales (November 10, 1986) called it "the first meaningful movie of the new season—intensely moving and gratifyingly consequential." At the same time, Shales sensed the network's hedging and safety nets. "Sayles' script leads only to a vicarious kind of climax. Neither that fact nor a wordy, wooden epilogue written by a team of lawyers blunts the impact of the film."

Aside from his directing, acting, and scriptwriting, Sayles would sometimes revert to doing pieces for print publication. "At Play: Pregame Jitters" (*Esquire*, June 1986) captures the kind of baseball games he played in his backyard on Sumner Avenue in Schenectady. His short story "The Halfway Diner" appeared in the *Atlantic Monthly* (June 1987). The narrative centers on an ethnically diverse group of women who stop at a diner halfway to and from visits with their husbands in prison. During this period, John also was recording a reading of his short-story collection *The Anarchists' Convention* (1979). That experimentation now complete, he turned once again to finding funding for the often postponed *Matewan*.

14

Matewan: The Sayles Production
Company and Its First Celebrities

I was happy with the whole film. I was also aware that we
had a chance to meet the people who had ancestors
involved with the mine wars. We were able to get some ideas
about what it was like in those days.

ACTOR JAMES EARL JONES, 1998

"IT WERE 1920," an old-time coal miner intones. With this opening voice-over, *Matewan* (1987) then plunges into the times and culture of Mingo County, West Virginia. Thus began the expansion of John Sayles's filmmaking onto a larger canvas. Centered on the town of Matewan, the coal miners' story was a film idea that first occurred to the director when, as a college student, he spent a summer on the road. In *Thinking in Pictures: The Making of the Movie Matewan* (1987), Sayles wrote, "In the late Sixties, I hitchhiked through the area several times and most of the people who gave me rides were coal miners or people with mining in their families." Through them, the twenty-year-old learned of the hardships in the United Mine Workers Union. In the early 1970s, they were facing the murder of a candidate for the UMW presidency and the refusal by the union leadership to compensate workers and their families for the repercussions of black-lung disease. "But every miner I

145

talked to, " Sayles recalled, "would shake his head and say, 'Buddy, this ain't nothing compared to what used to go on. I could tell you stories.'"

In 1977 Sayles had used those tales and his own research for his novel *Union Dues*. The bloody shootout in 1920 in the streets of Matewan was the central event of the coal miners' war that raged throughout the mountains of West Virginia and Kentucky. That encounter incited the most devastating and mortal confrontation between labor and government in U.S. history. In the minds of those beleaguered laborers, Matewan stood as their Alamo, a lost but heroic struggle. Recalled only in folk ballads, the Matewan massacre of 1920 was the story Sayles was determined to put on film.

Generally colored with the imagery of free spirits, loose living, and good times rolling, the Roaring Twenties were in fact years of economic turmoil, political unrest, and social intolerance of outsiders and troublemakers, foreign or domestic. With new ethnic groups pouring into the cities and African Americans streaming out of the South, bigotry and prejudice were rampant. The Palmer Raids, for example, rounded up European immigrants suspected of being Communists and deported them. The influx of veterans returning from World War I and the lack of jobs fomented the ongoing antagonism among races and social classes. Even when they had jobs, workers in many industries faced conditions approximating servitude.

To West Virginians, mine owners had for decades been ripping the money literally out from under their feet and kicking them off land that was rightfully theirs. In town after town, mining corporations reduced their employees to serfs. Docked from their miserable wages (doled out in company-store scrip) were payments for two-person shanties, tools, and fuel. As local stores continued jacking up prices, the owners lowered wages and demanded even more backbreaking work. Fourteen-year-olds went into the mines with adults to face disastrous accidents and dangerous diseases.

Sayles amassed the details for *Matewan* from historical manuscripts and from the oral testimony of eyewitnesses. In 1920, when the miners went on strike, the coal company owners sent in the notoriously cruel Baldwin-Felts agents to evict them from their homes. In an anomaly, both Matewan's mayor, Cabell Testerman, and sheriff, Sid Hatfield, sided with and deputized the workers.

Among the resisting forces was a hulking black miner known as Few Clothes. C. E. Lively was the spy who betrayed the miners' plans.

When the company gunmen tried to leave town, the Matewan shootout ensued leaving most of the agents, the mayor, and a few miners dead. The incident would lead to Sheriff Hatfield's assassination and the largest single armed conflict between labor and owners in American history. The fighting ended only after President Warren G. Harding sent in 2,500 troops and the air force bombed the "insurrectionists" into a submission that lasted into the 1930s.

In the murder of Sheriff Hatfield, the UMW saw the opportunity for propaganda and quickly released a 1922 one-reel silent film, *Smilin' Sam,* dramatizing the Matewan event. The short picture proved so effective that the Baldwin-Felts detectives stole and destroyed the lone print. More determined than ever, the union sought financing for *The Contrast,* a seven-reel feature. Without studio support, however, the project never materialized.

Sixty-five years later, Sayles's script on the topic also got bogged down in the Hollywood studio system. With the theme of underdogs fighting the bullies and the action building to a showdown between the sheriff and the thugs, the script hinted of *High Noon* (1952) revisited. For emotional impact and coherence, John had added two key fictional elements. The union representative, Joe Kenehan (Chris Cooper), is a pacifist organizing the miners' resistance, while Danny (Will Oldham) is the boy who witnesses the turmoil and grows up to continue the union cause. His is the narrator's voice heard in the film. While these characters personalized the battle, neither they nor the showdown climax could temper the leftist tack the project was taking. It sided with the workers and neither condemned nor applauded their violence. For Hollywood, the movie was not just liberal, it was radical.

Industry politics aside, the film would not wash in the 1980s, when the general populace was applauding President Ronald Reagan's tough-guy dismissal en masse of the striking airport traffic controllers. The projected *Matewan* also was bucking the Hollywood narrative tradition at every turn. The movie's pacifist hero was a resolute double loser who couldn't or wouldn't do "what a man's gotta do." The ending likewise limped. While a lot of "bad" guys got it, "good" guys died too, and their cause went with them. Instead of a positive hero, the film had Joe Kenehan preaching pacifism, then dying in the street. Instead of feeling good about the outcome, the audience was left to think about the events and their implications.

The studios had another monetary reservation as well. In a system that coddles high-cost celebrities, getting this epic in the can for $4 million was unimaginable, therefore unbankable. Thus, no deal!

■　　　■　　　■

In 1983 *Matewan* had come close to a real start but was abandoned when financing collapsed. Three years later, production costs (film stock, insurance, food and housing, union minimums, etc.) had nearly doubled, and the budget soared from $2 million to $4 million. Nevertheless, Red Dog Films, the company formed for the project, and co-producers Maggie Renzi and Peggy Rajski started drumming up the money. With the combined profits from *The Brother from Another Planet,* the movies he had scripted, and the Springsteen videos he had directed, John put up a third of the cash. The producers and the distributor, Cinecom International (who had also distributed *Brother*), then cobbled together a package that relied on outside investors: British investment bankers, foreign pre-sales, and home video pre-sales (to Holland's ATV Lorimar Studios), along with money from a dentist and, eventually, some of the cast. Renzi and Rajski now had to round up a crew who would make every penny count and who wouldn't ask for much pay in return.

Nobody was more economically efficient at the manipulating of reality into film image than production designer Nora Chavooshian. For just $5,000, she had delivered the design for *Brother*. For *Matewan,* she and art director Dan Bishop, a newcomer, would deploy $97,000 in constructing more than thirty sets. In that budget was a $7,000 line item for two days' rental of the ancient steam locomotive, which left just $90,000 for the other sets and props. Another Sayles regular, Cynthia Flynt, had moved up the ranks from wardrobe *(Lianna)* to wardrobe assistant *(Brother),* and now to costume designer. Her miracle, notes Dorothy McGhee in *American Film* (September 1987), was to dress 300 principals and extras with 1,400 different costumes and to keep the overall cost under $25,000. In the process, she visited the thrift shops and flea markets and "bought clothing by the pound."

To the union-member crew, the producers added many local residents, cutting the cost and creating good will in the region. As usual on a Sayles location, community relations were thoroughly mapped out. In the production packet given to each crew and cast member was a reminder of the production's "guest" status in West Virginia. After warning them about driving on the steep and narrow roads, heavy railroad traffic, white water-rafting safety, and lurking snakes, the letter emphasized, "We should respect and appreciate the ways of local people."

Throughout the summer of 1996 production, as Dan Bishop told me, "Maggie [Renzi] helped to involve the people. She's very personable and straightforward with everybody, including the community. In a small town like Thurmond [about seventy miles southeast of Charleston, West Virginia], people are really interested in being part of the production." Her efforts paid off. According to Steve Seidenberg in *Theater Crafts* (April 1987), the locals employed in the production taught the crew about the area and rounded up old mining paraphernalia, lumber, and even a caboose and some box cars. In the casting, twenty-three of the forty-seven speaking parts were given to locals. Of these recruits, Sayles later told the *New York Times* (April 6, 1987), "They brought their own passions and familiar memories to the roles they played." They also looked a lot more like Logan County, West Virginia, than Los Angeles County, California.

In a visit to the *Matewan* set for *American Film* (September 1987), reporter Dorothy McGhee discovered a crew composed almost entirely of people in their twenties. "I find myself waiting for the grownups to come back," she wrote. Even the department heads, many of them women, were young and possessed a key quality in Sayles's eyes. "The best possible people in a low-budget film," he had told a 1985 American Film Institute seminar, "are those who can work fast. There are plenty of DPs who can do beautiful stuff, but they do it by waiting for the light." *Waiting* is not in this director's lexicon. In their opening sermon to the crew, the producers reminded them that anybody could do it with money; they would get *Matewan* made with ingenuity and hard work.

The coup for Renzi was contracting two-time Academy Award winner Haskell Wexler (*Who's Afraid of Virginia Woolf,* 1966, and *Bound for Glory,* 1976) as cinematographer. Early in his career, Wexler had directed documentaries about coal mining in southern Illinois. In a 1999 interview, he recalled for me the negotiations. "John explained that the film was low budget and probably nonunion and asked if I wanted to do it. I said yes. In fact, I forced, intruded and prevailed upon him." Wexler would earn about a quarter of his usual pay. An officer in the International Alliance of Theatrical Stage Employees (IATSE), Wexler caught flak for working on a nonunion movie but stayed on the project because, as he said, "I liked what this film says about unions and about building our country and making it a better place." Ultimately, *Matewan* went with another union, the National Association of Broadcast Employees and Technicians (NABET), whose rules posed further production and budget problems.

Between Wexler and art director Nora Chavooshian, present-day Thurmond, West Virginia, was turned into the Matewan of the 1920s. (In 1986 Matewan itself looked too modern.) Like everyone else on the shoot, they lived in the Econo Lodge, and the motel chain's motto "Spend a Night, Not a Fortune" became a byword on the shoot. "The key idea," Wexler now says, "is that John did not have a motor home on location, probably the only director in the past fifteen years who has not. He was first on and last to leave the set. Usually during the shooting, a director will set up the camera shot, tell the crew to call him when they're ready, then go to the motor home. John stayed there and talked with people."

Over the next seven weeks, which included a lot of night work, the crew would translate Sayles's script into film footage. For Wexler this involved upgrading some of John's shooting practices, such as obtaining a camera truck to replace a station wagon. "I sorta won," he says. "I also wanted a 12 k [light], at least one. But I was going to do the picture no matter what. By not having all the goodies, power, and money, we had to improvise or go back to simpler ways of doing things, which adds to the excitement." The DP and director, nevertheless, disagreed often during the filming. According to Wexler, "John has a unique personality for dealing with arguments. He listens to you and you don't know whether anything registers for sure. But you never feel, 'OK buddy, shut up. I know what I'm doing. I don't need your input.' " In the end, Sayles credits Wexler for the visuals catching up with the dialogue in this, his fifth movie, and the cinematographer has since worked on two more projects with him.

Having scouted the territory, Chavooshian was now putting period fronts on the buildings along Thurmond's main street, giving a green-and-white color scheme to the Stone Mountain Coal Company properties, putting the right "dirt" over the asphalt roadway, and spraying the right mix of grime over nearly everything. Maggie Renzi's father, Ralph, a production assistant and extra on the movie, told me about warning a crew member not to remove a just perfect old sign from a building front. "I then learned that the sign had just come from Dan Bishop's art department. That's how good they were." For the mine scenes, the production borrowed the Beckley Exhibition Coal Mine and used Grandview State Park as the site of the miners' tent camp.

Set in a valley, Thurmond provided a sense of physical beauty with the feeling of entrapment. In his 1998 biography, *John Sayles, Filmmaker,* Jack Ryan notes how Wexler's camera picks up on that trapped theme in a crane shot framing the miners walking between the huge company coal cars to convey the dominating power of industry over them. The valley setting, the lines of boxcars, and the mines all created the right sense of claustrophobia. The location's downside was that the sun's late rising and early setting sliced an hour and a half off the shooting schedule, 70 percent of which was outdoors. Within the mines, the dim lighting sometimes called for precise camera focusing. In sum, this film called on all Wexler's feature and documentary background.

■   ■   ■

Casting director Barbara Shapiro had first gathered principals for the aborted 1983 production and now recruited another cast for the 1986 shoot. For the main character of Joe Kenehan, Chris Cooper brought lots of acting but little film experience. Yet he had the intangibles that the director wanted. "He can have a haunted quality," Sayles said. "He has the ability to seem like he has a past—and that it is a rocky one." In 1983, thirty-year-old Mary McDonnell looked too young for the role of Elma, the widow, but now she was just right to play opposite the thirty-five-year-old Cooper. Both would star in subsequent Sayles movies, McDonnell in *Passion Fish* (1992) and Cooper in *Lone Star* (1996). The Actors Theatre of Louisville (Kentucky) told Shapiro that Will Oldham was right for the part of Danny, the boy preacher turned union missionary. When Sayles suggested that fourteen-year-old Oldham should deliver sermons like a guy telling a story, the part and performer clicked.

When the production began in Thurmond, Kevin Tighe auditioned for a type of role he would play in two more Sayles movies: the heavy. As Hickey, the sadistic Felts agent, Tighe would have a sidekick, Griggs, a cruel sociopath played by Gordon Clapp. Like Clapp, David Strathairn was a Sayles regular and appeared as Sheriff Sid Hatfield. Nancy Mette was another Sayles favorite, here playing Bridey Mae. To save on Screen Actors Guild–level salaries, John leaped into the role of the screaming Baptist preacher and mine owners' shill. Finally, Maggie Renzi played an Italian mother. Scores of locals responded to ads for casting calls in state and local newspapers. The production fed them well, paid them little, and watched them grow close to each other. Some of them couldn't read, but they could tell stories, some of which were woven into the film.

The casting's real coup occurred almost as a lark. For the role of Few Clothes, Shapiro needed a hulking African-American actor who suggested the character's power to survive in the South and possessed the charisma to lead the black miners. James Earl Jones was mentioned but believed to be out of the production's financial league. Undaunted, Shapiro called his agent; Jones read the script and signed on. Asked about his reason, Jones told me, "Well, I liked what he did with *The Brother from Another Planet*," adding with a laugh, "and I was kinda broke at the time. I asked my wife if we could afford to do this for nothing. She said, 'This one you can afford to do for nothing.'" Jones was paid SAG scale (lowest wage) of $1,439 a week and earned every cent of it, sleeping at the Econo Lodge and slogging around in the mud like a noncelebrity. For an actor such as Jones, the tight shooting schedule worked to his advantage (and to Sayles's) in allowing him to take just six weeks for the film without giving up more lucrative projects.

Like the other principals in *Matewan,* Jones read the biography of his character provided by Sayles and then met with him to help frame the performance. "The biography," John has said, "gives the actors the backstory, what the relationships are that maybe aren't spelled out in the script. We'll talk about those things a lot before we go on the set." The device also reduces rehearsal time and costly retakes.

In retrospect, James Earl Jones remembers being concerned about the director's vision of his screen character. "John is very socially aware, and I was afraid Few Clothes would come off like a black activist of today, very hip. I don't think that would paint a clear picture of what was going on back in those days. I saw Few Clothes as an activist in the sense that he only wanted the best for the guys that came from Alabama with him. He knows if he talks back, he may get a noose put around his neck. There was no 'up against the wall.' It was 'yes sir and no sir.'"

The two agreed to keep Few Clothes in the context of the 1920s but did *not* concur on the film's closing scene. "Historically," Jones says, "blacks and Italians were part of the shootout in Mingo, but John chose to extract them and let the battle happen between the West Virginia people and the mining company. I wanted Few Clothes to be part of the encounter, but I accepted John's vision. It was an interesting choice, again putting the focus on the people who lived there and had the most to lose." Jones came to appreciate Sayles's creative vision. "It's always superimposed over you, and if you get off track, he'll help you. But basically he casts very accurately and then doesn't bother the actors."

■   ■   ■

With his outdoor sets supplied by the state of West Virginia and a cast and crew sprinkled with pros and lots of kids on their way up, the thirty-six-year-old Sayles launched the two-month, late summer production. Principally, the film story propelled itself into what he describes as a V shape with the forces of the miners and owners heading toward the collision in the streets of Matewan. Although labor appeared to be the major issue, the film embraced the uniting of genders, races, and ethnic groups to provide the bedrock of community, always a central theme of a Sayles movie. The trust and respect that binds these groups develops gradually in the film and takes solid shape in one pivotal scene in the miners' camp. In it, filming and editing reveal the possibility that this diverse group of locals, blacks, and Italian immigrants can unite. Mason Daring's score hints at, then cements the bonding of the miners and their families.

Heretofore, Daring had provided the music for *Secaucus Seven* and *Lianna* and the much-admired jazz score for *The Brother from Another Planet*. Musically, *Matewan* was more ambitious, and Mason worked with Sayles and Maggie Renzi to find the right mix of music, instruments, and performers. It was John, Daring told me, who recommended vocalist Hazel Dickens and invited her to sing Daring's "Fire in the Hole" and "Beautiful Hills of Galilee," the songs that open and close the film. In the scene where the young boy is buried, she appears on camera singing what amounts to a miner's resistance anthem, "The Gathering Storm," written by Daring. Herself the daughter of a preacher and sister of a miner too poor to afford a decent burial, Dickens let her voice echo all the long-held grievances of her own family. That authenticity allowed the scene to be shot in one take and left everyone in tears.

In building to the scene that will unite the disparate groups, Daring identifies each with certain instruments: blacks with harmonica, Italians with mandolin, and locals with guitar and fiddle. There was plenty of homework behind those choices. As Daring remembers, "John said, 'I'd like you to write something that will illustrate the combination of these three groups, and we're going to have that scene on camera in the tent camp.'" To capture the country music spirit, Sayles introduced his composer to Jerry Milnes, an accomplished West Virginia fiddle player. For further inspiration, Maggie took Daring to her uncle, an Italian guitar maker in New Jersey, who for a few hours played turn-of-the-century music from the old country. Out of that listening emerged Daring's *La Bella Noche* waltz, first heard offscreen coming from the Italians and played on the harmonica by John Hammond.

The theme of united workers emerges in a nighttime scene at the miners' tent camp. Recording the music tested the patience of Haskell Wexler, who was not used to having the composer present during filming. As Daring recalls, "A generator provided power for the eight-track remote, which played the previously recorded song in the ears of the musicians, some of them hundreds of yards apart." In the scene, the Italian mandolin starts playing *La Bella Noche,* with the melody picked up first by the West Virginians on guitar and fiddle, then by the blacks on harmonica. *Commonweal* (November 6, 1987) would later note the music's pictorializing "the eventual harmony among the victims [the miners and their families]" in what the critic called "one of the most dramatically integrated soundtracks in a nonmusical film."

■   ■   ■

In May 1987 *Matewan* played at the Directors Fortnight, a sidebar of the Cannes International Film Festival, and ecstatic French critics were comparing it to John Ford's populist film classic, *The Grapes of Wrath* (1940). Cinecom's distribution plans called for a limited release in October with the hope that good reviews and word-of-mouth publicity would send the film crossing over into the multiplexes. The strategy did not anticipate the glut of movies, both mainstream and art-adult, that reached the marketplace that fall, with an average of thirty pictures opening each month.

In that highly competitive arena, before a movie could get legs at the box office, it would be pulled off the screen in favor of a new release that might catch on faster. As Sayles said to the *New York Times* (August 23, 1987), "We didn't have time to get out word of mouth. We were yanked from some theaters in the third week when we were still doing good business." Cinecom was part of the problem. "We had a distributor with no clout. They couldn't say, 'Play *Matewan* or you won't get *Ghostbusters II.'*" Not surprisingly, *Matewan,* with a $4 million budget, made just a little under $2 million in American theaters.

Critics, however, applauded it as a breakthrough movie. "Sayles has finally got everything together," *Commonweal* judged (November 6, 1987), and the *Washington Post* (October 16, 1987) agreed that "Sayles had finally tapped the vein." *Rolling Stone* (October 8, 1987) welcomed the picture's social commentary. "In retreating from the present for the first time, filmmaker Sayles is paradoxically dealing more directly with the contemporary political landscape, where idealism is considered a quaint relic of the Woodstock Nation."

The Nation (October 17, 1987) picked up on the political theme, seeing "a stalwart, solid sort of movie without tricks or frills" but nevertheless flawed by "a canvas too large, the morals too clear . . . some excruciating shorthand about music, food and softball to express the eventual baptism into the melting pot." In *The New Republic* (September 7, 1987), Stanley Kauffmann admired Wexler's cinematography but questioned the characters' motivations: "Why do both the blacks and Italians become union supporters?" This question highlights *Matewan*'s demands on the eyes and ears of the audience. The cues and clues to motivation are there—in words.

The dialogue of the company boss who greets the newly arrived black miners describes without apology the horrific living and working conditions they will face and which will inspire mutiny in those characters. Later in the film—again through dialogue—Joe Kenehan learns the Italians, unaccustomed to this kind of labor, are dying like flies in the mine, providing that group with a motive for rebellion. Because of budget constraints and the large canvas, Sayles was doing what he did in *Secaucus Seven*: letting dialogue substitute for dramatic action. The result was both a perceived "shorthand" and missed clues as to the characterization and narrative, problems that would haunt John's next two films as well.

Despite these flaws, *Matewan* proved to be a powerful statement about American workers. In the summer of 1987, after screening the picture, the United Mine Workers Council sent a greeting (with edge) to the National Labor Relations Board: "Happy Labor Day—hope you get a chance to see this movie." In 1988 the film received the annual Independent Spirit Award for Best Cinematography. Leonard Maltin, in his *Movie & Video Guide 1999,* gives *Matewan* three and a half stars out of four and calls the movie "a compelling and compassionate drama about labor trouble. . . . Beautifully shot by Haskell Wexler." Among visitors to the John Sayles Web site, it ranks second in popularity only to *Lone Star* (1996).

One offshoot of the movie was the contribution to film studies that Sayles made in writing *Thinking in Pictures: The Making of the Movie* Matewan (1987). Using *Matewan* as his example and writing the book mainly during bus commutes between Hoboken and Manhattan, John charts the filmmaking process from financing to box office. Ironically, Sayles, who made a career of cutting classes, was now contributing to the university curriculum, the teacher's syllabus, and the students' academic burden. He was also cultivating disciples.

In the Sayles corpus, *Matewan* stands as a memorable picture about breaching barriers and crossing borders to form community. It also raises the issues of pacifism and violence that will recur in future films, notably *Men with Guns* (1998).

In one year, John both produced the movie and wrote the book. At the same time, he had rewritten the script for *Wild Thing* (1987), which brings a teenage Tarzan to the inner city to protect the little people. He is befriended by a social worker named—what else—Jane. Although Sayles included some of the humor found in his past horror film scripts, it was a bright idea for a not-so-hot picture. In the *Chicago Sun-Times* (April 24, 1987), Roger Ebert wondered why screenwriter Sayles settled for hackneyed heroes and run of-the-mill violence. Even for scripts like this, John was earning in the $75,000 to $150,000 range, money that would support his next project.

With *Matewan* in the can, the issue of men in dire straits was still on Sayles's mind, and he had a script ready to turn such thinking into pictures. A little later, Maggie would remind him about doing a film focused on women. That movie lay down the road. For the present, John was launching the second part of his planned triptych. Maggie's job was to find the money for a picture about the great American pastime. Neither the game nor her task was ever easy.

John (left) at three years old with his brother Doug, five, in 1953.
COURTESY OF DON AND MARY SAYLES

John (left, age seven), Doug (nine), and their mother, Mary, on vacation in
Hollywood, Florida, in 1957. COURTESY OF DON AND MARY SAYLES

The 1967 Mont Pleasant High School football team. John, offensive and
defensive end, wears number 80. COURTESY OF COACH LARRY MULVANEY AND
THE SCHOOL DISTRICT OF SCHENECTADY, NEW YORK

John's high school senior
portrait, 1968.
COURTESY OF DON AND
MARY SAYLES

With the sideburns of the
1970s, John posed for his
graduation picture at Williams
College in 1972, where he
earned a degree in psychology.
COURTESY OF DON AND
MARY SAYLES

John Sayles, Maggie Renzi, and her father, Ralph, caught between takes
during the shooting of *Matewan* (1987). COURTESY OF RALPH RENZI

Sayles takes a break from promoting *The Brother from Another Planet* (1984) during the 1984 Cannes Film Festival. COURTESY OF NANCY MORGAN/SYGMA

John and his producer
and life partner,
Maggie Renzi,
Christmas 1985.
COURTESY OF DON AND
MARY SAYLES

A 1993 reunion of the Sayles family (front row, left) Mary Sayles (mother) and her aunt, Betty Cooney; (back row, left) Donald Sayles (father), Doug Sayles (brother) holding his son, Andrew, and John.

Sayles directs Vincent Spano and Rosanna Arquette for their dance in the closing scene of *Baby It's You* (1983). COURTESY OF NANCY MORGAN/SYGMA

Limbo (1999) was an official entry at the 52nd Cannes Film Festival. Here, Mary Elizabeth Mastrantonio gets a touch-up while Sayles sits by.
COURTESY OF AP PHOTOS/RHONDA GALBRAITH

John Sayles at the Juneau, Alaska, production office where he was busy
rounding up boats and fishing gear for *Limbo* (1999).

15

Eight Men Out:
The Players and Their Pastime

It's about these big shots getting away with things and that

righteous phony, Kenesaw Mountain Landis, who was owned by

the owners. He represents them. They wanted a scapegoat,

so they got the players thrown out. Sure they threw the game,

but the other guys went untouched. He's right on the button.

That's what I like about [John] Sayles.

AUTHOR STUDS TERKEL, 1998

THE CAMERA ARCS ACROSS A BLUE, sun-filled sky. Like a lazy fly ball, it seems to drift up and over the unfolding film credits before slowly beginning its fall to the streets of Chicago, 1919. In the span of a few moments, the opening shot of *Eight Men Out* announces its subject, predicts the path the movie will follow, and visually describes the inexorable downward momentum of the events. Like the imagery in Leni Riefenstahl's Olympic diving sequence in *Olympiad* (1936), the filming here creates a dynamic interaction of the mythic, timeless, and ethereal quality of the heavens followed by the crass reality of the streets. As Jerry Roberts stated on the Cinemania Web site, both *Matewan* (1987) and *Eight Men Out* (1988) are period films about the "tainting of purity in the Jazz Age of the American past. After all, what has had more fiercely noble beginnings than the labor movement? And if the integrity of the national pastime couldn't be upheld, what was next?"

John Sayles had already employed the baseball setting in his short novel, *Pride of the Bimbos* (1975), which traced the journey of a barnstorming baseball team. He has spoken elsewhere of the game's preeminent status in American culture and its impact on his own life. While acknowledging the inroads made on the sport's popularity by basketball and football, he still maintains, "Little kids play baseball first. You're doing it like a big leaguer. It's fun. I think little kids like the rules, like the rehearsals. The endless arguments (*New York Times*, August 28, 1998)." As a kid, he passed his summers playing Wiffle ball in the backyard on Sumner Avenue and listening to Pittsburgh Pirates games. As a college student, John cultivated an appreciation for the writing of Nelson Algren, including his stories about the Chicago White Sox and how they threw the 1919 World Series against the Cincinnati Reds, thus creating the infamous "Black Sox" scandal.

In 1978, when John was first trying to convince the Hollywood studios that he could write for the movies, he submitted a complete shooting script based on Eliot Asinof's 1963 book, *Eight Men Out*. Over the years, he teased himself with the prospect of shooting the project, but *Eight Men Out* was seemingly the movie that just wouldn't get made.

The first incarnation was a script Asinof wrote in 1959 for David Susskind's television production for *DuPont Show of the Month*. NBC benched that project when Ford Frick, then baseball commissioner, intervened, arguing that resurrecting the bribery scandal was not in the best interest of the national pastime. The cancellation gave Asinof time to intensify his research and eventually write the book based in part on interviews with members of the White Sox.

Asinof's investigation had helped discredit in his eyes the view of that infamous World Series as simply a sellout by the eight players. "It was only after I saw how the whole thing unfolded and why," Asinof told *Esquire*'s Charles Siebert (August 1988), "that I realized they were victims. I came to realize how the political system in America works and how things get covered up. Sayles understands that. It's in his script." (Sayles had written his script knowing that the rights to the book were not then available.)

Among the factors contributing to the fix was the double-dealing of White Sox owner Charles Comiskey, which reduced the players to indentured

servants, as well as the intervention of gamblers (most notoriously Arnold
Rothstein) who capitalized on the athletes' financial needs and their antagonism toward Comiskey. Chicago sportswriters (co-opted by Comiskey) exacerbated the real story first by idolizing and then vilifying the accused Sox
teammates. The fix itself was followed by a collusion of the gamblers and
owners bent on concealing the crime by ensuring the players' acquittal, then
banning them for life from the sport.

After the publication of *Eight Men Out,* onetime Cincinnati pitcher Dutch
Reuther sued Asinof in a $2 million libel case for repeating an accusation that
Reuther was drinking the night before the Series' opening game. That legal
skirmish scuttled a planned Twentieth Century-Fox film production. Ten years
later, David Susskind perpetuated the curse on the project by suing Asinof for
$1.75 million. According to Hal Erickson in *Baseball in the Movies* (1992),
Susskind sued Asinof "for not accepting $20,000 to give authorization for
Susskind's own adaptation of Asinof's 1959 teleplay, which the writer felt
Susskind had falsified in the rewriting process." The nasty and seemingly endless legal battles would lead Asinof to write still another book—this time,
about the lawsuits—*Bleeding Between the Lines* (1979).

By 1980, however, producers Midge Sanford and Sarah Pillsbury had
acquired a six-month screen option on Asinof's book. Sayles too was now pursuing the screen rights to the baseball story. For Sayles, the Black Sox scandal
was an intriguing, multileveled conspiracy story. The combination of labor
problems, the baseball setting, and the sheer complexity of events were the
story ingredients that first attracted him to Asinof's book. Knowing that
Sanford and Pillsbury held 25 percent of the rights to the book, he contacted
them and agreed to a partnership. Sayles bought the remaining 75 percent and
the project was launched.

According to John, he got along well with his female partners
(women producers being not uncommon in the film industry). In 1980 the
co-producers were predicting that they would get *Eight Men Out* done
right away. It would be five years, however, before shooting started. At the
time, the producers lacked in filmmaking experience, and baseball had yet
to become a "bankable" screen subject. By 1986, however, Pillsbury and

Sanford had delivered the offbeat comedy *Desperately Seeking Susan* (1985) for Orion Pictures and the disturbing teen-centered *River's Edge* (1986) for Hemdale. As they peddled *Eight Men Out* around Hollywood, the baseball movie genre underwent a film resurgence that started with *The Natural* (1984), followed by *Bull Durham* (1988). With $25 million and $22 million, respectively, in domestic rentals, the two pictures punctured the industry axiom that baseball was box-office poison.

To these baseball-on-screen success stories and their own recent history, the producers could now add Sayles's track record of making feature films on time and within budget, especially a large-scale effort like *Matewan* (1987). The group turned to Orion Classics, an autonomous division of the director-friendly Orion Pictures that twice had rejected the Sanford-Pillsbury proposal for *Eight Men Out* but was now reconsidering. When the studio questioned the $6 million budget for a period movie with an ensemble cast, Sayles reminded them about his doing *Matewan* for less, and the studio agreed to finance *Eight Men Out*. Still, there was little enthusiasm from Orion. None of the five owners liked the baseball material. Executive producer Mike Medavoy would begin meetings saying, "Well, before you start the pitch, baseball to me is like watching paint dry. OK, go ahead, tell me the story." In these script sessions, John played down the sports, a trick he passed along to students at a 1996 American Film Institute seminar: "You type it so baseball doesn't look that big—a montage of shots looks less like baseball but isn't."

However effective the sleight of hand, the investors had to accept certain nonnegotiable realities. There was no big-name star like Kevin Costner and, unlike the fireworks that attended Robert Redford's home run that ended *The Natural,* the climax here takes place at a rundown minor-league field in Hoboken. Orion still needed assurance about the box-office potential. Finally, this "cursed" film got lucky.

In the mid-1980s, Hollywood was bursting with young male actors eager for work and faced with nothing but the then in vogue war movies as vehicles. The ensemble cast needed for *Eight Men Out* provided a viable alternative, and the negotiations started. If the studio had to live without a big star, would the filmmaker include a few hot young properties to create a big box office?

The two sides finally agreed on and signed three rising and athletic stars: Charlie Sheen (*Platoon,* 1986), John Cusack (*Broadcast News,* 1987), and D. B. Sweeney (*Gardens of Stone,* 1987). They were self-confessed jocks who willingly traded reduced celebrity status for the chance to play baseball on camera.

Sayles then addressed Orion's other concern about the film's projected length and agreed to make it less than two hours. (It came in at 1:59.48.) As Sayles told the AFI seminar, "They knew I wasn't going to hand them a three-hour epic, then embarrass them in *Variety* for their beating up of this filmmaker." With agreement on those two "concessions," John could keep the final cut. In Orion Classics, Sayles, Sanford, and Pillsbury had found a company that specialized in low-budget films and could, if those entries proved successful, lateral the distribution to the parent company and into mainstream theaters. With that hope in mind, they turned to the story.

For years the Black Sox scandal seemed cut and dry. "Shoeless Joe" Jackson, star outfielder and Baseball Hall of Fame shoo-in, joined seven teammates in throwing the 1919 World Series against the Cincinnati Reds. Although the court found the players innocent of the conspiracy charges, baseball commissioner Kenesaw Mountain Landis banned them from the sport for life. Legend had it that as the accused Jackson left the courthouse, a little boy called out, "Say it ain't so, Joe." The boy's plaintive cry became part of American parental parlance. For years fathers used the Black Sox scandal to warn their children about the evils of cheating and lying.

The passing years continued to simplify the story, and when Asinof approached the subject, he was predisposed to condemn the players as bums who deserved to be forever banned from baseball and, in Jackson's case, from the Hall of Fame as well. In researching this inglorious chapter in sports history, the writer tracked down the still-living members of the two teams. As so often happens while investigating cases of conspiracy, Asinof began "following the money." The path led him to the baseball owners, a godfather, gamblers, and the courts. Each step uncovered complicating motivations, unsavory alliances, and dirty double-dealings.

■   ■   ■

In tackling the scandal, Sayles knew the difficulty involved in gamblers getting a group of rough-and-tumble young ballplayers to do their worst at what they did best. Behind all the curveless curve balls, the overthrows at first base, and the inept base running, there had to be reasons. In *Box Office* (September 1988), Sayles asked the film's key question: "How do you fix that many guys? How can you get enough guys to make sure they lose a baseball game . . . ?" In its opening scenes, *Eight Men Out* starts answering those questions and reviewing the myths of youth and innocence, of hard work and the American dream, and, as in *Matewan,* the central myth of the 1920s as the fun-loving Jazz Age.

In the opening scene, two boys, having just finished selling newspapers idolizing the city's baseball heroes, race through the streets to Comiskey Park to see the players in action. Once inside, the camera cuts to Charles Comiskey's office, where the club owner is feeding the press a buffet of food and a barrage of baloney about the family feeling on his team.

Out on the field, those same players are winding up the American League pennant and enviously ragging on Eddie Collins, the "college boy" second baseman smart enough to be making $15,000 a year while they each earn $5,000. In the stands, like twin Greek choruses, two gamblers estimate which players might cooperate in a World Series fix while the two boys plead with their heroes for a hit. With the game over and the pennant won, the Sox pour into the locker room looking for the bonus promised by Comiskey. The "bonus" turns out to be a dozen bottles of stale champagne. In a few minutes, the sequence identifies the forces that propel the players to their crime and that allow Comiskey to cover up the subsequent events through public relations ploys and the compliant media.

To convey the tension behind the fix, Sayles was looking for three basic character groups: the players, the gamblers, and the media. For the ensemble cast, he called again on his stable of stars. David Strathairn, Gordon Clapp, Jace Alexander, and Kevin Tighe all returned from *Matewan,* with Maggie Renzi and John playing key roles. In the supporting parts were veteran character actors Clifton James, Christopher Lloyd, John Mahoney, and John Anderson.

The key name actors that satisfied Orion came gifted with the look and coordination of professional athletes. John Cusack, who played Buck Weaver, adapted his softball skills to the bigger diamond. Though it took twenty-three takes, he made an on-camera, major-league, diving catch at third base. Prior to a motorcycle injury to his knee, D. B. Sweeney, who took on the role of "Shoeless Joe" Jackson, played ball for Tulane University and earned a minor-league baseball contract. Preparing for the *Eight Man* shoot, he spent six weeks with the Kenosha Wisconsin Twins learning how to bat left-handed in the manner of his character. When Sweeney crossed paths with actor Charlie Sheen in New York, Sheen, the former Santa Monica (California) High letter winner, instantly pursued the chance to play ball again and in front of the cameras, this after his starring role in the Oscar-winning Vietnam War film *Platoon* (1986). (When first casting this long-delayed picture, Sayles had wanted Martin Sheen—Charlie's father—and Stacy Keach; both, however, were now in their mid-forties.) Seeing mime Bill Irwin on stage convinced John that he had the body control of a ballplayer, and he cast him as White Sox second baseman Eddie Collins.

For James Read, the role of "Lefty" Williams came via an interview with Sayles in New York City. During the course of their discussion, Read recently told me, he alluded to his and Sayles's hometown, Schenectady, and to playing baseball for Niskayuma High, a cross-town rival of Mont Pleasant High. When the topic turned to pitching, James spoke of his career on the mound and got the role. He also took a pay cut. "I certainly made more money in TV mini-series like *North and South* [1985]."

■　　　■　　　■

For Read and the other onscreen ballplayers, *Eight Men Out* meant a triple dose of instruction. First, Sayles provided each actor with a short biography of his character followed by a face-to-face meeting with the director. "He kinda did our homework," Read says. "In the discussions, he wasn't looking for my input; he was looking for me to reflect his vision and for my character to help create the larger picture. John wanted 'Lefty' Williams to be a guy who's more interested in his wife and spending time with her, and he's embarrassed to admit that to the guys. That's what causes him to act the way he does at the end of the Series."

John also screened old-time newsreels of how baseball looked in that bygone era. He then showed the actors James Cagney as a boxer in *City for Conquest* (1940) to let them hear how athletes might have talked back then. Read says, "John wanted the staccato, machine-gun delivery, a tough, brawny, unsophisticated American style of the Roaring Twenties." The director also wanted an attitude. In *Past Imperfect* (1995), Sayles told historian Eric Foner, "Back in 1919, white athletes were poor kids, and they were in your face. 'We're gonna kill those guys tomorrow. They don't have a f***in' chance.' They didn't say 'f***in',' but there was the same cockiness that you see among black players today."

Two weeks before shooting started in September 1987, the actors began the final stage of their indoctrination. They moved into the Riverside Apartments in Indianapolis. With all the young athletes, the comfortable apartment complex began to resemble a dorm and bred a collegiate, fraternal atmosphere with nightly card games and visits to the nearby Westbrook Bar. Along with local ballplayers now added as extras, the cast commenced "spring training" camp. With typical insistence on authenticity, Sayles brought in Ken Berry, a former major-league outfielder and at the time a minor-league coach for the White Sox. He would run the camp.

Charles Siebert, a Sayles recruit from a Manhattan softball field, was in the cast and wrote about the ritual for *Esquire* (August 1988). "Every morning at 8:00, we'd pile into a van. . . . Our practices had the look of normal early-season training: stretches, sprints, and warm up tosses, infield, outfield, and batting practice." Berry was a coach of the no-nonsense school and was well respected. As expected, shaping up hurt physically. "After the first three days of throwing," Read remembers, "I couldn't pick up a fork."

What complicated these practices even for the most athletic actors was adapting to the baseball bats and cleats of 1919. With the cooperation of the Louisville Slugger Company, they were swinging replicas of the bat models used by Eddie Collins and Joe Jackson. The "rookies" also were trying to catch with old-fashioned gloves in order to get into the long-forgotten style in the field.

"Catch with an old-fashioned glove for a while," Siebert told *Esquire*'s readers, "and your arms and legs get a jerky rockabye cradle motion going. A big chaw of tobacco starts growing in your cheek. Your hair gets short, your uniform baggy, a goofy smile appears on your face, and your ears stick out. You're an old time ballplayer." Both the gloves and bats used in the movie, including Joe Jackson's "Black Betsey," now reside in the Film Memorabilia Collection at the Baseball Hall of Fame. Alongside them are the uniforms once worn by Robert Redford (*The Natural,* 1984), Tim Robbins (*Bull Durham,* 1988), Ray Liotta (*Field of Dreams,* 1989), and Geena Davis (*A League of Their Own,* 1992).

■   ■   ■

While the actors were perfecting their game, the cinematographer and the art department were creating a ballpark—or two. The producers chose Bush Stadium in Indianapolis because, like the old ballparks, it had a single deck. Now, with the removal of the light standards and a papering of the plastic orange seats with "wood" covering, a period look began to emerge. Adding a few well-placed beams in the stands and varying the advertising signs on the outfield wall ("No Gambling in this Park" being one) could quickly turn the Indianapolis Indians' minor-league ball yard into either Chicago's Comiskey Field or Cincinnati's Redland Field.

As usual in a $6 million movie trying to look like a $30 million movie, the crew was called on for continual improvisational creativity and stamina. When not enough extras showed up to fill the stands, for example, cinematographer Robert Richardson (an Oscar nominee for *Platoon*) would switch to a narrower lens, and the production assistants would fill in the empty seats with Paul Marcuses. Paul Marcus was the film's location manager. As Sayles told *Variety* (July 20, 1994), "Bob Richardson worked out exactly how many people we needed to fill the stands with a 75mm lens doing the shot. . . . We didn't have the money to get a lot of people." Dan Bishop's art department took

Marcus's picture in period costume, then blew it up and made 400 hundred life-size cardboard cutouts. "With a hat or a scarf on and stuck among the real extras," he told me, "a hundred Marcuses completed the background for the game shots."

A new covering of reddish dirt, a lowered pitcher's mound, and the keyhole-shaped lane between the mound and home plate helped turn the clock back to 1919. Shots from the dugout used a coach in the foreground to conceal the remaining light standard on the left-field foul line. (No lights were used during night games in the 1910s.) The crew faced other, less predictable obstacles. Bishop told me that the *Eight Men Out* shoot was made more grueling by the weather. "One time a windstorm blew down a section of the outfield wall. John got them to fix one part and let one section go. We just shot around it."

With training camp over and the ballpark prepared, the players finally got on the diamond. One visitor, Sayles's brother, Doug, jokingly told me about the "dangerous" set. "Some of the semiathletes couldn't throw accurately, couldn't catch. Everybody was getting beaned, and you didn't have enough eyes to cover the places the balls were coming from." Testosterone and adrenaline also were running high, as many of the players were feeling the hype of the re-created World Series. The new "Lefty," James Read, tried to remember that he was pitching in a movie, but with "fans" (the crew and extras) all around, he excitedly thought, *I gotta throw strikes.* He then would pitch a fastball into the camera shield—well off home plate. Eventually Read and the rest of the players settled down and looked like a solid ball club, not major league but far better than the usual Hollywood version.

When the plotline turned from the game to the gamblers and the fix, the players appeared in a new and less legendary perspective. They became the little fish that everyone fed on. In baseball, a "reserve clause," a legal loophole in the monopoly law allowed by the courts, bound them to one owner. On their own, the players could not go to another club and negotiate a new salary as they might today. As the film shows it, they were extremely underpaid and virtually owned by Charlie Comiskey who treated them like chattel.

In 1919, while anger and cynicism were mounting among the Sox players, gambling was becoming commonplace and baseball's purity was up for grabs. As columnist and baseball fan George Will observes (October 6, 1999), "When the government closed the racetracks during the war [1917–19], gamblers turned to baseball, America's biggest entertainment industry. Hotel lobbies where teams stayed teamed with gamblers. 'Hippodroming' was the nineteenth century word for throwing games, and in postwar America, there was a new brazenness by the gamblers." Unlike the unseen coal barons of *Matewan,* the villains of this film are on-screen: owners, gamblers, league officials, commissioners, and the press exploited athletes too naïve and gullible even to hire their own lawyer.

Resentful of their imposed "slave" status, the ballplayers are an easy mark for the gamblers who range from small-time con artists to middle-level crooks. The kingpin, Arnold Rothstein (Michael Lerner), gives the go-ahead to fix the World Series and waits in New York for news of the first pitch of game one. Starting White Sox hurler Eddie Cicotte (David Strathairn) deliberately hits the Cincinnati Reds leadoff hitter, signaling that the Sox players are throwing the Series. The fix is on.

Like Comiskey, the gamblers are playing for high stakes, and they are soon cheating the seven players out of the promised payoff. (Third baseman Buck Weaver takes no money and plays to win.) In jeopardizing their careers and the integrity of the game, five of the White Sox receive less than $5,000 each, peanuts compared to the well over $100,000 raked in by Rothstein. Meanwhile, his intermediary, Joseph "Sport" Sullivan (Kevin Tighe), skims $20,000 off the players' payoff money and, comparing the players to horses, says, "You give them just enough to let them know they're hungry." In both baseball and gambling, the ballplayers lose.

On the evening prior to the closing game, a Rothstein henchman visits a Chicago restaurant, sidles up to starting pitcher "Lefty" Williams, and coolly reminds him that should he win the game, his wife will be killed. The following day, as the band plays the national anthem, Williams looks up at the Comiskey Park stands to see the hitman sitting directly behind his wife. He then proceeds to groove his pitches, and the Reds pound out the hits, easily winning the game. The sequence closes with the stands emptying out and a lone bugler (Mason Daring) playing taps for the Series, the eight players, and, as some would have it, for baseball and American innocence.

■   ■   ■

Sitting outside Jerry's Famous Deli in Beverly Hills, actor Michael Lerner recollects his learning about the Arnold Rothstein role through his friends, producers Sarah Pillsbury and Midge Sanford. The quality of the script and the chance to work with Sayles overcame the veteran actor's aversion to auditioning on videotape and to working for little salary. Lerner got the part and, in keeping with his "thinking-man's actor" reputation, arrived on the set ready to portray the notorious criminal. "John knew I had done my homework. I had read the biography written by Arnold Rothstein's wife. [In 1934, Mrs. Carolyn Green [Rothstein] wrote *Now I'll Tell*.] As I saw it, he was a Jewish mobster who kept his hands clean while his minions did the dirty work."

The veteran actor came to admire Sayles's ability to cast correctly and direct sparingly. "The really strong directors trust themselves. They cast well. Even Studs Terkel, who's no great actor, was a great stroke. With somebody like John Mahoney, Chris Lloyd, and me, he just trusts your instincts. He may have said something to me in the scene where I'm eating and talking on the phone. He might have suggested a little faster, slower, bigger, but mainly he just lets you do your work. He directs like a writer. He lets the script speak."

In *Eight Men Out*, Sayles uses a pair of reporters, Hugh Fullerton (Studs Terkel) and Ring Lardner (Sayles), as a choruslike commentary on the action. The pair also serve four specific narrative purposes. First, they investigate the rumors about the Sox sellout, keeping tabs on each player's performance. Second, they chide their newspaper colleagues (a.k.a. shills) for ignoring the problems on the team. "Sportswriters of the world unite," Lardner shouts to them. "You have nothing to lose but your bar privileges." Third, Lardner especially tries to induce the players to come clean, then taunts them when they continue the fix. Finally, despite Lardner's warning that the readers will hate him, it is Fullerton who blows the whistle and sends the case to court and to their eventual acquittal and expulsion. All of these incidents were based on Asinof's factual account.

For the role of Chicago reporter Hugh Fullerton, Sayles could not have made a more popular choice. No celebrity is more closely identified with that town than journalist and media personality Studs Terkel. For years host of his own shows on radio and then television, Terkel knew the Black Sox story and the personalities involved in it. In a phone call, the renowned commentator and authority on the worker in America told me of his experience as a film actor. He had already interviewed Sayles for TV but was not expecting to be asked to perform for the camera.

"John called me up and said, 'I'm doing a film of *Eight Men Out* by Eliot Asinof. How'd you like to be Hughy Fullerton, the sportswriter?' I said, 'No, I can't.' He says, 'You gotta. I'll give you good cigars.' I said, 'That does it.' That's how I came to work with John. It was quite an experience." Author of the bestseller *Working* (1974) and several other books, Terkel was primed for the invitation—he had seen and admired *Matewan*.

Once on location in Indianapolis, Terkel had plenty of journalistic company. While *Esquire*'s Charlie Siebert was playing the part of Cincinnati Reds catcher Wingo Ivy Brown, he could look up at the stands and see the animated conversations going on among Terkel, Asinof, and Ring Lardner Jr. As a tribute, Sayles cast Asinof as 1919 National League president John Heyler. It was a courtesy deeply appreciated by the writer. "A gesture of respect if you please," he wrote in *DGA Magazine* (December 1997/January 1998). "In all his interviews, he would never speak of the filming without reference to me and my book." Lardner Jr., meanwhile, enjoyed Sayles's uncannily accurate depiction of his father.

■   ■   ■

In the spring of 1988, rounding third base and finally heading to theaters, *Eight Men Out,* the "cursed" film, encountered distribution problems. For the second time, Sayles had difficulties dealing with a studio and the release of his movie. He described the crisis to the *New York Times* as a case of "monopoly capitalism." Independent theaters were being bought up or driven out of business by chains, and Orion Pictures had bigger, hotter films on its list that fall and would not make room for Sayles's entry.

When *Eight Men Out* finally made it to the screen, critics raved about its realism but questioned the film's focus. Three *New York Times* articles cited the movie's authenticity. George Vecsey (August 28, 1988) wrote, "The action is realistic enough because Mr. Sayles practiced and filmed entire sequences rather than faking segments of the same play." While he noted that "Eddie Collins" was swinging from the wrong side of the plate, Wilfred Sheed (May 14, 1989) loved the double play. "The slickest by a hair [ever performed for the camera] comes in *Eight Men Out,* courtesy of the funny little 1919 gloves which make the difficult seem impossible." Less enamored by the sport's technique, *New York Times* reviewer Janet Maslin (September 2, 1988) saluted Sayles's talent for "drawing striking performances from actors who have never been nearly this memorable in other roles." She then decided that "for Mr. Sayles, whose idealism has never before been more affecting or apparent than in this story of boyish enthusiasm gone bad in an all too grown up world, *Eight Men Out* represents a home run."

In reviewing several baseball movies, *The New Yorker* baseball guru Roger Angel (July 31, 1989) found the film's idealism less effective than the tough-minded cynicism of Asinof's book. Nevertheless, he too enjoyed the convincing caliber of the baseball action. Having cited Cicotte's "smooth, effortless windup and delivery," and Joe Jackson's "flat bat, left-handed cut at the ball," Angel concluded, "I can't think of any other baseball film or cast of baseball actors that pulls this off." In the course of his review, however, Angel also cited various problems. In his eyes, there were too many players who looked alike, and there was too much difficulty keeping track of the bribes and deals.

Other critics cited the same confusion and suggested that concentrating on a single character would have tightened the film's focus. In *Sports Illustrated,* Steve Wulf (September 12, 1988) wrote, "Every time Weaver or Cicotte enters the picture, though, the film comes alive, which suggests *Eight Men Out* might have been better had it been told from one point of view." *Time* magazine's Richard Schickel (September 12, 1988) allowed that "the aspiration to dramatize a historical incident in all its complexity is not an unworthy one—and rare enough in movies. . . . Whatever failures result from this ambition, there is something likeable as well as commendable about this movie."

Eight Men Out cost approximately $6.6 million. By 1998 the movie's box office for the PG-rated picture reached $5.7 million. With its baseball plot and American intrigue, there was little hope for foreign gross. Aside from home video, the movie did realize some profit from a tie-in with Pacific Trading Cards of Edmonds, Washington, which was selling cards of the 1919 Sox and Reds players at $9.95 for a box of 100 and using the film for promotion.

While writing, directing, and publicizing *Eight Men Out,* Sayles had published two short stories, "The Halfway Diner" (*The Atlantic Monthly,* June 1987) and "Treasure" (*Esquire,* March 1988). In the course of his promotional interviews for *Eight Men,* he was promising a third epic, this one about the Abraham Lincoln brigade, which fought against the Fascist general Francisco Franco in the Spanish Civil War. The prospective director for the project, however, was not him but Bille August of Denmark. Sayles foresaw the production as the end of his historical cycle.

After back-to-back big-scale, ensemble movie productions, he was hoping for a rest. In September 1988, he and Maggie embarked on a working vacation, combining appearances at film festivals with downtime in Alaska and Australia. Ten years after the start of his film career and now thirty-eight years old, John seemed in no hurry to start another project. Still, the trip to Alaska would sow the seeds for a film a decade in the offing, and Sayles's resolve to slow down on writing and directing would be tested.

16

Shannon's Deal, Los Gusanos, and City of Hope: The Sayles Disciples and Community Issues

I suspect that always in John's films there's an exploration or looking for a distinct sense of community and how people act in groups. That's another thing that distinguishes him as a writer, director, and filmmaker. He's interested in people in groups, not just in a hero or heroine. That's almost un-American.

SCRIPT SUPERVISOR FRANCES DOEL, 1998

NOW APPROACHING FORTY YEARS of age in the late 1980s, Sayles had just devoted three years to completing *Matewan* (1987) and *Eight Men Out* (1988). Both projects were epic in scope and shot on location with large ensemble casts and hundreds of extras. As usual John had guided the films from concept to script to screen, writing, directing, editing, and promoting the releases. While Maggie Renzi handled the financing of the film, it was the filmmaker who had to work around the constraints of a low budget.

His energies depleted by his endeavors, he decided—after returning from his trek to Alaska and Australia—to step back from the rigors of moviemaking and redirect his creative energies. Yet, more than at any period in his professional life, this three-year period (1989–91) captures the range and depth of his creative talents. Leading up to the making of *City of Hope* (1991), he wrote an epic novel, a screenplay, a television pilot and two episodes, and an article for the *New York Times*. As an actor, John performed in three films and co-directed a music video for PBS-TV.

During this period, Sayles would break with some of his own policies and practices. Perhaps the most notable departure occurred in his 1989 decision to allow someone else to direct a Sayles screenplay, *Breaking In* (1989). Nine years earlier he had ended negotiations with a production team he simply did not like; now he renegotiated. "I didn't feel I was the one to direct it," he told the *New York Times* (September 18, 1988). "But I didn't want to sell it to be directed by just anyone. I really wanted to place it."

Sayles and the producers, the Samuel Goldwyn Company, agreed on Bill Forsyth, a Scottish writer/director respected for his light, insightful comedies and whose *Local Hero* (1983) was voted by many critics as one of the top films of the 1980s. Though he was unhappy directing somebody else's script—even one by Sayles—Forsyth turned what might have been a caper film, or simply Burt Reynolds's comeback movie, into a comedy about the relationship between a lonely sixty-year-old burglar (Reynolds) and a teenager (Casey Siemaszko) learning that illicit trade. Sayles appreciated the job Forsyth did, and Roger Ebert (*Chicago Sun-Times,* October 13, 1989) admired both contributors: "It's simply a well-written, well-directed picture." The ninety-four-minute release, however, realized a domestic gross of only $1,878,000.

While Sayles had felt uncomfortable at the prospect of directing *Breaking In,* he did lend his expertise to Marta Renzi (Maggie's sister) when she directed the music video "Mountainview" (1989). He wanted to repay her for two earlier favors: the dancing and choreography she provided for *Lianna* (1983) and introducing him to Bruce Springsteen in 1984. Produced for Boston's PBS affiliate WGBH-TV, "Mountainview" uses the music of Springsteen, Aretha Franklin, and Marvin Gaye in a narrative dance film. Renzi choreographed the story, set in a dingy, resort bar where each night the young customers come to dance out their feelings. As he said in *Sayles on Sayles,* the director certainly recognized that theme. "A lot of what Marta was getting at was community and the contributions of various characters through dance." John wrote the grant proposal that secured the funding, then stepped forward to co-direct the program, suggesting techniques that made the performance less stage-bound and more oriented toward the TV cameras.

■   ■   ■

Outside the family connections, other prospective moviemakers were drawing Sayles's attention and earning his support. Scores of young director wanna-bes, especially women, got their first chance to work on his movies. One of them was Nancy Savoca. Both Sayles and Jonathan Demme contributed to the tiny $750,000 budget that helped produce her first movie, *True Love* (1989). She would go on to direct *Dogfight* (1991) and *24-Hour Woman* (1998). Back in 1983, it was her office assistant's job at Sayles's Anarchists Convention head-quarters for *The Brother from Another Planet* that started her in the film business.

From her home in Rockland County, New York, Savoca remembers that opportunity. "Peggy Rajski hired me because I could type. . . . Breaking in was really important because I wanted to direct, and I had a script. Very ner-vously, I gave Peggy a copy, and she passed it on to Maggie, then John." About five years passed, and then at dinner with her and Maggie, John inquired about the *True Love* script and learned it was going nowhere. As Savoca recalls, he told her, "'Look, if you want to make the film real low budget, real guerrilla, I'll be your first investor.' If he hadn't done that, I don't think I'd have gotten my first film made.

"After John got the ball rolling, my husband [co-author Rich Guay], [pro-ducer] Shelly Houis, and I turned the film financing into 'celebrity investors.' We called every director we ever worked with and got the money. I asked John if he wanted the usual executive producer credit. He said, 'No, that's not necessary. I don't need that to happen.'"

At the 1989 Sundance Film Festival, *True Love* won the Grand Jury Award as Best Picture. Early in her career, Savoca had adopted Sayles's credo. "For John, 'independent film' means it's his movie under his creative control. That stance marks his entire career, and his integrity has been an inspiration to me as a director."

A few years later, John was assisting another first-time filmmaker. Having shot several documentaries, Robby Henson was directing his debut feature, *Pharaoh's Army* (1995), a Civil War story set in the Cumberland Mountains of Henson's native Kentucky. The movie starred Chris Cooper *(Matewan)* and Kris Kristofferson, and it was Cooper who invited Maggie and John to Henson's apartment in the Village to screen the film. As Henson told me, "They watched the rough cut of the movie, then stayed for three or four hours talking about some nuts-and-bolts things like the choice of music and editing, what slowed things down, what didn't work. I was very surprised. John was very realistic, saying things like, 'Yeah, getting distribution is really hard,' which is not what I wanted to hear. . . . I later heard that he fought for us to be included at Sundance. That was also nice to hear." In 1995 *Pharaoh's Army* was broadcast on PBS-TV.

Over the past twenty years, Sayles has jump-started the careers of dozens of young movie professionals whose admiration and affection endures. Typical of the first experience is Kevin Boyd, who would land his first film job as a production assistant for *City of Hope.* Today he recalls thinking, *I'm a tool. I know it and they know it, but they treat me with respect.* Having just served as video assist operator for *Lone Star* (1996) and *Limbo* (1999), Boyd told me about the good vibes on a Sayles set and about the freedom to work. "John lets people do their job. You might get tired or homesick, but there's never any of that 'let me get the hell out of here' feeling."

Patrick Cady also found his first job on *City of Hope,* working in the production office. On long days, he crashed on a mattress at Sayles's house in Hoboken. When he later attended New York University's film school, Cady would return to the Sayles compound for dinner and professional advice. Then he would walk home to the apartment John and Maggie found for him and where he still lives. Today a cinematographer, Cady recalls the old days. "It was pretty amazing, especially to be learning from 'The Guy' and from a group of people who were time and again making these great films."

In the late 1980s, John revisited the acting part of his career, though not in the United States. Though barely mentioned in *Sayles on Sayles* and unnoticed by American reviewers, he had, for reasons unknown, acted in David

Ferrario's *La Fine della Notte* (1989) and for Japanese director Go Takemin in *Untamaguru* (1989), winner of the 1990 Caligari Award at the Berlin Film Festival. (Sayles played a military high commissioner who tours the base with a pig in the back seat of his limousine.) Back in the United States at the 1989 Virginia Festival in Charlottesville, Virginia, he and Maggie led a panel discussion for the eight hundred people that attended a special screening of *Eight Men Out*. As Bob Gazzale, the festival's organizer, told me, "John brought a great sense of youthful energy to the event that year, especially since most of the festival was devoted to film history. We had tributes to Jimmy Stewart and Gregory Peck and a symposium on the blacklisting of the 1950s. We brought John in to present him with our Distinguished Filmmaker Award."

■   ■   ■

In 1988 Brandon Tartikoff, president of NBC-TV's entertainment division in Los Angeles and responsible for developing pilots and programs for the network, asked John to conceive a pilot for a television series. Sayles liked and admired Tartikoff and had enjoyed writing the script for and acting in NBC's venturesome and highly acclaimed movie *Unnatural Causes* (1986). Viewing programs such as *Moonlighting* (1985–89), *Miami Vice* (1984–89), and *Hill Street Blues* (1981–87), Sayles was convinced the networks were now working with complicated narratives, multiple plots, and looser formats. "They realize that they are competing with more players," he told *Interview* magazine (May 5, 1990), "There's Fox and HBO and home video . . . it's actually liberated the networks." He signed on with Tartikoff as writer and creative consultant. Presented with three of Sayles's ideas for a possible series, Brandon liked *Shannon's Deal*, with its story line about a Philadelphia lawyer trying to make a comeback from a morally corrupting corporate law career and a family-wrecking addiction to gambling.

Having gotten the green light, John began writing the two-hour pilot. In contrast to *Perry Mason* (1957–66; 1973–74) and *L.A. Law* (1986–94), the hero of this series was a blue-collar attorney, shrewder than he was smart. Despite the network's suggestions, nobody carried a gun, and Shannon's success depended on his wheeling and dealing, bluffing, manipulating, bending, and compromising so his clients never had to go to court. Setting aside courtroom theatrics, the show focused on justice as sought by the middle- and lower-class clients. For expertise, John consulted executive producer Stan Rogow, who in the 1960s worked as an attorney for a community medical center in Roxbury, a working-class section of Boston.

Shannon the antihero is humanized by his past. As a "good" company lawyer, he had callously trampled over justice in the name of corporate greed. As a husband and father, Shannon let his gambling end his marriage and damage his relationship with his daughter, Neala. In the series, it is Neala and his secretary, Lucy Acosta, who provide the human support that moves him beyond his guilt and away from his addiction. Shannon's past also brings to his office a series of misfits worthy of *Guys and Dolls* (1955), including a good-hearted bill collector of old gambling debts, the shyster lawyer down the hall, and, as the client in the first episode, a thuggish husband (Sayles) out to bilk his wife.

Lacking the glamour of *L.A. Law* and the courtroom showmanship of *Perry Mason,* the show was aimed at the more sophisticated, later-viewing audience. As with David Lynch's *Twin Peaks* (1990–91), *Shannon's Deal* started with a respectable film director's name attached, partly as a signal from NBC to encourage other established film writers and directors to follow Sayles to the small screen. In a *Los Angeles Times* interview, Rogow addressed the entertainment industry. "While you're waiting to sell your next Broadway play or direct your next $20 million movie, why not do a little television. . . . We're doing a little movie here each week. All we ask is that you use our characters. The rest is up for grabs."

Some talented Hollywood veterans took the bait. Lewis Teague (*Alligator,* 1980) and Allan Arkush (*Hollywood Boulevard,* 1976)—both Sayles collaborators from his horror film days—directed *Shannon* episodes, as did Joel Oliansky (writer/director, *The Competition,* 1980), John Byron (writer/director, *The Razor's Edge,* 1984), and Tom Rickman (writer, *Coal Miner's Daughter,* 1980). To the team Rogow added jazz trumpeter Wynton Marsalis, who composed the music for the series.

Although Sayles traditionally took a very proactive role in the selection of his casts, for *Shannon's Deal* the producers chose the young star, Jamey Sheridan, anticipating that the series would run ten years and that he would age nicely with it. The cast members recommended by Sayles were Elizabeth Peña, (Lucy Acosta), Jenny Lewis (Neala), and Richard Edson (Wilmer, the debt collector). In his role as creative consultant, Sayles also scripted two other episodes for the first season. NBC ran the pilot in the summer of 1989, then aired it again to introduce the six-part series in the spring of 1990. While the filmmaker enjoyed the TV fling, he was guarding himself against extended involvement. For the second season, John left the series in the hands of the writers, but agreed to help out by consulting with the producers or submitting script revisions when and if the show got in trouble.

The network had misgivings about *Shannon* ("too smart for prime time"), but they liked the characters and the drama. Of the pilot, television critic John O'Connor of the *New York Times* observed (June 4, 1989), "Clearly there's a new attitude abroad in the land: No matter what you may think of television, this is where the money is. Besides, you actually may be able to get away with something substantial." For the pilot, Sayles received the Edgar Allan Poe Award for Best Television Feature of 1990 from the Mystery Writers of America.

Reviewing the show's first season, the *Washington Post* (May 16, 1990) continued the kudos: "Sayles isn't slumming. . . . He's helping the effort to bring film quality to TV." Critics rewarded the producers' confidence with reviews applauding almost every element of the show. The *Baltimore Sun* saw *Shannon's Deal* as "the most engaging and richest hour of weekly drama in prime time. . . . [It is] as good as some of his [Sayles] best work." In the hero, some saw shades of Raymond Chandler's Philip Marlowe, minus some macho. "Call him soft-boiled," *Film Comment* (July 1990) said, then added: "It may be a back-handed compliment, but Sayles thrives in the tighter medium."

Despite the good notices, *Shannon's Deal* went off the air after a second, slightly abbreviated season. By that time John was on to other projects. One was his adaptation of Michael Dorris's 1988 novel, *Yellow Raft in Blue Waters,* the story of three generations of a Montana Indian family, a project that for some reason fell by the wayside. Sayles then returned to his desk in Hoboken and to a project he had been working on for twelve years: completing his third novel, *Los Gusanos.*

■   ■   ■

Sayles's initial interest in the story of the Cuban community in Miami began with his boyhood vacation trips to his maternal grandparents' home in Hollywood, Florida, in the mid-1950s and periodically in the 1960s. A lifelong baseball fan, his grandfather, Frederick Rousch, would take Doug and John to minor-league baseball games in Miami, exposing them to the city and the impact of the immigrants who fled Fidel Castro's Cuba. Sayles speaks of how he saw the exile community growing and Miami changing from a sleepy southern Jewish resort town to a vibrant international city with Spanish as its primary language.

The early exposure sparked a twenty-year study of the language and the Spanish-speaking community. Through his Hoboken neighbors and the media (including Cuban films), John picked up ideas and feelings that defied translation but were part of the story of Spanish-speaking Americans. "My neighbors spoke Spanish," he told *Venice* magazine (April 1998), "and I got into it . . . to find out who are they? How do they think? How come they're here?" His research included some seventy books, about twenty of them Cuban novels. In 1980, *The Atlantic Monthly* asked him to write an article about the boat lift that allowed thousands of Cubans to flee the country and the Castro regime. The assignment took him to interview the refugees at the Orange Bowl in Miami, where the escapees were being detained. The article was never published, but the conversations deepened John's grasp of the Cuban-Miami continuum and antagonism. In 1989 he put his moviemaking on hold and took the year off to travel the United States and Australia and write.

When *Los Gusanos* neared completion, Sayles opened a unique chapter in his own life and in the annals of American publishing. Rather than using his literary agent, he put the novel out for bids himself. Very shortly, he who so often had to scrape for support of his films was entertaining four competing bids.

He told the *Hollywood Reporter* (July 30, 1991), "I was interested in more than an advance. I didn't want to take any chances, wanted to know how many copies would be printed, what kind of budget there would be, how the book would be marketed. . . . I asked for approval of cover art and jacket copy, and I'm happy with the job they've done."

The auction led to Harper Collins acquiring the publishing rights. The NewYork firm gave Sayles a six-figure advance and agreed to his two key conditions: no major editing changes, and the inclusion of untranslated Spanish without italics. In John's mind, italics signaled "not normal." The insistence that Spanish be included without translation also sprang from Sayles's research on the mixture of Spanish and English spoken by Cubans in the Miami area. In practice, the use of Spanish did not pose a barrier. The English answers helped "translate" the Spanish questions and vice versa, thereby retaining the language without stalling the action or losing the reader.

A sprawling epic, the 475-page *Los Gusanos,* published in 1991, encompasses the period from the 1930s through the 1980s. Included are characters from veterans of the Lincoln Brigade who fought the Fascists in Spain, to rebels of the 1960s who failed to overthrow the Communist regime through their invasion of Cuba at the Bay of Pigs. Around the novel's central event— another even more ludicrous invasion of Havana—John involves scores of characters and stories radiating out from a core family group, the Cruzes. Marta Cruz is involved in the attack to avenge her brother's death and earn her father's respect. She is surrounded by her uncle Feliz (a former Castro gunrunner), a renegade priest, and a former member of Cuba's secret police. Dozens of other characters take the spotlight, each with a point of view about Cuba, usually appearing in flashback sections. The novel's title, taken from the phrase Castro used to describe the exiles, "The Worms," becomes increasingly applicable to people on both sides of the gulf.

Critics responded enthusiastically but with some reservations. In the *Washington Post* in mid-1991, Gustavez Perez Firmat cited the narrative's derivative glitter, borrowed from the 1980s TV series *MiamiVice* and from the Al Pacino feature film *Scarface* (1983). That qualification made, Firmat called the novel an "inspiring pastiche" with results that "were often compelling."

The *New York Times* (July 16, 1991) found it "an energetic, fierce, melodramatic and ironic adventure." The *American Book Review* (August 1992) disparaged the book as "more Harold Robbins than Joseph Conrad," but the *Library Journal* (April 15, 1991) cast it as "an exciting, instructive and highly readable novel." A paperback edition followed in 1992.

■   ■   ■

Unlike the thirteen-year gestation he allowed *Los Gusanos,* Sayles took *City of Hope* (1991) from conception to fully realized script in an amazingly short time—about eighteen days. He had ample memories from which to draw inspiration and documentation for his ideas about contemporary urban life. In its "Hudson City" setting, the picture alludes to Hoboken and Jersey City (both in New Jersey's Hudson County). A resident of one and commuter through the other, John certainly knew these urban landscapes, but his post-college days also had shown him the dark side of politics in Albany, East Boston, and Atlanta. Only the names of the politicians differed, but all of them might have been the models for the unseemly government officials in the film. Sayles told *Daily Variety* (July 20, 1994) that he checked his script's realism by scanning the *Jersey Journal* and the *Hudson Dispatch.* "Every day, there were headlines right out of the movie: a mayor went to jail, the son of another politician was charged with drunken driving, a construction boss was indicted, a rally was held to protest police brutality."

To finance *City of Hope,* Maggie Renzi turned first to the Hollywood studios but anticipated their rejections. As always, Sayles's insistence on creative control, casting rights, and final cut turned off the majors. As Renzi described to the *Washington Post* (October 20, 1991), "They say, 'Well, you know we can work all that out.' And then they start proposing actors for it that are not the right actors—and you begin to see what's happening." John himself felt that the studios of the early 1990s were resisting any kind of narrative complexity in screenplays. As he told *Pulse* (March 1993), "Studio executives and story editors attended screen writing seminars that reduce everything to formulas . . . so scripts that rely on intelligent dialog rather than buttocks and breasts are not in great demand." Sayles joked that he was going to title the movie *Sex, Lies and Urban Renewal*. This allusion to Steven Soderbergh's *sex, lies and videotape* (1989) came with a hint of envy, respect, and gratitude for a movie that went against the grain and helped make the studios more daring in their productions.

Under the management of Larry Estes, Columbia–TriStar Home Video had backed the $1.5 million Soderbergh movie and watched it gross $25 million at the box office. In *Spike, Mike, Slackers & Dykes* (1995), agent/author John Pierson states that *sex, lies and videotape* "had totally redefined the off-Hollywood world at mid-decade." The studios refused the picture, the independent distributors didn't bid enough, and home video stepped in as a new partner for independent filmmakers. TriStar was now looking for more films like it.

Of her meeting with Estes, Maggie recalled in *Sayles on Sayles* that she said, "'We think we can make it for three million dollars, very quickly,' and he said 'great.' That was that, one stop shopping, terrific. And we agreed that we would look for the right distributor later on." Little wonder that *Premiere*'s Terri Minsky (September 1991) calls *City* a landmark in Sayles's career, "The Movie That Was Easy to make. It took him two weeks to write the script, a month for Renzi to make the money, five weeks to film on location in Cincinnati, and a screening at Sundance Film Festival to line up a distributor." As with the television and book contracts, financing a film had suddenly become easy for the veteran moviemaker—at least for now.

Most of Sayles's energy was tapped for the production of a script that, even for him, was daunting in the number of characters, settings, plots, subplots, and themes involved. Promoting the picture, the Goldwyn press kit would include a who's who of the thirty-eight key characters. The British *Sight and Sound* (December 1991) devoted a full small-print column attempting to summarize the story. The *Washington Post*'s Rita Kempley (November 5, 1992) later suggested that the story "doesn't call so much for an ensemble as a congregation."

Several preproduction choices (cast, location, crew, and a documentary-style camera technique) helped ease the directing problems. In the scripting,

John wrote parts for his company of players: Vincent Spano (Nick, the alienated young man), Joe Morton (Wynn, the emerging politician), Chris Cooper (Riggs, a construction foreman), Jace Alexander (Bobby, a small-time hood), and David Strathairn (the mentally unbalanced Asteroid), supported by Kevin Tighe (the exploitative O'Brien), Mason Daring (Peter, a young man), and Maggie Renzi (Connie, a concerned parent). This community emphasis prevailed on and offscreen, even as Sayles saved a juicy character part for himself: Carl, the sadistic car mechanic. It is Carl who has the film's most authentic line (overheard by Sayles at a Hoboken garage): "Benny, you fat, f***in' hemorrhoid, get in here."

In the summer of 1990, Sayles, the crew, and the actors returned to Cincinnati and to the funky neighborhood previously used in *Eight Men Out*. Diverse enough to provide the needed forty locations and small enough to move around in quickly (sometimes twice a day), the city provided another plus: it suffered from none of the jet traffic and street noise of Newark or Hoboken.

With customary attention to detail, Sayles created Hudson City for the camera. Production designer Dan Bishop told me about one instance of the director's eye for the right props, the basketball sneakers hanging from the telephone wires—alluding to urban teenagers' way of discarding their worn-out sports shoes. "John knows New Jersey from living there, so the sneakers were his idea, just like the sign 'Garden State Brick Face and Stucco.' We kept good community relations by taking down the sneakers when we finished."

To tell his 129-minute narrative of urban strife and convey the theme of interconnectedness among citizens, John introduced new equipment and employed novel filming techniques. Fresh from *Eight Men Out*, cinematographer Robert Richardson convinced the director to employ super 35mm, widescreen film and to make the master shot (which covers the full panorama of the scene) the basic and recurring shot of the movie. Having settled on this format and tactic, Sayles combined them in a technique he calls trading. Familiar from the films of Robert Altman (*Nashville*, 1975) and today a staple of TV hospital and police series, trading has the camera follow one group of characters to another, then shift and follow the new group. In *City of Hope*, the constant shifting gives the movie a relentless force as the action is shunted from one urban problem to another, all to the driving beat of Mason Daring's contemporary urban, blues, and jazz score.

Director Joe Dante told me, "*City of Hope* represents a tremendous departure in John's camerawork, very fluid and with great use of the wide screen." The price for the use of these long-take techniques was paid for in the rehearsals to perfect the choreography of cast and camera movement. The payoff came in the format's allowing for several characters, foreground and background, to trade the action and in the technique's eliminating cuts, thereby saving time in the editing room. With the $3 million budget imposing a tight shooting schedule and the need to switch locations and set up fast, Sayles adopted Garrett Brown's invention, the Steadicam. It eliminates tripods and dollies and lets the photographer "wear" the strapped-on camera as he shoots. As Dan Bishop says, "It helped with the problem of shooting on the run."

As the movie's title suggests, the central character here is the city. As Sayles depicts it, "tribalism" has brought the metropolis to the end of its rope. Each generation has seen a new ethnic group rise to power—the Irish followed by the Italians, followed by the African Americans and Puerto Ricans. In the background of abandoned warehouses, dilapidated apartments, and barricaded store fronts stands the evidence of past governments' success in taking funds from the public till. With the Irish fleeing to the suburbs and the Italians following their lead, the Italian mayor sees one last chance to gouge the city by razing low-income housing and selling the land to Japanese interests under the guise of urban development. After that the blacks can have city hall and take what's left.

Nick, the closest thing in the film to a hero, is the Hamlet of Hudson City. He condemns his father, Joe (Tony LoBianco), for letting Nick's older brother go to his death in Vietnam, and bristles at the havoc the city fathers have wrought on the town, physically and morally. Slacking off on the job on Dad's construction project, Nick sets the movie's cynical mood by inhaling cocaine. It is Nick's gambling debts that drive him to join his friends in a botched burglary. Having been fingered by Carl the mechanic, he is saved from jail by his dad, who cuts a deal with the mayor. The price for Nick's rescue is equally high. To make way for the administrator's renewal project, Joe arranges the burning of the slum apartments he owns and unwittingly kills a young mother and child. At the end of the movie Nick is dying of a gun wound, and Joe is standing by his son, shouting in vain for help.

Within *City of Hope,* no help emerges from the self-serving bureaucracy, but Sayles allows slight glimmers of hope, as seen in a concerned mother, two honest cops, and a black politician (Joe Morton) who may stem the tide of rampant tribalism. The *New York Times* (August 10, 1992) saw the story's grim side but also perceived something affirmative in Sayles's "amusement at each of the minor characters' flamboyant presentation of self that imparts an under-current of optimism . . . like the goofy pair of housewife-complainers who makes up the film's nitwit chorus."

After premiering at the Sundance Film Festival in January 1991, Sayles's movie won the Grand Prize at the Tokyo International Film Festival. The R-rated film also found a distributor in the Samuel Goldwyn Company. When *City of Hope* opened in October 1991, reviews ran the gamut as critics admired the ambition of the screenplay, cited flaws in the picture, and saw promise for John's future. Several recognized a similarity in theme to Spike Lee's *Do the Right Thing* (1989), and Sayles admits that his film was in part a response to that provocative and controversial motion picture about black and white tensions centered around a white-owned pizza parlor in a Brooklyn, New York, neighborhood. The *Episcopal News* (December 1991) identified the story framing as the difference between the two movies. "*Do the Right Thing* was a horizontal slice of life in one city block. *City of Hope* is a vertical slice of three days in the life of the city." While Lee's movie ends in a riot, *City* alleviates the bleakness through the black councilman's resistance to the white corruption and to the spirit of African-American separatism. (Also released in 1991, *Boyz N the Hood* is John Singleton's sober look at a black father living in south-central Los Angeles and trying to steer his son away from the gangs and toward decent moral values.)

New York magazine (October 28, 1991) called *City of Hope* "a kind of slap-dash, TV-movie project . . . in which most of the ideas seem generalized and secondhand." Georgia Brown (*Village Voice*, October 22, 1991) saw "an old-fashioned, rub-your-nose-in-it slice of sordidness." The *Los Angeles Times* (October 25, 1991) labeled it "the most ambitious film of the year" and admired it for having "the temerity to address major social issues and the pizzazz to do it in a dramatically involving way." That energy also won the applause of the *Christian Science Monitor* and excited renewed expectations for Sayles "orchestrating elements of plot, characterization, and cinematic style into dynamic and unpredictable structures." Most reviewers applauded the attempt to bring to the screen genuine social concerns without pat conclusions. In his end-of-the-year review for the *New York Times* (December 12, 1991), Vincent Canby judged it "The Most Spectacular Modestly Budgeted Film of 1991."

Sayles felt that of all his seven films at that time, *City of Hope* got the best reviews ever, but too many critics included the word *grim*. He would have added *despair, futility, malignant cancer*, and *dark* to the list of phrases that turned off most moviegoers and left the picture with a paltry box-office gross of $1.3 million.

While the film's earnings were slight, it did have an impact in promoting discussion. In 1989 a number of screenings of *Do the Right Thing* had unfortunately been marked by riots outside the theaters. Sayles's feature generated more cerebral exchanges of viewpoints. When *City of Hope* opened at the Avco Center Cinema in Los Angeles, a panel discussion followed, with city officials and social workers discussing the movie's themes as they pertained to their city. In Hartford, Connecticut, People for Change staged a Progressive Party benefit around the screening of the film and a discussion with Sayles. Later that year, at the Fourteenth Annual Denver International Film Festival, Sayles won the John Cassavetes Award as "the individual who has made the greatest contribution to American independent filmmaking during the calendar year."

In her 1996 book, *Reel to Real: Race, Sex, and Class at the Movies*, African-American film scholar bell hooks cited John's contribution to an authentic understanding of black culture, then added, "There are black images in works by white filmmakers like Jim Jarmusch and John Sayles that are more radical than black images in Spike's work."

For his 1995 book *Past Imperfect,* Columbia University historian Eric Foner reviewed contributions to the history genre of motion pictures. He discovered a gender issue in Sayles's movies. "Most of these films are about the male world. *Matewan* is basically a male world. In fact *Eight Men Out* is a completely male world. Why can't filmmakers make films about women's history?" Back in 1991 Maggie Renzi had wondered why one filmmaker in particular (Sayles) couldn't make a second film about women. After two period films and the big-canvas urban movie, John agreed. He was now seeking both a gender and a structural change of pace—from men to women, from large canvas to small.

17

Passion Fish:
Some Critical Conversions

I acted in Passion Fish *because it was an opportunity to work with John Sayles. I had seen a couple of his films,* Matewan *being the most influential. I enjoyed the subject matter, things of the heart, emotions, not a lot of shooting and cursing, all that kind of thing.*

PLAYWRIGHT/ACTOR JOHN HENRY REDMOND, 1998

THROUGH THE EARLY 1990S, Sayles continued to exercise his performing muscles on television and in film. In 1991 he appeared on A&E's documentary series *Naked Hollywood* discussing his experiences in the movies. In 1992 he made one appearance on "Mathnet," a serialized segment of PBS-TV's *Square One Television* produced by the Children's Television Workshop. The "Mathnet" episode used various celebrities to show children that arithmetic was cool. John played Roy "Lefty" Cobbs, a kidnapped baseball player who loved math games.

As a devotee of the sport and the writer/director of *Eight Men Out* (1988), Sayles provided his insight into the game's history as part of Ken Burns's nine-part TV documentary entitled *Baseball* (1994).

On the big screen, Sayles seemed to be helping his friends rather than forging a career as an actor. Perry Lang, who had acted in *Alligator* (1980) and

Eight Men Out, had turned to directing. His film *Little Vegas* (1990) featured Anthony John Denison and Catherine O'Hara in a comedy about the Mafia trying to take over a trailer camp and create a little Las Vegas. Sayles had a one-minute cameo as a trailer owner, and both he and Maggie Renzi got special thanks in the closing credits. In 1994 Lang directed the direct-to-video adventure *Men of War.* Based on a Sayles script, the movie starred Dolph Lundgren as a member of a group of mercenaries trying to take a mineral-rich island from the natives.

Sayles also appeared briefly in three comedies: *Straight Talk* (1992), *My Life's in Turnaround* (1993), and *Matinee* (1993). A comedy directed by Barnet Kellman and starring Dolly Parton, *Straight Talk* featured John in the opening scene as Don, a dance-hall owner who fires Parton's character for not dancing with enough people. Co-directed by and costarring Eric Schaeffer and Donald Lardner Ward, *My Life's in Turnaround* found John on familiar turf in a loosely knit farce about making a low-budget movie. Playing against reputation, he appears as a "marginal producer" who becomes incensed when prospective filmmakers pitch him an art film. Like *Turnaround, Matinee* was another comic send-up of the movies, this time a nostalgic salute to the films of William Castle (1914–77), the schlockmaster of the horror genre, here renamed Lawrence Woolsey and played by John Goodman. Directed by Joe Dante, a friend from the Corman years, the film had Sayles playing Bob, a man bent on sabotaging the sneak preview of Woolsey's new hit, *Mant*—"Half Man, Half Ant, All Terror."

Joining scores of other New York City–based actors, Sayles pitched in on Spike Lee's *Malcolm X* (1992), appearing in a cameo as a wiretapping FBI agent. In the old days, John would have used the performance money to support his productions. These acting stints, however, were done as favors or in fun, and for a change Sayles didn't need the money—just yet.

■   ■   ■

With *Matewan* (1987) and *Eight Men Out* (1988), *City of Hope* (1991) completed a three-picture cycle of big movies addressing social problems both historical and contemporary. Simply as a relief from the onus of making large-scale movies with a low budget, a return to a simpler kind of film about personal issues made sense for him. Easing the pressure and changing the scope of his features, however, were not the only motivations for his next project. As Sayles told *Sight and Sound* (September 1993), "What influenced me most was . . . the fact that I'd done three 'guy' movies, which is what basically politics consists of. . . . Maggie asked me if I had any stories for women, so I thought we'd do the hospital one next."

Ostensibly, in turning to "women's movies," Sayles was also setting aside the commentary his three pictures had made about corporate and political greed. These pictures had reverberated with an antagonism toward the Reagan administration philosophy, wherein companies were kings and unions got clobbered and city problems ignored. John's next two films seemingly stepped back from their attacks on the establishment; in truth, the examination of American values seems not so much dropped as shifted in focus. From the macroeconomics of national and local governmental policy, Sayles now looked to the microworld of personal lives lived in the "Me Generation." These forthcoming productions would examine the human havoc wrought when materialism is the preeminent norm for judging personal growth and success.

Not unexpectedly in these independent-minded Sayles entries, the characters defy traditional Hollywood notions of women and children as sweet but plucky. In *Passion Fish* (1992), the former soap opera star May-Alice is not just attractive looking and physically impaired. Even in a wheelchair, she is sometimes selfish, mean, and unlikable. She also shows that like men, women can really, as Sayles says, "f*** up" and "f*** people up." The child hero of *The Secret of Roan Inish* (1994) is equally three-dimensional, having a grit and self-starting work ethic that dispel and defy the "cute" roles so often saddled on young girls in films.

While different locations and stories provide each of these two projects with unique textures, they share the usual Sayles community theme. Both films question the advantages of physical relocation for money and success when traded for community heritage and family traditions. In these women-related features, money has separated the characters from their roots. For different economic reasons, the TV actress and the orphaned girl have both been cut off from their homes, families, and cultures and, therefore, themselves. Now they turn to those roots in need of the physical and emotional healing found in their respective settings.

These roots are truly restorative. Back in their old homes, the woman and the girl can recoup from the failures, setbacks, and disillusionment each found in the city. Far from the urban glitz and busyness, each finds her spiritual home in the native dialects and folk customs of her community. In adopting this smaller scale, Sayles's economy and focus in his writing would provide rich dividends for his casts and for both movies.

■   ■   ■

In referring to *Passion Fish* as the "hospital film," Sayles alludes to the movie's inspiration. Back in the 1970s, his job as an orderly in hospitals and nursing homes in Schenectady, New York, showed him the kinds of relationships that emerge between two dependent people, such as a nurse needing a job and a patient requiring care. That kernel of an idea launched this script about a New York soap opera star who, while on her way to a beauty parlor to have her legs waxed, gets run over by a cab and turned into a paraplegic needing a full-time nurse.

Passion Fish finds May-Alice (Mary McDonnell) returning to southern Louisiana. There she reopens the home she had abandoned for her career. Now confined to a wheelchair, the forty-year-old resists therapy and instead turns to the twin narcotics of alcohol and TV. Her tart tongue drives off three nurses before meeting her potential savior, Chantelle (Alfre Woodard). Chantelle is an African-American nurse from Chicago, also about forty and suffering her own paralysis—drug-induced in her case—that has led to a dead end. May-Alice's house may represent her last chance, and in turn she may hold her boss's only hope for recovery. Chantelle has a low tolerance for self-pity, a quick wit, and the professional experience to handle May-Alice's outbursts. Rarely leaving the confines of the estate, the movie develops the strident but promising relationship between the celebrity and her nurse. The film also complicates their characters' lives through visits from family, friends, and once and future lovers, all of whom bring revelations about the past and possibilities for the future to the ailing nurse and her patient.

In the spring of 1992, Sayles's production team arrived in Jennings, Louisiana, and established its production residence at the local Holiday Inn and its headquarters at the former Jeff Davis Beauty Salon. The movie still had no title. What it did have was an ample budget (by John's standards), an Academy Award–winning cinematographer, and a first-rate cast.

The "Louisiana Project" did not get its final release title until a contest among the crew members led to *Passion Fish*. In the narrative, the phrase refers to a Louisiana tradition in ways that would be followed up in *Roan Inish*. Here the local folk legend alludes to the little fish sometimes found in the innards of bigger fish. These are the passion fish, so the myth has it, that promise romance and love to finders.

The financing for *Passion Fish* flowed from the $3 million in its home video pre-sales, and the production this time had a distributor, thanks to John Sloss. As Sayles's new legal representative and executive producer, the Manhattan-based lawyer hammered out film contracts with backers and then haggled with the distributor, Miramax, to preserve the film's lengthy running time (135 minutes).

Beyond the upfront production money, the projected home video sales would open the film to an audience outside the usual art-house circuit. More immediately, the generous financing deal gave *Passion Fish* the same $3 million budget as *Matewan* and permitted a longer shooting schedule than *City of Hope*. With this backing, Sayles wished to step up the quality of the movie imagery through his investment in a cinematographer of the same caliber as Haskell Wexler and Robert Richardson.

Having just wrapped *Air America* (1990), director of photography Roger Deakins brought his entire British film crew to Jennings and with them created the languorous mood of backcountry Louisiana. Later a favorite of the Coen brothers (*Fargo*, 1996) and Martin Scorsese (*Kundun*, 1997), Deakins was two years away from his Oscar nomination for *The Shawshank Redemption* (1994). Responding to the suggestion that Sayles's film should become more visual and less script-bound, Maggie Renzi would tell *Sight and Sound* (September 1993), "There's no minimizing the difference money makes."

In casting this intimate movie, Sayles found the two leads from his professional past. Mary McDonnell had worked with him in *Matewan,* and Alfre Woodard had starred in the Sayles-scripted TV film *Unnatural Causes.* These two seasoned actors brought extraordinary credentials to John's new outing. Just two years earlier McDonnell, playing opposite Kevin Costner, had her breakthrough performance as Stands-with-a-Fist in the Oscar-winning *Dances with Wolves* (1990). Woodard, a veteran of the stage, had already been nominated for Best Supporting Actress Oscar for Martin Ritt's drama *Cross Creek* (1983). She was equally successful on the small screen, taking home Emmys for her strong performances on *Hill Street Blues* and *L.A. Law.*

McDonnell and Woodard had just costarred in Lawrence Kasdan's *Grand Canyon* (1991). Now, in a year marked by a dearth of opportunities for women in movies, John provided the duo with roles written expressly for them. Still, some observers felt they faced risks in working in a low-budget, independent project. In *Passion Fish,* however, Woodard's and McDonnell's performances would disprove any such imagined risks and would lead to Oscar and Golden Globe nominations.

Casting, as always, was key. Playing Dr. Blades, Chantelle's father, John Henry Redmond witnessed the outstanding acting qualities on the set. He told me, "You have to understand the time and financial constraints. You need to get things done as quickly as possible. You don't need someone around taking up your time being a star or a diva." With comic exaggeration, Alfre Woodard offered her view of the demands of *Passion Fish* for *People* magazine (March 8, 1993): "Whereas most movie sets offer elegant catered meals . . . my family lived like vagabonds crouching on the floor of the Holiday Inn over a steamer eating rice."

McDonnell stated the salary issue more directly in *People* magazine (March 8, 1993). "You don't do a Sayles movie for money. You do it for the incredible text and for what you know will be a great movie." As for Woodard and her vagabonds, Thurmond fondly recalls dining with her and her husband and learning how to crack and eat Cajun-cooked crayfish.

This family feeling on the set, which was a lakeside home outside Jennings, Louisiana, owned by parents of Jimmy McDonnell, a musician associate of Sayles, evolved partly from the democratic regime of the Sayles shoot and the respect for all parties involved. While businesslike, a convivial spirit prevailed and reflected the care with which Maggie and John always cast each film and selected their crews. Having auditioned for *Matewan* and lost the part to James Earl Jones, Redmond this time was offered and took the part of Chantelle's father. "Without a doubt ego plays into it," he says. "But, if somebody hands you a role with no audition, you don't want to turn that down."

On the other hand, Elaine West, an acting professional and Baton Rouge, Louisiana, resident, got the chance to test, thanks to Sayles's practice of using videotape and hiring locally. "If you live in parts unknown," she informed me, "taping auditions gives you a chance. That's how I got the part, and I liked the set. There was no psychodrama, no back-stabbing, no room for anything except being a good person and getting your work done."

As a first-timer, camera assistant Pat Cady got paid per diem and thought it was great. "I bailed out of grad school at New York University and drove a truck down there with six Steenbecks. Every day I'd do something completely wrong," he says with a laugh. "But I learned a lot of 'don't-evers' and took a lot of professionalism back to class." Joining the ranks of Cady and other young production assistants were Maggie's father, Ralph, and his colleague from Williams College, Dr. James Stenson, both in their sixties. "We were a couple of $200-a-week gofers in crafts and services," Ralph recalls. "You pitch a tent, bring the groceries, serve the food, then you find diapers at three A.M. for somebody with a kid screaming bloody murder. At times we were a couple of tired old dogs, but Sten told me it was a highlight of his life."

Both characters in the film are facing midlife crises. For May-Alice, the sudden loss of her celebrity status has left her emotionally stagnant, and her home is barren of family and friends. Chantelle's life seems equally bereft. Her past includes drug abuse and an ex-husband, as well as a young daughter now in the custody of Chantelle's father.

In the earlier scenes of *Passion Fish,* May-Alice's drunken despondency turns the nicely appointed family home into a stark chamber. After the arrival of Chantelle, however, the narrative moves out to the lawn and introduces new faces. The visitors provide a commentary on the relationship between patient and nurse. May-Alice's boozy uncle Reeves (Lee Burmester), for one, sadly confides in her about his unfulfilled dreams. Yet, in leaving May-Alice the key to his photographic lab, Reeves provides a way out of her own malaise. For Chantelle, a visit from her former husband and from her father and child reminds her of the need to reshape her life—and also to keep her job so she can get back the daughter she loves.

May-Alice's other guests evoke similar insights and reflections. With the arrival of her former high school classmates, she recognizes the cultural and professional rut she avoided by leaving town. By contrast, her conversations with the visiting cast of the soap opera reveal how superficial her celebrity life had become. Meanwhile, Chantelle has a romance with the much married Sugar LaDoux (Vondie Curtis-Hall), and a chance chain of events brings local handyman/fisherman, Rennie (David Strathairn) onto the scene. It leads to his reunion with Mary-Alice, the dream woman of his high school years. Thus, both Sugar and Rennie help to escort the women from the sidelines back to the dance of life.

At the end, the film eschews any big, "music-up" happy resolutions. While the characters reach an understanding, there is a lingering distance among them and doubts about their futures. For Chantelle, Sugar's easy-living style, while refreshing, may not provide the stability she needs. May-Alice's relationship with Rennie is likewise problematic because he's married and has children. In her last onscreen meeting with Rennie, she advises him that he is always welcome to come see her. The lightness of tone serves well in concluding a movie in which Sayles had balanced a serious drama about personal values with refreshing comic dialogue and action.

■   ■   ■

Hardly a year passed between the fall 1991 opening of *City of Hope* and the December 1992 release of John Sayles's eighth movie, the R-rated *Passion Fish*. A few critics found the latter too languorous and tolerant of thematic excursions not carefully enough tied to the plot. Most reviewers, however, welcomed back the quirky humor that characterized *Return of the Secaucus Seven* and found the film, as the *Washington Post* (January 29, 1993) did, "more fun and less pedantic." *Sight and Sound* (September 1993) admired the movie's resistance to sentimental stickiness through "its crisp, acute writing" and "above all the acting—especially by the two principals." *Newsweek* (January 11, 1993) struck the same chord: "The soap opera framework remains, but the suds have been replaced with smarts and the emotions ring true." After admiring *Passion Fish* and its Cajun music score, Georgia Brown of the *Village Voice* (December 8, 1992) conceded, "This is a movie for those who don't like Sayles's movies. And it's probably (though I wouldn't know) for those who do."

Brown was not the only critic won over by *Passion Fish*. In a remarkable coincidence and journalistic anomaly, two reviewers apologized in print for neglecting the movie's debut. Admitting he had not seen the film before writing his Ten Best List for 1992 for *Film Comment,* Andrew Sarris confessed in the May 1993 issue, "I was frankly embarrassed to discover that Sayles had chosen the inopportune moment [mid-December 1992] to deliver his masterpiece." For Sarris, this new admiration started with the first scene. In it, the comatose May-Alice awakens in the hospital, sees her prerecorded soap on TV, and shouts, "They've stolen my f***ing close-up!" As Sarris wrote, "It's a writer's line of Norma Desmond proportions. . . . From there I followed Sayles wherever he wanted to take me at whatever pace he desired."

In *New York* magazine (February 15, 1993), David Denby offered his own regrets. "I would like to make amends for not reviewing until this date one of the best films of 1992. . . . This is the real one, the living breathing one—the work of art you have to see." Still unimpressed by Sayles's earlier political movies, Denby proposed his theory: "Since *Passion Fish,* Sayles's best movie yet, has a small subject, the principal in his directing career has become clear. . . . When he works small, he discovers, he deepens, he enlarges."

Despite all the critical plaudits and the enthusiastic receptions at the Vienna, Dublin, and Munich film festivals, *Passion Fish* stumbled at the box office. It grossed just under its $5 million production cost, but this was, after all, a picture funded by home-video money. Fittingly, video and DVD may be its chief source of income. It is now a given that most people do not see Sayles's movies in theaters.

While sluggish at the box office, *Passion Fish* was Sayles's first multiple-award winner. Perhaps responding to the urging of the critics, the Academy of Motion Picture Arts and Sciences nominated the film for Best Original Screenplay (won by Neil Jordan for *The Crying Game*) and Mary McDonnell for Best Actress (won by Emma Thompson for *Howards End*). Though neither received a Golden Globe Award, both McDonnell (Best Actress) and Alfre Woodard (Best Supporting Actress) were nominated, and Woodard won the Independent Spirit Award for Best Supporting Actress.

The most enthusiastic accolades for *Passion Fish,* however, came from the people of Jennings, Louisiana, where it premiered. More than four hundred guests turned out for the gala. As actress Elaine West recalls, "They had everybody bring food and things, and John and Maggie were there. Thanks to that benefit, the city was able to refurbish its little theater." In Maggie's eyes, the greatest tribute was the pride that everyone in Jennings felt in making the movie.

■   ■   ■

Sayles would soon wish that the response to *Passion Fish* had stopped with the critics and the box office. What stunned him was the copyright lawsuit that challenged his integrity and cost him hundreds of thousand of dollars.

Filed in 1993 by Virginia Towler against the production companies (Atchafalaya and Esperanza), the distributor (Miramax), and Sayles, the suit charged that the defendants allegedly had infringed on her copyrighted screenplay, "Crossed Wires or Bobbie and Wendy Were Neighbors." Judge Claude M. Hilton of the U.S. District Court for the Eastern District of Virginia at Alexandria presided at the hearings. Having refused to dismiss the case, the judge established a two-prong test for the plaintiff's claim: (1) whether Towler had proven that Sayles had received the script and read it, and (2) whether the *Passion Fish* script was substantially like her script.

Towler testified that she had sent her screenplay to Tracy Strain, an employee at SCS Films. The company was named after chief executive officer Steven Clark Swid, but Towler mistakenly thought its initials stood for Secaucus Seven. She also claimed that Strain had promised to send the script to Sayles. In the courtroom, the plaintiff's lawyer could not establish Sayles's contact with SCS, nor was there proof that the script was ever sent to him. After reading Towler's work, the judge concluded there were neither internal nor external substantial similarities between it and the film. In January 1994, saying there was not a scintilla of evidence, Hilton dismissed the case.

Towler then appealed and the case dragged on for two more years. Finally, on February 23, 1996, the three judges of the U.S. Court of Appeals for the Fourth Circuit in Richmond, Virginia, also dismissed the case. In 1998, sitting in the living room of the Sayles home on Sumner Street, Mary Sayles explains one consequence of that suit. "People ask us to have John look at a script, but you have to say no. That's why it's difficult to get to John; even his address can be used against him. Now somebody's coming after him about *Lone Star.*"

The lawyers' fees had drained the filmmaker's resources. Fortunately, John could recoup those losses by writing scripts. In 1991 he had started work on a screenplay for a Jonathan Demme epic about the Japanese sinking of the USS *Indianapolis* in the Pacific Ocean during World War II and the ensuing shark attack on the surviving sailors. At the time Sayles worried that Orion, the production company, would itself sink. It did, and with it went what he calls "that floating-head movie." With it also went part of the bankroll for his next film. After the ease of financing *City of Hope* and *Passion Fish,* he might now have to dig into his own pockets to make *The Secret of Roan Inish.*

18

The Secret of Roan Inish:
A Gift to Maggie Renzi

Who else could make us fall in love with a cranky, self-pitying
soap opera star? Or renew our childish wonder with
the magical, mystical tale of a toddler in a remote Irish village?

WRITERS GUILD FOUNDATION
PRESIDENT JOHN FURIA JR., 1998

THE IMPETUS FOR MAKING John Sayles's first family-oriented, lyrical children's film goes back to the Renzi household of the 1960s in Williamstown, Massachusetts, and to the weekly trips young Maggie made to the town library. The favorite book of her girlhood was the 1957 novella *The Secret of Ron Mor Skerry* by the Scottish author Rosalie Fry.

Some years later, Maggie returned to that library and bought the book for a quarter at a book sale. She carried it around for a while, as she told Margaret Moser of the *Austin Chronicle* (September 26, 1996), "and then proposed to John that we do it as a movie. And he said, 'yeah, maybe sometime.' Then right before we were set to go down and shoot *Passion Fish* [1992] he said, 'I'll write the script, then when we get back to cut, you and Sarah can go to Ireland and start scouting for it. That'll be the next one we do.'" As Sayles's brother, Doug, told me about this quirky film, "John did it because Maggie loved the story.

That was his gift to her." Had he known the price tag beforehand, Sayles might have kept on shopping.

With the project undertaken, John did some adapting of the text. Growing up Catholic in Schenectady and familiar with the Irish from his days of living in Boston, Sayles decided to transpose the setting of the story from Scotland to Ireland, specifically from Ron Mor Skerry to Roan Inish, Gaelic for "seal island." He read autobiographies of men who lived and fished on the famed Aran Islands off the rugged Irish west coast. Most of those tales were written in Gaelic, and in the film that language becomes one of the links of post–World War II Ireland to its ancient heritage. As John explains in *Sayles on Sayles* (1998), "I found that [language] to be a good metaphor for Fiona [the movie's girl hero] and the way she was living now with the world that came before, when seals and people were more symbiotic, when they lived a natural life and made their living off the sea." To the language connection, Sayles would then add Fiona's own mystical rapport and communication with the sea, the seals and gulls, and with the mythical half-seal, half-human creature, the selkie.

Perhaps the foreign location and the novelty of the haunting film explain the difficulty producers Sarah Green and Maggie Renzi experienced in connecting with investors. The search for *Roan Inish's* financing dragged on through most of 1993, while the opportunity to shoot the picture was fading. Finally, with Ireland's inclement fall weather still in the offing, Sayles put up a third of the movie's $5 million cost, sent the equipment, cast, and crew to County Donegal, Ireland, and started the late summer production.

The funding came from the savings Sayles had accumulated from his scripting-for-hire. In 1992 he had developed screenplays for a Martin Scorsese-Steven Spielberg remake of the 1946 RKO thriller *Bedlam,* and for a Dolph Lundgren vehicle called *A Safe Place.* Like so many other movie projects, neither of these scripts was filmed, but John earned his writer's fees. His aggressive investment of those earnings in his ninth movie soon had the filmmaker and the production over a barrel.

Supposedly, the rest of the financing was to come from Jones Intercable of Denver. That company reportedly grew cautious, however, and started investigating Sayles's credit rating and renegotiating their investment in the film.

As Sayles told an American Film Institute seminar in Los Angeles in the mid-1990s, "They were able to keep changing the deal in their favor, while all my money down to the last dollar was invested in the film. I liked the people, I liked the movie, but the economic situation was stressful." For two weeks the shooting continued on the northwest coast of Ireland in the village of Rosberg, about 120 miles from Belfast. The crew worked under the threat that, without the financing, the producers would have to tell everyone to go home. According to veteran cinematographer Haskell Wexler, the crew was confident: "I knew we were working before they had the money, but nobody would have left or said 'f*** you, I'm going home.' That's because Maggie gets people who want to work with John."

After the money started coming in, the production would go so smoothly that it came in under budget, and in the end, all hands received a $650 bonus. ("That's *never* happened before," Wexler told me.) Along the way, the production team had to convince the County Donegal villagers that the filmmakers really were not Mormons determined to convert the Irish children. The hiring of local cast, crew, and musicians alleviated them.

Once again, Sayles's longtime producer and lifetime partner was at the production helm, organizing the local cast and the crew. Occasionally, John teases Maggie saying that her role of creative producer is an oxymoron, but the two have developed a viably successful professional and personal relationship. Renzi does not aspire to writing or directing; what she takes care of are all the other things the movie and the filmmaker need. As she told the *Austin Chronicle*'s Moser, "I'm close enough to John and he trusts me enough that it's possible for me to say 'We really need you to reconsider location . . . to think about changing your schedule because we can only get this actor for two days.'"

What neither Maggie nor John care to discuss publicly is the private understanding they have about their life together that, without benefit of marriage, has lasted for more than twenty-five years. The reasons for their choice of sharing life without children remains private, with the exception that Maggie admits that, though she loves youngsters, she has never felt the need to be a parent.

■   ■   ■

As controller of the budget, Renzi appreciates that Sayles does not count himself in the above-the-line expenses that cover the salaries of writers, directors, and actors. She implicitly believes that the film that emerges will come in on time and on budget, look expensive, and be worth the trouble. Modest, forthright, and universally admired by those who have worked on a Sayles project, Renzi was once asked about her film school training and laughed. Her film education, she reiterated, came from watching her mother host a party, making everyone comfortable, sparking the conversation, keeping the gathering congenial and the glasses full. As with any good party, the number of guests who don't want to leave attests to the success of Maggie's capabilities. In the case of *Roan Inish,* even with a crew from both the Protestant Ulster of the North and the Catholic Irish Republic of the South, she kept the peace, maintained the production pace, and threw the parties.

In rounding up the actors for *Roan Inish,* Renzi and Sarah Green employed the local expertise of Ros and John Hubbard, who had cast several recent Irish features. For the leading roles, they found Mick Lally, a popular TV actor, for the grandfather, Eileen Colgan (*My Left Foot,* 1989) for the grandmother, and John Lynch (*Cal,* 1984) for Tadhg Coneely, the mysterious connection to the family's past. Finding the right ten-year-old girl to play Fiona and a fifteen-year-old boy to play her cousin, Eamon, took notices on TV and turned up thousands of candidates, including newcomers Jeni Courtney and Richard Sheridan, who won the parts. The rest of the cast were locals, likewise the crew, which included some specialists. One was the new associate producer, Paul Miller, who teamed with Green and Renzi.

A graduate of the National Film and Television School in London, Miller met Sayles and Renzi through his job at the Waterstone Book Store. After an afternoon of John's signing copies of his then new novel *Los Gusanos,* a dinner followed. Miller spoke with the couple about his background in wildlife filming and his interest in making movies. He told me, "I was hired especially to assist with the nature parts of *Roan Inish.* Then I started using my professional contacts in England and Ireland."

For the magical seals who "speak" with Fiona, Miller turned to John Yeadon, director of an Irish sanctuary that rehabilitates injured seals and then sets them free. Between their recuperation and return to the ocean, some of these mammals would become film stars. For the gulls who look after the little girl, Miller sought out Birds of Prey, a company that trains birds for movies. Jeff Goodman, a natural history cameraman, shot the footage of the seals, and Lyons Model Effect of Bristol, England, created the animatronics for the transformation of the mythical selkie into a woman. As with *Matewan* and *Passion Fish,* the local production team helped educate Sayles about local language and customs.

For the cinematography, Sayles brought back Haskell Wexler, and the two men resumed their sometimes combative but constructive modes of shooting. Like a chef, Wexler has great respect for preparation but puts little stock in cookbooks, in this case Sayles's storyboards with each shot carefully drawn. "They're for the birds because things change," Wexler told me, "but once I decided to subjugate my usual attitude of being God's gift to creativity, John loosened up." The photographer brought to bear his special talent for shooting outdoors and keeping the lighting consistent despite the vagaries of the maritime weather. To that expertise, Sayles added settings designed by Adrian Smith to capture the necessary rustic feeling. As Wexler told the author, "For the people who carved their home out of the land, fire becomes the focus, natural light from the sky the key."

The other American on the shoot was composer Mason Daring, who arrived on the worst day of the August–September 1993 production. Sitting on his porch overlooking the ocean at Marblehead, Massachusetts, Daring later recalled the crisis for me. "I walked on the set, and it was a low point. They had already had trouble getting financing, and now some loony burned down the three cottages [for the set] that had taken days to build and thatch. Bam, they're gone. Everybody was so depressed. Then they were spending all their time with the seals and the goddamned water was freezing. That shoot was murder, but they kept trucking and made the movie." (The "loony," who had a drinking problem, mistakenly thought he had not gotten his overtime pay and set the fire as revenge. Insurance covered the damage, but the rebuilding delayed shooting.) Daring spent three days recording with the Irish musicians, who were equipped with native instruments: flutes, tin whistles and pennywhistles, pipes, fiddle, bouzouki, and bodhran (a tambourine-like drum).

With fondness for his Irish peers, Daring remembers the recording sessions at Dublin's Windmill Studio, home base of the Irish rock group U2. "The first day we got to know each other; the third day we knocked off overdubs. The second day we did a ton of music. They'd play some public domain, authentic Irish reels, then we'd show them the scene. We'd add a couple of instruments and shape the music to it. Everything came together. Sometimes, God taps you on the shoulder and says, 'This is your day.'" Once back in New England, Daring gathered his own band and completed the film score.

Like *Passion Fish, The Secret of Roan Inish* centers on a woman, a girl in this case, Fiona Coneely, who is coming back to her community. Even the seals come out to greet her as the boat brings her from the city back to the Irish coast of the late 1940s. Standing on the ship deck, Fiona conveys the determination she will need to bridge the gap between the spiritually impoverished present and the rich heritage of her family. That legacy unfolds in the tales told by her grandfather about their real home, the island of Roan Inish. Even as his wife cautions him about sinful superstitions, she is lighting a fire and murmuring a druid prayer. From their rented cottage, Fiona can see Roan Inish and feel the triple pain of loss: her mother, her baby brother Jamie, and her roots.

Through her haunted cousin Tadhg, Fiona learns of the Coneely connection to Roan Inish, the Island of the Seals, and hears of the mysterious disappearance of her brother when his cradle was carried out to sea just as the family was leaving the island for good. With her teenage cousin Eamon, Fiona goes to the island and there finds signs of life there, including the baby footprints of Jamie. The girl vows to the seals that in exchange for her brother's return, she will restore the three abandoned cottages and bring back her family. Meanwhile, faced with eviction and a choice of moving inland or back to Roan Inish, her grandmother resolves to return to the island. At the close, the elders and children witness the seals pushing Jamie's cradle back to the shore and the gulls chasing the lost child up the beach and back to "the other branch of the family." It is all just as Tadhg had foretold.

Having overcome the financing crisis and survived the challenge of shooting footage at sea, *Roan Inish* deserved a lucky break that, unfortunately, did not occur. The film seemed ill-fated, this time by the movie's resistance to easy promotional strategies. *Variety* (May 9, 1994) warned about the inherent problems: "Short on the lush atmosphere its fanciful story calls for . . . presents a marketing problem . . . too talky and sophisticated for kids, too mild to lure adult customers."

When Sayles got back to Hoboken, he was dead broke, and his new film was going nowhere. Initially, Jones Entertainment thought they had a possible crossover hit and gave the studios first shot. There were no takers. As a favor to Wexler, John Calley, president of Sony Pictures, looked at the movie and liked it, but told him, "I don't think we know how to market it." A full year would elapse between the film's screening at the 1994 Seattle Film Festival and its return to that city for commercial exhibition in 1995. The movie also had been screened in July 1994 as part of an Irish film festival at the Walter Reade Theatre in New York City. Finally in late 1994, First Look Pictures stepped in. A small unit of Overseas Filmgroup Inc. of Los Angeles, First Look agreed to handle the domestic distribution, with Overseas doing the foreign sales.

According to Robby Henson, who at the time was trying to get his first film, *Pharaoh's Army* (1995) distributed, Sayles warned him about how difficult finding a distributor could be. In retrospect, Henson told me, "Maybe his comments were coming out of his problems with *Roan Inish*. He could not get Sony Classics or Samuel Goldwyn, so he ended up with First Look Overseas, but that's like sixth on the list of distributors." Despite the ranking, the small distributor would, as Henson says, "kick off Sayles's career again." Though First Look had little money, it understood the movie. With a smart distribution plan behind it, *The Secret of Roan Inish* commenced its charmed life with a special premiere in Williamstown as a benefit for Renzi's hometown library, where she had first read the original Rosalie Fry story.

The release started with a limited exhibition, then, as word of mouth spread, expanded to other cities and screens. Box-office figures in Portland, Oregon, epitomize *Roan Inish's* track record nationwide and point to the kind of patience Sayles believes most of his films require from distributors. Opening in February 1995 without radio or TV advertising, *Roan Inish* began its life as a cult hit, and in the *Sunday Oregonian* (July 9, 1995) Shawn Levy traced its exhibition history.

Owner of Portland's Cinema 21, Tom Ranieri worried about showing a "kids' film" in his art house, but the movie had a strong two-week run before it moved to another art venue, Cinemagic. At the time this little theater was on verge of closing, but *Roan Inish* had legs enough to keep business brisk. Over the next several months, the movie caught on and eventually grossed more than $100,000 there.

Portland was not the movie's only marketing success story. On St. Patrick's Day, six weeks after the film's opening, First Look expanded the exhibition to 100 screens in the United States. By April, as it surpassed the $3 million mark, *USA Today* was calling it "the little movie that could." At the end of its run, the $5 million film that barely got financed had grossed $200,000 in Minneapolis and $250,000 in New York City and reached a box-office total of $6.2 million, topping *Eight Men*'s $5.7 million and making *Roan Inish* Sayles's most popular release at the time.

John's own perspective on the success was positive but subdued by distribution reality. As he told London's *Independent* (October 6, 1996), "There are whole states where we have never played. You're gonna play South Carolina on video because there's not a place that shows non-Hollywood movies, and in Wyoming you won't even be able to get the video except by mail order."

■   ■   ■

In branching into the family film genre with the PG-rated *Roan Inish,* Sayles maintained his cool, antisentimental stance and magically eschewed the "leprechaun" cuteness of so many American movies about Ireland. Brief by Sayles's standards, the 103-minute feature also avoided the saccharine quality of many kids' pictures. *Entertainment Weekly* (February 10, 1995) marveled at its restraint. "Only when the last seal has looked squarely into the camera do you realize how notably unsentimental and casually magical *Inish* is." Sayles's authenticity and camerawork caught the eye of the *Wall Street Journal* (March 2, 1995). "The ride has a lulling rhythm, enlivened by richly observed details of Irish seaside life—its workaday rituals and fireside legends. . . . Wexler captures with great elegance the many colors and textures of the sea."

Roan Inish's unique place in Sayles's diverse body of work was noted by Philip Kemp in *Sight and Sound* (August 1996) and by Kenneth Turan in the *Los Angeles Times* (February 3, 1995). Kemp cited " a concern with people trying to gain (or regain) control of their lives often by coming to terms with who they are and where they started out from." Turan linked the film's lyrical quality to "situations that cross the line into myths," as in *Matewan* and *Eight Men Out* and concluded that in this film, "Sayles's matter-of-factness makes the magic seem all the more plausible and real."

In 1996, John addressed AFI students about crunch times in movie-making. "*Roan Inish* had been so tooth and nail," he said, "that I really didn't have another movie ready to go. I had to work for a lot of other people just to pay the rent because I had used all my money to throw into that film and hadn't gotten any back yet." For *Rolling Stone* he wrote "Keeping Time," a short story about musicians, and he continued scripting. Director Joe Dante recalls "The Mummy," a project reportedly in trouble at Universal. "I told them only one guy can service the screenplay this quick, and John wrote a fabulous script, funny and contemporary. Steve Spielberg took it to his friend, producer Sid Sheinberg, but he rejected it. Sheinberg said he didn't like *The Mummy* as modern and that he wanted it as a period piece."

With some regret, Sayles told a Screen Writers Guild gathering (February 13, 1998), "I wish they had made *Mummy*. . . . [It] would have been a good Joe Dante picture." As it turns out, both Sheinberg and Sayles were right: someone (Universal Studios) was developing the film, and it worked as a period piece. In 1999 *The Mummy* was set in the 1920s and featured Brendan Fraser in the lead. After four months, it was an enormous $142 million hit. While not acknowledged in the credits, John has said that he wrote parts of the feature. The screenplay credit went to Nina Wilcox Putnam.

When Ron Howard's space-mission movie *Apollo 13* (1995) ran into script problems, Sayles stepped in to restore its realistic edge. Together with Tom Hanks and Howard, Sayles put back into the script the scientific tone of astronaut Jim Lovell's 1994 book. According to *Esquire* (June 1996), the film's grateful producer, Brian Grazer, paid Sayles his salary and added his name to the screen credits as a bonus. However, the Writers Guild stuck by its percentage-of-the-script rule and would not allow Sayles's name in the official final credits.

Between screenwriting jobs, John and Maggie took a vacation on the Texas border and the setting reminded Sayles of a film project he had been mulling over for years. John recalled in an online, published interview with Mike Frogely and Matt Symond about the making of *Lone Star,* "I was just poking around the border. I said, 'Well, I've had this border idea for a long time. Why don't I do that next?'"

19

Lone Star: A Big Score, a Second Start

Eagle Pass is a little Texas, and Texas is a little United States.
There are all kinds of groups there, different people working
together. But they keep building prisons to solve their problems.

ACTOR KRIS KRISTOFFERSON, 1999

BETWEEN THE WRAP OF *The Secret of Roan Inish* in the summer of 1993 and its distribution in February 1995, John and his production team returned to filmmaking. Immediately after leaving Ireland, Maggie Renzi and Paul Miller, now a full-fledged producer, scouted Central America, seeking locations for John's next movie, *Men with Guns*. Faced with the political turmoil in Mexico, the project's limited commercial appeal, and Sayles's depleted coffers, they postponed that production.

Sayles focused his efforts on refilling his treasury through his "job" of writing and doctoring scripts for other people's movies even as prospects for his own productions reached an all-time low. In the past, he could always resort to funding a film himself, but his currently reduced savings made that a last resort.

With help from friends, the forty-four-year-old Sayles worked and played himself out of the financial-creative crisis. As loyal collaborator and creative catalyst, Maggie nudged him toward his next movie. Over the years she has acquired a sense of the gestation period for a John Sayles project, a time that combines private pondering and public recounting of the plot. She described her role in that creative process to the *Austin Chronicle* (June 28, 1996). "Sometimes my job is to say, 'John, tell the story about the soap opera star . . . [or the one about] the sheriff on the border' because the more he tells it, the more he finds out if this is gonna be the next movie he makes or if it's not quite working out." Perhaps aware of the "border story" brewing, she stoked the fires by arranging a work-vacation at the home of friends in Austin, Texas. As Renzi recalled, "We spent about four days driving around Lake Amistad [on the northern tip of the Rio Grande], the border, and about a week after we got back home, John said, 'Let's make the Texas one. I'll write it.'"

Meanwhile, at Castle Rock Entertainment, Sayles was working with co-owner/producer/director Rob Reiner on a script about the 1960s that was subsequently dropped. At the time, however, the filmmaker-friendly studio was recruiting directors, and Rob asked John if he had a project in mind. With lots of concepts but no money available, Sayles was fast in responding to that opportunity. He later told *Sprocket*'s Mike Frogley about his proposal for the border movie. "Three weeks later I showed it to Castle Rock, and they said 'yes' which is about the quickest I've ever raised money." By early 1995, he had completed the script (labeled "Forget the Alamo") and the production went on location in April. At the same time, the deal hinted of potential problems between studio financing and Sayles's insistence on creative control.

As John saw it, Reiner and Castle Rock stood between him and the interference from whatever studio would distribute the film. At a 1996 American Film Institute seminar in Los Angeles, John spoke with students about Castle Rock: "They basically get to do what they want to do and get studios to release the pictures. They don't have to take notes the studios give, and they pass that freedom along to the directors. It wasn't 'You have to do this cut or cast this actor.'" In the final phase of the production and after screening a rough cut for Reiner, Sayles listened to some suggestions and made a few changes, but sometimes told the company, "This does not really apply to the story I want to tell."

To finance the film, Castle Rock acquired a few million dollars upfront through the pre-sale deal for cable showings on TNT and TBS. Sayles was resigned to this latest kind of arrangement, telling *Filmmaker* (Summer 1996), "You just can't fart in this country without working for [media tycoons] Rupert Murdoch or Ted Turner." When *Lone Star* (1996) reached cable, *Variety*'s John Dempsey (January 27, 1997) would note the advantages of the agreement. "[Sayles] won't have to chop 40 minutes off for the [broadcast] net's two hour time slot." Further, the film would be able to run for its full 135 minutes as an event. "With multiple showings," Dempsey concluded, "Sayles will pocket just as much money as he would have from broadcast."

■   ■   ■

The script for *Lone Star* (1996) reflects the expertise Sayles learned from both his large-scale and small, personal films and seems like a second start in his career. Every bit as complicated as his three large-canvas movies (*Matewan, Eight Men Out,* and *City of Hope*), the new entry has the sturdier narrative spine of his smaller pictures, most notably *Passion Fish* and *The Secret of Roan Inish.*

John may have learned how to synthesize plot complexities into a straightforward story-line progression from his experience writing for the NBC-TV series *Shannon's Deal.* The discipline imposed by network TV's prime-time constraints addressed a problem in the bigger Sayles movies, where character and plot motivation sometimes got lost in the welter of marginally related incidents, minor characters, and variations of themes. By contrast, in *Passion Fish* and *The Secret of Roan Inish,* the necessity of reaching the immediately stated goal gave momentum and closure to the action. In this way they seemed to prepare John to incorporate the more traditional movie hero with a unifying psychological motivation, as personified in *Lone Star.*

For the multiple-plotted, time-shifting, fifty-character *Lone Star,* Sayles found the central theme in one sentence suggested by his research into "Texas talk." He told critic Amy Longsdorf (August 11, 1996), "There are three major things that Texans say. 'Well, there you go,' 'He needed killing,' and 'There's family involved." And sometimes you can use them all in the same sentence. In *Lone Star,* there was family involved, Charlie Wade needed killing, so there you go."

The old narrative staple of a murder mystery set against the American West gave this upcoming production cohesiveness. The story line is omnipresent even in the midst of thematic forays into differing time periods and contrasting cultures. In integrating his own community-centered purpose with classical film structure, Sayles seemed to chart a new course.

While in part *Lone Star* was inspired by John's boyhood watching of Davy Crockett and the television version of the Battle of the Alamo, the filmmaker drew on other, less nostalgic sources. The border setting, the interaction of Mexicans and Americans, and a legendary lawman hero owe something to Orson Welles's film noir classic *Touch of Evil* (1958). The theme of a border lawman accepting illegal payoffs also emerges in Tony Richardson's *The Border* (1982), which starred Jack Nicholson as a patrolman smuggling immigrants. *Border Incident* (1949) and *Borderline* (1950) had depicted illegal trafficking on the Texas/Mexico border.

Sayles's visits to the border area provided other contemporary social ingredients. Both Anglos and Mexicans spoke Spanish there, and Mexican and U.S. currency worked on both sides of the international border. Yet, for no evident reason, a line had been drawn dividing these people from a common culture. It thus made the Anglos much closer in language, customs, and concerns to the border Latinos than to the Anglos in San Antonio or, certainly, Houston.

For no reason other than tradition, these border people continued to be separated into ethnic and class factions. As Sayles told *Premiere* (July 1996), "I noticed that the Daughters of the Confederacy who were all white and the Daughters of the Alamo who were all Latino were still fighting for their version of history." As usual, the filmmaker also looked for the cultural influences found in regional literature, particularly in the *corridos,* or Mexican ballads, in which the bad guys became heroes by fighting the vicious Texas Rangers. In fairness, Sayles also interviewed border patrol officers to hear their views. His research revealed that in most of the border towns, political power had already passed from the Caucasian, English-speaking Anglos to the Spanish-speaking Latinos.

There remained, however, lingering resentment, especially toward people still coming over from Mexico. This resentment was surprisingly strong from immigrants of only one generation ago, who saw the newly arrived Mexicans as "others."

On the border, John found a complicated metaphor for the entire United States. He set out to produce an adult movie that would salute neither American nor Texas history, much less further lionize its legendary heroes. Instead, through the eyes of his lawman hero, *Lone Star* would undertake a scrutiny of the border's past on both public and personal levels. In the movie, an investigation begins in the 1990s, when two GIs find a rusty sheriff's badge and a Masonic ring in the sagebrush on their Army base. Beneath these symbols of status lie the remains of Charlie Wade, the sheriff of the town of Frontera in the 1950s. The task of solving this mystery and possible murder falls to Sam Deeds, a local called back by the citizens to be their new law enforcer. The evidence, especially in Sam's mind, soon points to the likely killer as his father, Buddy Deeds, the 1960s lawman in whose shadow Sam now lives and works. On the eve of Wade's sudden disappearance, it had been Buddy, then a deputy, who publicly confronted Charlie in the local cantina, challenging his graft-taking and staring down the sheriff's threats.

While retracing the crime, Sam unearths the history of the region that continually pits Anglos against Mexicans, whites against blacks, and children against parents. In the past, what contained those simmering conflicts was the abusive domination by Wade, followed by the adroit political skills of Buddy. What now seems to unify the diverse groups is the view that Sam, as lawman, pales by comparison to his father. As one constituent tells him, "Sheriff Deeds is dead, honey. . . . You just Sheriff junior."

It was Buddy, the World War II hero, who took the reins from Wade and whose control moved from the tyranny of the ruthless racist to a wheeler-dealer style where nobody got hurt and everybody got something. With the Anglo population controlling the town, Buddy took care of himself and his friends without neglecting the Mexicans and blacks. Now, with the minority population growing, the Mexicans and blacks seem eager for their turn to control and reap rewards.

The film is a complex narrative with two basic strands: (1) the relationship between parent and child (generation to generation), and (2) the connection between people and their own culture and other cultures. The unity in *Lone Star* is provided by Sam's public search for the killer and by the film's examination of the private (and sometimes public) lives of three families, including Sam's. Personifying these strands is Delmore Payne (Joe Morton), another native son returned to town. His success is measured by his appointment as the first African-American commander of the army base. He must now cope with Otis (Ron Canada), his father, who abandoned him as a child and who now owns the local tavern where the soldiers find entertainment. Payne also must deal with a son at home and with a black woman soldier on the base, both of whom are bewildered by Delmore's alienation from his own race.

In juxtaposition, the Cruz family has a three-generational battle in progress to match that of the Paynes'. Like Delmore, Mercedes Cruz (Miriam Colon) has distanced herself from her culture. As owner of the town's cantina, she insists that employees speak English and is known to report illegal entries of Mexicans to the police. Ironically, her daughter, Pilar (Elizabeth Peña), clings to the heritage the mother rejects and teaches it to her history students. A rebellious teenager herself, she now confronts a son heading for trouble. Pilar also must deal with her love for Sam Deeds, rekindled since his return.

These families hold the secrets of the past that Sam must reclaim. In negotiating and renegotiating their relationships to their parents and children, the central characters enact on the personal scale the community's attempts to assess its inherited myths, customs, and taboos, and their roles in framing the present. In Bunny (Frances McDormand), Sam's ex-wife, and her compulsive love-hate relationship to her dad, the movie depicts the trap of living in the past and how it ruined her marriage and her life. Her counterparts, Sam, Pilar, and Delmore, seem on the verge of redeeming themselves from a similar fatal perspective. Delmore discovers a pliable father who has changed from family deserter to pensive custodian of black history, including his son's military achievements.

In the closing scene, the dilapidated drive-in theater where Sam and Pilar made love in the 1970s hints again at their connection with the past, as Sam and Pilar acknowledge the ties that bind them. The couple are a metaphor for a realization as applicable to Texas as it is to Belfast, to Bosnia, and to those thousands of places around the world still clinging to ancient divisions. In a conversation with *Entertainment Weekly* (January 14, 1996), Sayles stated, "Not only are their lives intertwined, but they are of the same blood, and they better admit that there's no huge difference between an Anglo and a Mexican. People create things to separate themselves from each other. Sometimes we need that, but sometimes it's really destructive."

■   ■   ■

In casting *Lone Star,* Sayles started with a principal character: the setting. Seeking authenticity, the producers resisted the conveniences (airport, film services, and nightlife) of shooting in Austin. Instead, the production unit moved to the Mexican border. As producer Paul Miller told me, "We looked at two Texas border towns. A lot of films had used Del Rio. So we took Eagle Pass. In a low-budget film, we needed the support of the town which would respond to the novelty." The town of 20,000 sits 150 miles southwest of San Antonio and is linked by an international bridge to Piedras Negras, a Mexican city of 200,000 people. As Sayles explained later, "Eagle Pass had what we needed. The river is here; the desert is here. The people are here, and for the fifty-five speaking parts, we used twenty people from Texas."

The extras already had the right accents, the local stores had the right props; and the town itself had the sought-after class and cultural themes. The wealthy Anglos owned estates on the river, while the economically challenged Latinos were so desperate for work that, seeing the film's realistic restaurant set, they applied for cooking and service jobs. The shoot certainly boosted the town's economy. As Miller says, "We employed a lot of locals as drivers, and the art department used a class of high school kids to construct a drive-in theater, both as new and abandoned. For some scenes, the producers had to bus in African Americans from the United States Air Force Base in Del Rio, about fifty miles north."

For the cast, Sayles corralled three cowboy country natives: Chris Cooper, Matthew McConaughey, and Kris Kristofferson. Raised on a Kansas cattle ranch, Cooper easily adapted to wearing a hat and strolling the streets of *Lone Star*. Back in 1987 he launched his film acting career in *Matewan,* and the Sam Deeds role, written for him by Sayles, jump-started a career that was faltering. As John says, "This is a guy with a past." In the part of Buddy Deeds, McConaughey was playing a father who, seen in flashbacks, is more handsome and younger than his son. Buddy's self-confidence contrasts with Sheriff Wade's cocky machismo and the bland, sad, and self-doubting Sam. Sayles saw in the twenty-six-year-old McConaughey a masculine self-assurance that even in soft voice could confront a Charlie Wade without flinching.

For the fifty-five-year-old Kris Kristofferson, the Charlie Wade character provided a homecoming and film career comeback. "I was born and raised in Brownsville [Texas] and felt like an old dog going back home," he told me. "As soon as I turned on the car radio and heard the mariachi music, I knew where I was." A country music and film star of the 1970s, Kris had fallen into a professional limbo, going without a leading role for ten years.

Behind Kristofferson's rebirth in *Lone Star* was his appearance in Robby Henson's Civil War movie *Pharaoh's Army*. "In that film," the actor says, "I got a small role as a settler and had a 'stare-down' scene with Chris Cooper. John saw me while he was helping to edit the film and then refamiliarized himself with my work." Later, at a dinner meeting in Manhattan, Sayles, Renzi, and Kristofferson talked about *Lone Star* and the Charlie Wade character. "When we talked about the part, John said, 'Charlie Wade never blinked first.' He saw Wade as a hit man with a sense of honor in keeping his poise and position. I saw Charlie as border trash working his way up the system. He's like a high school kid who doesn't want to lose." The dinner was audition enough for John, and Kris got the role.

Having already worked with Sayles on the TV series *Shannon's Deal,* Elizabeth Peña jumped at the opportunity to play Pilar. As she told the *Houston Chronicle* (June 30, 1996), "When my agent called, I said, 'Great. Close the deal. If it's John Sayles, I don't care if it's one scene.'" For Frances McDormand, one scene is exactly what she played. A Best Actress Oscar winner for 1996's *Fargo,* she spent one day playing Sam Deeds's ex-wife, Bunny, and as John said, "came through like a locomotive." For his part as the African-American army colonel,

Joe Morton—a Sayles veteran from *The Brother from Another Planet* and *City of Hope*—could draw on his experience as an army brat raised on military bases in both the United States and Germany. (Sayles cast himself as a border patrol agent, but when he was editing the movie, he found the sequences confusing and unnecessary, so his performance ended on the cutting room floor.)

As experienced actors familiar with his directing methods, the cast helped Sayles economize on the shoot and give credence to his claim that as a director he was now getting more for the money. He told *Filmmaker* (Summer 1996), "With a $3 million budget, I can be a little bit more ambitious . . . we can get really experienced people, both actors and technicians. That translates into a high talent to time ratio." No less important in that formula was the caliber of the crew. As Miller said to me, "Maggie and John tend to use the same crew. We just work with the agents, and they hire the production heads who will bring their team with them." Most conspicuous among those returning to the *Lone Star* crew were production designer Dan Bishop, set decorator Dianna Freas, and composer/orchestrator Mason Daring, each with multiple Sayles film experiences to their credit.

Sayles also continued his pattern of employing the best cinematographers of the industry, here New Zealand's Stuart Dryburgh, who had already earned an Oscar nomination for Jane Campion's acclaimed *The Piano* (1993). For the first time, John Powditch (a.k.a. J. P.) joined the crew as assistant director and was much admired by his assistants.

One of the squad answering to Powditch was Nate Fitzgerald, a camera production assistant. He was representative of the other essential component of Sayles's crew: the young, the energetic, and the low paid. Just a few years out of the University of Notre Dame with a degree in communications, Fitzgerald had already acquired industry experience in Austin. What got him the *Lone Star* assignment, however, was his Spanish-speaking ability, polished during a year spent studying in Madrid, Spain, and a year as a Jesuit volunteer in Tijuana, Mexico. On the shoot, he used his Spanish in working with the extras, many driven in for the day from Del Rio, Texas, and paid a flat rate.

Fitzgerald still remembers the Texas heat, which reached 115 degrees and sent a few people keeling over during the production. He also had to adjust to night shooting and to a reversal of daytime and nighttime. "You turn into a vampire," Fitzgerald told me, "and put up tinfoil in the motel windows to block out the sun." The shooting would stop at daybreak, followed by a few hours of winding down then sleeping until 5 P.M., which was "breakfast time" and the start of another "day" on the set. Now a film editor in Hollywood, Fitzgerald remembers more than just the heat and inconveniences. "I was making $500 a week, not much by Hollywood standards. But with the apartment and the meals, I thought it was great. In my five years, it was the best experience overall. The crew was so much fun, and then it's so rare that you get to work on something you're really proud of."

The atmosphere of John Sayles's sets, with its "no yelling" professionalism, relaxed camaraderie in the after hours, and pride in the final product seemed to reach its apotheosis at Eagle Pass. Caroline (Hall) Otis, Maggie's college friend and a freelance writer, negotiated downtime from her husband and two teenage sons. She joined the set as a cable puller on the sound crew. Like everyone else, Otis spent the ten weeks living at the La Quinta Motel. For her the housing reflects the entire atmosphere. "Most sets are hierarchical," she says, "John's was flat. That's the John and Maggie culture."

Caroline's job on the shoot started at 6:30 A.M. to help wire the actors for sound, connect microphones, wrap cable, load boxes, insert microphone batteries, and hold the second boom pole. During the shoot, she dealt with the withering heat, mosquitoes, a sprained ankle, and accidentally conking Chris Cooper's head with a boom mike. Still, she came away with memories of postshooting pool parties with live music by Kris Kristofferson and Joe Morton, Maggie Renzi's homemade margaritas, midnight rodeo disco in nearby Piedras Negras, and inner-tubing down the Frio River. She even had a few minutes on camera as an Anglo mom in the school board meeting scene. While rejecting a lifetime in moviemaking, Otis enjoyed its exhilaration and the camaraderie. "It's like living in a college dorm with everybody taking the same class. It's like camp but with beer."

Kris Kristofferson shared those sentiments. "People are here because they love the movie, not because they want a lot of money," he told me. "John's like Martin Scorsese; he gets good people to work for him. Everybody's excited.

In *Mean Streets* (1973) and *Lone Star,* everybody in the film is good. It's not just a couple of stars." Like so many crews and casts before them, Otis and Kristofferson left the Eagle Pass shoot admiring Sayles's visible but unobtrusive directing and Maggie's knack for keeping the crew happy. Back home in Minneapolis, Otis concluded, "Would I do it again? In a heartbeat."

While Kristofferson was making his comeback in *Lone Star,* costar Matthew McConaughey was making a significant splash in the film industry. Seen as the next Paul Newman, the Texas native had just finished *Boys on the Side* (1995) and was being groomed for his first starring role as the defense attorney in *A Time to Kill* (1996). In his role as Buddy Deeds, McConaughey matched the sadistic-lawman performance of Kristofferson with his own riveting charisma, suggesting that beneath the good looks lay a veteran steeled by war and not ready to blink. Recognizing the box-office lure of the fast-rising young actor, the *Lone Star* promotional posters featured the faces of Kristofferson and McConaughey in the foreground, with Chris Cooper about half that size, and Elizabeth Peña half of that.

As a film showcasing and reviving talents, *Lone Star* suggests the reasons why actors sometimes set aside salary to participate in a Sayles film.

■   ■   ■

For *Lone Star* Sayles compiled his own library of gospel-and-blues, country-western songs from the United States, and the ranchero, bolero, and *conjunto* music from Mexico. The songs helped the story progress and complemented its narrative theme. As *Filmmaker* (Summer 1996) would note, "The social and historical intercourse finds its most effective expression in the blues, Tejano, and country music that underlies the action." Chiefly atmospheric, the music comes to the foreground in the dance of Sam and Pilar to Freddie Fender's "Desde Que Conosco." The problem for the score's composer, Mason Daring, was that John wanted the lyrics in Spanish. Maggie tracked down Fender, Mexico's first rock and roll king in the 1950s, and sent Daring back to Boston to record the needed music. Once the tape was done and Fender was located in Corpus Christi, Texas, Mason flew there and recorded Freddie's Spanish lyrics. "After twenty minutes," Daring told me, "I left the studio with a new recording, and we didn't have to buy it. The dance and the song left the women on the set weeping and helped create Cooper as a romantic lead."

The film's score would draw appreciative comments for its dual purpose in capturing the diversity of the borderland groups and for dramatizing the idea that cross-cultural communication often begins with music. Both Daring and Kristofferson, with a combined fifty years in the business, now contend that Sayles knows more about music than they do. "I thought 'Honest Sam' would be a good song for the film," Kristofferson says, "so I played a couple of chord progressions. John said, 'Is that by the same guy that wrote such-and-such?' It was Paul Siebolt, who used to play in the Village back in the seventies, and not many people knew him."

For the distribution of *Lone Star,* Sayles and Castle Rock turned to Sony. That left them with the choice of the corporation's Columbia Pictures or Sony Pictures Classics division. As Sayles related to AFI students, "Columbia was very honest with us. They're much more a major studio, and *Lone Star* was the kind of movie that would open in no more than three theaters in Los Angeles." Sony Pictures Classics was better suited to the small film. Sayles was reunited with Sony's Tom Bernard and Michael Barker, who, while at United Artists Classics, had promoted and distributed *Lianna* before moving on to Orion Pictures where they handled *Eight Men Out.*

Now, with nine features to his credit, Sayles felt confident in the Sony team's ability to market a small movie, and their success corroborated his trust. Still, the film that critics saw as Oscar material did not receive a wide release, and in most markets played in only a single theater. Writing about Dallas's twenty-four-screen AMC Grand multiplex, the *New York Times* (August 4, 1996) noted a sad irony. "If they [filmgoers at the multiplex] wanted to see *Lone Star,* the new art movie by John Sayles about life in Texas, they would have been out of luck. It's not playing here."

The good feelings accorded the shoot by cast and crew anticipated the accolades of critics. In the *Los Angeles Times* (June 21, 1996), Kenneth Turan saw this picture as reason to include John Sayles in the top tier of American filmmakers. "The triumph of *Lone Star,"* he wrote, "is how well it integrates

Sayles's concerns with the heightened tension and narrative drive the thriller provides." Citing the twenty significant characters, each with a story to tell, critics compared *Lone Star* to a compact Charles Dickens novel. Others said its emphasis on family ties was akin to Greek tragedy. In an extraordinarily laudatory review, Janet Maslin (*New York Times,* June 21, 1996) wrote, "Gratifyingly complex, beautifully told, the tale explores a huge array of cultural, racist, economic and familial tensions. . . . Plain and forthright as it looks, *Lone Star* winds up with a scope and overview rarely attempted in American film today which makes its success that much more exemplary."

The reviews found something and someone to praise at almost every level, making it the most critically acclaimed work in Sayles's oeuvre thus far. The *Times* of London (October 13, 1996) opined: "*Lone Star* packs a shocking plot twist that puts *The Crying Game* [1992] to shame, and has at its center a spit-vicious star turn from Kristofferson who plays the baddest, bada** sheriff in Frontera's history." In the Wade-Deeds confrontations, the *San Francisco Chronicle* (June 21, 1996) admired McConaughey's "laconic finger in your eye style."

As the guilt-encumbered Sam Deeds, Chris Cooper was compared to Gary Cooper (no relation), Oedipus, and Hamlet, although some found his "haunted past" performance too subdued, especially in the presence of the "crackling, curt" Elizabeth Peña (*Entertainment Weekly,* June 21, 1996). Although Frances McDormand was on screen for less than five minutes, her appearance as the manic-depressive Bunny was a poignant showstopper in a "cameo of knife-edge hysteria" (*Sight and Sound,* October 1996).

■   ■   ■

Opening *Lone Star* at the Directors' Fortnight series at the Cannes Film Festival, John and Maggie started the hype machine, and subsequently John did more than two hundred promotional interviews. As *Variety* noted, "Yet contrary to his bohemian image . . . the director is keenly attuned to the marketplace for his movies. So tirelessly does he work to promote them that one imagines he must know every filmgoer personally." With vigorous pushing by Sony, enthusiastic endorsements from the critics at Cannes, and strong word of mouth, *Lone Star*'s numbers steadily rose on the charts. By 1998 it had realized a domestic gross of nearly $13 million, doubling the earning of *The Secret of Roan Inish,* at that time the second most popular Sayles movie at $6.2 million.

The film's script won nominations for the Golden Globe, Independent Spirit, and Writers Guild awards; it earned Sayles his second Academy Award nomination (the first was for *Passion Fish*), also as screenwriter. At the Oscar ceremony in March 1997, Sayles for the first time in his adult life put on a tuxedo. (The Best Screenplay award that year went to Ethan Coen and Joel Coen for *Fargo.*) Both Sayles and Renzi accepted a special tribute at their alma mater from the Williams College Black Alumni for Distinguished Achievement. The award recognized the positive images of African Americans found in *The Brother from Another Planet* (1984), *Passion Fish* (1992), and *Lone Star* (1996). Once again, Renzi and Sayles used a film premiere and their presence to support regional theater, this one benefiting the Old Castle Theatre in Bennington, Vermont, where Renzi's mother, Helen, is a board member.

■   ■   ■

Before and after the production of *Lone Star,* Sayles was scripting films for several projects, most of which never made it to the screen. As he told *The Journal* (July 1996), "So many of these things don't get made, or you don't get credit that I actually forget what I've done. But I've probably written ten or twelve movies in the past two years for other people." The list of unrealized projects includes *The Gold of Exodus* for Castle Rock, *The Fifth Child* (now on its third director), *Tom Mix Died for Your Sins* for director Sydney Pollack, *Oh, Carolina* for the Fresh Produce production company of Seattle, Washington, and *Brother Termite* for filmmaker James Cameron.

The idea of the high-principled Sayles teaming with the director of the mainstream blockbuster *Titanic* (1997) may horrify independent purists, but they forget John's writer-for-hire pragmatist side. Sayles and Cameron both come from the same Roger Corman stable, one as the fast writer, the other as art director for *Battle Beyond the Stars* (1980). In addition, Sayles, as the low-budget director, appreciates the technical research done by Cameron for *Titanic* and the impact on cost saving that the devices used in the film (especially the computer-generated imagery) could have for future filmmakers.

Prior to undertaking *Lone Star*, John had assisted with the scripting for the Sharon Stone Western *The Quick and the Dead* (1995), confining his efforts to solidifying Gene Hackman's dialogue for a script that faltered in far too many other places. Both Sayles and Steven Soderbergh (*sex, lies and videotape*, 1989) attempted a script-doctoring for Guillermo Del Toro's cockroach movie, *Mimic* (1997), and both successfully fought to escape the credit list.

Virtually the senior statesman now of independent filmmakers, the forty-seven-year-old Sayles accepted membership on two advisory boards: Aperture Pictures, a nonprofit group that awards grants to new filmmakers for short films, and Next Wave Films, formed by cable's Independent Film Channel to provide completion money for film projects by emerging filmmakers. On his own, John provided 30 percent of the money for *Santitos,* a Mexican film that won Sundance's 1998 Latin American Cinema Award. Ever the actor, he also squeezed in another critically unnoticed cameo for actor/friend Vondie Curtis-Hall (*Passion Fish*) in his directing debut, *Gridlock'd* (1998), an urban comedy about two drug users (Tupac Shakur and Tim Roth) looking for rehabilitation.

As happened with *Return of the Secaucus Seven* (1980) but on a far greater scale, John Sayles now found himself a "hot" director. *Lone Star* proved emphatically that with a few million dollars, he could make magic happen with a camera. Stars worked for him for scale, towns rolled out the carpet, filmmaker wanna-be's got their feet wet, and at the box office the picture could bring in quadruple its cost. With industry nominations and awards, memberships on boards, and directors clamoring to hire his scriptwriting skills, John once again faced the choice to play with the major studios or stick to his own working philosophy. Fifteen years in filmmaking had distanced him from the neophyte that Paramount Pictures pushed around during the making of *Baby It's You*. Scriptwriting for other producers and directors had further educated him, and his two latest screen projects reflected how deft he had become in financing, producing, and distributing. He now had the reputation, the clout, and the cunning to make the leap into the big time.

20

Men with Guns:
Financing the Sayles Film

Independent film is not just low-budget poverty chic.
It's a relentless vision peculiar to one person who has something
unique to say, every time out. It's John Sayles.

FILMMAKER NANCY SAVOCA, 1999

WITH *LONE STAR* (1996), his eleventh feature film, John Sayles, the American movie industry's best-known contemporary maverick, rode out of the art houses and into the malls. In the multiplexes, his newest release eventually grossed more than $14 million and demonstrated that he could produce as well as write movies for the mainstream. John attributed part of the financial success to the people of Texas and their deep fascination with the rich history of their expansive state. While the moderate popularity of the movie (by Hollywood norms) did not make Sayles a household name, it did reposition him in to the eyes of the major studios. As the *Los Angeles Daily News* (March 12, 1998) noted wryly, "Colleagues and studio executives loved his film, and Sayles could have parlayed its success to make just about any movie he wanted, even one with a budget totaling more than, say, $5 million."

There were models, after all, for taking the big-budget bait. Directors such as Francis Ford Coppola, Martin Scorsese, and Spike Lee had made arrangements with the A-list studios that balanced the corporate interests with their own and would trade the necessity of making *The Godfather* (1972) for the means to direct *The Conversation* (1974). This time, however, the maverick stayed the maverick. *Lone Star* was not his audition piece for Hollywood, nor was he forging a "career move." Doug Sayles told me about his brother John's unchanged stance in the later 1990s toward the industry. "He says, 'If I'm going to take a year of my life, it's going to be for what I like doing.' That's why there's such a difference between what he scripts so rapidly for others and makes huge bucks for and what he'll do with that year that's for him."

The director's response to the opportunity to go establishment could not have been more idiosyncratic, exotic, or as film guru John Pierson puts it, "bizarre". For Sayles the next challenge meant simply getting back to unfinished business, namely the Latin American/American film *Men with Guns* (1998). The production had a history dating back to 1994, according to producer Paul Miller. "Right after *Roan Inish,*" he told me, "they were scouting in Mexico, but at the time they did not think it was feasible, especially if John, as planned, was going to shoot in different countries." Sayles had visited Guatemala, seen the backcountry, and heard the stories of oppression. As he continued looking for locations in Mexico, the Zapatista rebellion erupted. Those battles prohibited a visit to his potential site, Chiapas, for the film and forced the shelving of *Men with Guns* in favor of *Lone Star.*

With *Lone Star* done, Sayles once again turned his attention to *Men with Guns.* Maggie Renzi almost quit. The proposal seemed to her to be laden with an overly ambitious formula for a low-budget catastrophe. They would have six weeks to shoot the movie, primarily in the jungle, in three Mexican states as far from each other as New York, Indiana, and Wyoming. The potential for disaster was further abetted by what looked to Renzi like a calculated blunting of box-office attraction.

Featuring only two Americans in cameo roles, the picture would have no stars or even box-office names. It had instead a downbeat story about an old man, genocide, and the use of subtitles, the last of which meant certain death at the box office. Not only was the project fighting a declining interest in foreign films at the U.S. box office (about 1 percent of the receipts), it was breaking the American filmmaker mold. Unlike their counterparts elsewhere, Hollywood directors do *not* make foreign films. Friends joined Renzi in warning Sayles that the film was a folly and impossible to accomplish. As producer, Renzi felt that this time she could not possibly do a good job.

Renzi later described her feelings to Ruthie Stein (*San Francisco Chronicle,* March 8, 1998): "John had this fantasy that everyone would just pile in a van and drive around Mexico." She thought the film would cost $5 million to shoot; he estimated $1 million. For what was perceived as a far-fetched undertaking, however, Sayles was ready to adopt practical limitations. He told the *New York Times* (March 9, 1998), "I started with the idea that nobody would want to finance it, so I'd have to make it on my own nickel, in 16mm and shoot it in four weeks instead of six." To that practical approach, he added his passion for the idea and a determination that obstacles merely challenged one to find solutions. If he did not make this film about oppression of the poor, nobody would do it, especially nobody in Latin America, where the cinema is state-supported and the "shit list" of political protestors is long and lethal. He said, "I had the money to do it, and maybe I would take a couple of years to finish it, but I would finish it."

After reading the script, the dubious Renzi had a change of heart. She told Stein, "I loved the story and couldn't bear the thought of missing out. . . . I don't like to miss out on anything and to miss out on one of these life experiences with John wasn't a good idea." Having worked in Harlem, Matewan, and County Donegal, Maggie now agreed to produce Sayles's first "foreign film" in Mexico.

■   ■   ■

Producer Paul Miller remembers the ease of financing *Lone Star* and, in contrast, the arduous challenge of finding money for a subtitled, starless movie bogged down with location worries. "We sent it out to the studios, but forget it. They just had zero interest." With financing at a standstill, Doug Sayles provided a helping hand. In the summer of 1996, he was lunching in New York with James DeNardo, a Dartmouth College classmate, occasional visitor to the Sayles home, and now professor of political science at UCLA. As Doug relates, "When I heard John needed financing, I thought about Jim's contacts in Hollywood and gave him a call. I told him about this quirky movie that was not going to be a box-office killer and asked if he knew anybody that might be interested. J. D. said, 'Well, let me knock it around, call a few people, and pitch it.' "

Sitting in his campus office at UCLA, DeNardo described for me the chronological development of financing *Men with Guns*. At the time of Doug Sayles's call, the educator was founding Willow Community, a progressive grade school that brings together upper- and low-income kids. One of the school's fellow pioneers was Lou Gonda, a Forbes 200 executive and co-founder of International Release Finance Company. In reading the script sent by Doug, both DeNardo and Gonda saw a "Holocaust film in Spanish with a lot of different themes and an absorbing story."

It was the kind of content that had a double appeal for Gonda, who was raised in Venezuela and whose family had helped launch the Holocaust Museum in Los Angeles. Already involved in the feature film business through his company, Lexington Road Pictures, Gonda agreed to DeNardo's suggestion of a follow-up talk with producer Paul Miller. From the start of the discussions, what was not on the table was artistic control. "It was take it or leave it," DeNardo says. "What they offered us was territorial rights to the proceeds of the film, in our case the U.S. That's when we started talking about the cost of the film [$2 million to $3 million], the division of the pie, and the order of return on the proceeds."

Renzi, Miller, DeNardo, and Doug Sayles were the "lieutenants" working up the deal and reporting to John Sayles and Gonda. All of them were alert to the time constraints that were dependent on the Mexican weather, the political climate, and Sayles's other commitments. In the budget, DeNardo saw the hand of Sayles the pragmatist. "Instead of letting artistic considerations reign, the budget was calculated to fit the expected box-office return." Gonda was about to finance the entire film—just as it was drawing interest in other quarters. Foremost among these others was Clear Blue Sky Productions, owned by

Microsoft co-founder Paul Allen, with his sister, Jody Patton, as president. Suddenly, Clear Blue Sky and Lexington Road were pressing the producers with competing bids for the U.S. territorial rights.

With European interests in the movie's financing unexpectedly starting to wane, the producers wanted both companies to come on board. As Miller says, "We decided to have each group, Allen's and Gonda's, finance it for $1 million each. They really wanted to be involved in this film, and we felt that down the road they might provide future support for other projects." That decision placed the competitors in a mini-bidding war. "At a certain point," DeNardo says, "it had to be decided: do you want it to be fifty-fifty? When Clear Blue Sky and Gonda said yes, that started the communication between the two groups about mutual concerns."

To codify the agreement, Sayles's lawyer and executive producer John Sloss met with attorneys for the two firms and worked up the contract. As DeNardo explains, "John Sloss is a cottage company that specializes in independent films, and he knows what a contract needs to look like to get legal coverage and insurance for the film. *Men with Guns* was a 'back-end' deal with everyone's take, including John's, contingent on the proceeds from the movie."

Whatever the mixture of altruism and profit motive behind their financing of *Men with Guns,* each of the two companies was now supporting a project on which Sayles had already started production with his own money. According to John Pierson's book on independent filmmaking, *Spike, Mike, Slackers & Dykes* (1995), starting the shooting before completion of the financing step was becoming standard practice. "More low budget features are started with partial budgets intended to get it in the can. . . . Companies like mine have encouraged and implicitly endorsed this rash behavior. The key personality elements in most cases are a writer/director who is almost overconfident and a core support group that feeds the wonderful delusion that come hell or high water the film will be made."

Sayles's self-assurance got a well-timed boost from Sony Pictures Classics, which acquired the distribution rights for North America and Latin America. With some modesty, Sony Classics co-president Tom Bernard told me, "We were a piece, I think, that completed the financing." What DeNardo remembers about Sony was " a generous advance that presented the revenue strength already being generated by the film and eliminated some of the risks for the financiers."

Following the Sony deal, IFC Productions, an arm of cable's Independent Film Channel, indicated they would help fund the picture for theatrical release in exchange for the right to show it on television. *Men with Guns* would be IFC's first venture. Combined, these sundry sources backed *Men* in a hybrid deal that was part "negative pickup" (since the film was already under way) and part upfront "equity owners" risking their investment with the hope of proceeds to follow. Still to be sold were the territorial rights to profits in Europe and Asia. At the top of the credits, the names of these companies would be listed as producers and distributors. Far, far down on the roll are the names of the two key people who got the deal started: Doug Sayles and James DeNardo.

The $2.3 million budget, paltry by almost any standard in the 1990s and certainly by Hollywood's, would go farther in Mexico. As Paul Miller notes, "When the peso dropped, the time was ripe. Originally, John thought about a documentary, road-type picture, but we decided on just a low-budget movie." For what would be his most ambitious project, Sayles settled on a schedule that had one week in Mexico City, five in Vera Cruz, and two more in Chiapas, with fifty-three different locations in all. In the use of the foreign settings, the production faced three major challenges: physical safety, technical support, and communication.

■   ■   ■

As events at the time had indicated, the Chiapas region of Mexico was a dangerous hot zone, and U.S. citizenship guaranteed no protection from the two warring factions: revolutionaries and government troops. As Sayles related to the *Chicago Tribune* (April 27, 1998), the violence portrayed on camera was never far from the set.

"It was not unusual to see a pickup full of guys not in uniform, with semi-automatic weapons."

Along with Doug Sayles, Jim DeNardo visited the set and saw the film's ideas playing out in reality. "The day before we got there," he remembers, "some crew guys traveled down a road. They met about a thousand peasants who were carrying two-by-fours with spikes in them. They were collecting tolls to raise funds for the revolution. Subsequently, there were massacres in that area." For the scenes of the military caravans, the producers negotiated with the army to obtain and use fake and disabled weapons.

The jungle scenes posed a double problem: finding them and then shooting near them. Renzi told the IFC filmmakers who were making a documentary about the *Men with Guns* production that the Mexican jungle was "disappearing as the words leave my mouth." The art and location crews were constantly racing ahead to new locations and establishing the connections that would, as Doug Sayles notes, "link camera to generator, generator to truck, and truck to the road." After they bulldozed their way into the jungle and the location was opened, the cast and crew would arrive, exhausted after a twelve-hour bus trip. Giving new meaning to the term *guerrilla filmmaking,* the production then had to be wary of real guerrillas and ready to fend off the tarantulas, leeches, scorpions, and venomous insects that inhabited the terrain. Added to what Sayles calls a "balls to the walls" shooting schedule, the physical challenges posed by the location made *Men with Guns* the director's most difficult feature undertaken so far.

Working with a Mexican crew posed no special problem for the bilingual director, but Spanish was just the first of many linguistic barriers. With each mile beyond the city beltways, John and his team were discovering new cultures and languages as well. They found places where, to the natives, Mexicans were just as foreign as Americans and where some crew members had never seen a movie, much less a call sheet. The different tribes were adding more than local color to the film; they were making it allegorical and moving it beyond an association with any particular country. To keep the movie's Spanish generic, Sayles enlisted a Peruvian to purge it of Mexican idioms. The inclusion of Mayan, Tzotzil (also Mayan), Kuna (Panamanian), and Nahuatl (Aztec) languages further detached the film from Mexico, while the use of dialects led to an honor system with the actors. The Indians in the cast had to translate the Spanish script into their own dialects, then, if they fumbled their dialogue on camera, had to tell Sayles about their mistake.

On the shoot, the only real breakdown in communication occurred when the director and his Polish-speaking photographer, Slawomir Idziak, disagreed about how the movie should be lighted. The cinematographer was resisting the use of the hard white sunlight that the director favored. Their standoff was unresolved, giving the movie a look that neither wanted but which Sayles begrudgingly said was "fine." While acknowledging Idziak's talents, the director later told *Indiewire Interviews* (March 6, 1998) that he got the job because Haskell Wexler dropped out at the last minute and because, at the time, the "good Mexican photographers were all working in the States."

In employing the several dialects, Sayles wrote his dialogue to fit the subtitle format of thirty-two characters per line. What evolved was a screenplay style he describes as part haiku and part catechism. His statement hints at the poetic, mystical, and didactic feelings found in this journey-movie, with its wide-ranging literary and cinematic allusions to Joseph Conrad's novel *Heart of Darkness* (1902), the film classic *The Wizard of Oz* (1939), and Ingmar Bergman's *Wild Strawberries* (1957). *Men with Guns* has similarities especially to Bergman's film, in which its doctor hero goes on a journey of self-discovery.

Like that physician, *Men with Guns'* Dr. Fuentes recognizes in his wife's death his own impending mortality and confronts the question of the legacy he will leave behind. To that personal crisis, the movie adds a political detective story as the doctor decides to track down the medical students he has sent into the jungle to treat the natives. Sayles got the inspiration for this angle from novelist Francisco Goldman, who told Sayles of an uncle in Guatemala who trained his medical students for a special United Nations program that sent them to Indian villages, where the military killed almost all of them. (Goldman himself was given screen credit as creator of the Dr. Arrau/Dr. Fuentes character in his 1993 novel, *The Long Night of the White Chickens*.)

■   ■   ■

The opening scenes of the 126-minute *Men with Guns* immediately lays the thematic groundwork for this road story, establishing the doctor's ignorance about the plight of the country and himself. In his office, the physician is probing a growth in a patient's prostate. With the examination complete, the patient puts on his general's uniform, complaining about the country's troubles and blaming them on Communist propaganda and a few troublesome guerrillas. In the first of many incidences, Dr. Fuentes is advised of his ignorance. "You are like a child, Humberto," the general tells him. "The world is a savage place." In just a few strokes, the scene has established key ideas: the invisibility of the native people talked about but unseen, the cancerous growth in the military, and the hero's naïve indifference to both realities.

Going on vacation, the doctor decides to visit his former students in their villages. Prior to setting out, however, he meets one of them, Bravo, who has abandoned the medical mission for the drug trade. Fuentes's exchanges with both the general and Bravo introduce the issue of responsibility and push the doctor to confront his own guilt.

His exploration takes him first into territories identified by the peasants simply by their type of labor, namely the salt people, the corn people, and the sugar people. Later, Fuentes's meeting with two American tourists indicates that despite the language barrier, they share an abysmal ignorance of the effects that their class, their corporations, and their governments have on the people in this country. As he continues on his way to the villages, Fuentes uncovers progressively more dehumanizing perversions taking place: a school turned into a torture chamber and a doctor's instruments used to make people talk and then peddled on the street corner for money or food.

Guiding him through these nightmares is ten-year-old Conejo (Rabbit). The offspring of a woman raped by a soldier, the boy tells Fuentes, "I'm as f***ed as the rest of them." But it's much worse. The rest of his village looks on him as a dog who "takes the scraps the real people leave."

With his dog-boy companion, the doctor discovers the death of his disciples and is stripped of his comfortable illusions about his program and legacy. He meets three parable-like wayfarers, each with a tale to tell. Domingo, the renegade soldier, was forced to stab unarmed peasants, and Padre Portillo, a priest, fled from a village knowing a peasant would replace him as the next victim of an army death squad. The last to join the group is Graciela, a now mute victim of sustained rapes by the soldiers. Arriving in Cerca del Cielo,

Fuentes finds that his hope of locating at least one village doctor there as his legacy is denied. In the end Fuentes dies at that village, bereft of any last-minute consolation. What cold comfort the ending offers is provided by Domingo (Sunday), who reluctantly steps forward, picks up the doctor's bag, and goes off to treat, as best he can, a native child. Otherwise both the low-land and hill country of the Indians stand shorn of any of the teachers, doc-tors, and priests who might help them.

As Sayles has noted, for these natives the land and God are one; if they lose the land, they have lost their past and their future. Shortly after the film-ing ended, life in Chiapas began imitating art. By the fall of 1997, forty-five villagers had been executed and paramilitary groups were roaming the entire region, driving thousands of natives from their homes, razing entire villages, and intimidating the locals with random shooting sprees. The tragedy in Mexico, the continued escalation of violence in the Balkans, and further tribal government massacres in Africa gave *Men with Guns* a true resonance. As if confirming the film's theme of blissful but culpable ignorance, audiences wished the headlines away and avoided the movie.

■   ■   ■

To prime the marketplace, Sony Classics screened the movie at the Telluride Film Festival in August 1997. The film also had a fall screening at the Toronto Film Festival and, in December 1997, another one to a packed house at the Festival of New Latin American Films in Havana, Cuba. In March 1998, when the R-rated movie debuted in the United States, its business fell below even the modest expectations of its producers. Discouraged but game, Sayles spent the spring on promotional tours, flying everywhere in the United States with Maggie, then making special forays into Mexico, Argentina, Colombia, and Brazil. Faced with countries that had few if any cinemas, he was always hoping to have the film picked up by one of the Latin American television conglomerates.

According to Doug Sayles, the scuttlebutt in Los Angeles indicated that the brunt of Sony Pictures Classics' promotion went to another Sony release, David Mamet's *The Spanish Prisoner* (1998). Doug told me, "I don't think anyone's going to retire on the profits." By 1999, however, James DeNardo was more optimistic, feeling that after the year 2000, video and cable would enhance the earnings.

Critical opinion was clear across the spectrum. While the *New York Times* (March 9, 1997) saw the film project as part of a wave of Latin-themed movies (*Selena, Zapata,* and *Zorro*), it predicted that "*Hombres Armados* may be too difficult for even John Sayles to pull off." In *Show Biz,* the review scorched the film and the director: "*Men With Guns* is yet another well-intended but tedious essay by Sayles." The *Chicago Tribune* (March 27, 1998) was disappointed: "The movie needs a strong visual style. . . . Why didn't he bring back [Haskell] Wexler, who may have been born to shoot *Men with Guns.*" (When Sayles asked Wexler, he was unavailable.) The *Christian Science Monitor* (March 13, 1998) agreed, seeing *Men with Guns* as a "socially responsible drama" but "more like a photographed screenplay than a truly cinematic work." Several other critics credited Sayles for the courage to make the film, then added a "but." The *San Francisco Chronicle,* for example, cited John for "daring to explore the territory" but found the movie "murky with implications that are at once disturbing and a little pat."

For the *New York Times* (March 6, 1998), however, the movie continued a great tradition. "John Sayles is the most courageous and decent storyteller working in American films today. . . . *Men with Guns* . . . brings the quiet integrity of Mr. Sayles's *Lone Star* to bear on even more uncompromising material." The *Chicago Sun-Times* (March 27, 1998) applauded the picture as "immensely moving and sad, and yet, because it does so much, it is an exhilarating film. It frees itself from specific stories about this villain or that strategy to stand back and look at the big picture, at societies in collapse because power had been concentrated in the hands of small men made big by guns."

While *Men with Guns* struggled at the box office, the moviemaker himself was having industry recognition heaped on him. The Writers Guild Award for career achievement came as a special surprise. "It's a great honor," he told the *New York Times* (February 20, 1998), "but I honestly don't feel like I've been out there long enough to get that, and I have things I'm still doing." On February 13, 1998, at the Writers Guild Theatre in Hollywood, he appeared on stage for an interview with film historian Leonard Maltin and a tribute from his colleagues. As *Variety* (February 17, 1998) reported, "It was easy to observe that Sayles—a native of Schenectady, New York, dressed down in a faded denim shirt, his sleeves rolled up—was a little uncomfortable with the hyperbole."

The kudos started with the citation read by John Furia Jr., president of the Writers Guild Foundation. "That's one John Sayles," he said, "the quirky, randomly curious, wondrously original writer who not only marches to his own drummer but plays the drum himself and hums harmony. The other John Sayles is in constant demand to write or rewrite mainstream movies and has done so with a keen appreciation for the 'well-made narrative,' sparkling dialogue, and characters who create quick and powerful empathy." Furia also reminded the audience that the relatively young honoree had written twenty-two screenplays.

Further accolades came from veteran producer Robert Wise, cinematographer Haskell Wexler, Stu Robinson (Sayles's agent), and Kris Kristofferson, who added a lighter note to the evening. "I was trying to express my gratitude for John's resurrecting my acting career. I said, 'Anytime you can use me, I'll work for scale.' He looked at me and said, 'If you work for me, you'll be working for scale.'" In accepting the honor, Sayles joined the ranks of esteemed screenwriters Robert Bolt, Billy Wilder, Oliver Stone, and Ruth Prawer Jhabvala. His thanks were addressed especially to Maggie Renzi and the regular crew of his many movies.

The following evening Sayles was again sitting on a dais, this time at the Martha Heasley Cox Center for Steinbeck Studies at California's San Jose State University. He was following his friend Bruce Springsteen as the second recipient of the John Steinbeck Award. Addressing the dinner assembly, Dr. Susan Shillington, director of the center, said, "The subtitle on the award 'in the souls of the people' comes from *The Grapes of Wrath*. Steinbeck said that the only reason he wrote was to make people understand one another. I think John Sayles does that in film after film." The award kicked off a weeklong Sayles retrospective that began with *Men with Guns*.

In the fall of 1998, the former member of the French Honor Society at Mont Pleasant High School and self-taught Spanish-scriptwriter returned to his roots to accept an award from the High School Teachers of Foreign Language of New York. Arriving moments before the presentation, John first met his father, who was relieved at not having to substitute for him. John then rolled up his shirtsleeves and accepted the plaque for his contributions to the appreciation of the study of foreign languages. Later that year John joined the honorary advisory board for the first San Diego International Film Festival, participating with directors Atom Egoyan and Ang Lee on the independent film subcommittee.

The multiple honors were signs of Sayles's evolving relationship with the film industry. At the American Film Institute's Lifetime Achievement Award ceremony honoring Robert Wise, held on February 19, 1998, in Los Angeles, the television camera panned across the faces of the film celebrities gathered to honor the director/producer of such classics as *West Side Story* (1961) and *The Sound of Music* (1965). Among them for the third time in two years was John Sayles, *sans* denim and in tux. In his acceptance speech, Wise saw better days ahead for American motion pictures and referenced the new generation of filmmakers such as John Sayles and James Cameron as reasons for his optimism. The presence of Sayles among the Hollywood establishment and the respect they showered on him anticipated the dramatic shifts in his dealing with the major studios that would attend the making of his next feature film.

21

Limbo and the New Deal

I'm always afraid that Hollywood will seduce
John into doing their thing, not by logic or agreement—they'll
never do that—but by seduction.

CINEMATOGRAPHER

HASKELL WEXLER, 1999

IN THE FALL OF 1997, after wrapping *Men with Guns* (1998), John Sayles once again stepped into the marketplace to hustle "our" (never "my") film at festivals and premieres and to give hundreds of media interviews. On the surface, these promotional activities continued a familiar pattern of writing, directing, and publicizing that marks his twenty-year term as dean of the independent school of American filmmaking.

Still, some seismographic shifts were taking place in the Sayles modus operandi and evoking apprehension, especially among his crew and his cult following. They worried that the maverick might one day be lured by the establishment into its moviemaking system. Haskell Wexler told me of his advice to the director: "If working with a lower budget gives you the independence, don't take the studio money. There are already enough films made by focus groups and by producers who don't know shit about filmmaking or marketing."

Behind this realignment of Sayles and the system lie the economic realities facing both the independent filmmakers and the studios. Numbers tell the
story. Over the past five years the average cost for producing a movie has
gone from $26 million to $53 million, with marketing costs rising another 80
percent in the same time frame. Meanwhile, box-office receipts, which
accounted for 35 percent of film revenue in 1990, dropped to 25 percent in
1998. Coincidentally, home video business has slowed, and the next big source
of revenue, DVDs (digital video discs), is just getting started. Film business
veteran Michael Ovitz to the *New York Times* (June 13, 1999) explained one
major impact of all this on the industry's current economy: "With risks so
great it's just much easier for a studio to say no to anything they believe is not
very commercial."

One result of the industry's caution is a declining ratio of produced to
exhibited films. Further, without the massive advertising packages behind
them, even those films that make it to the theaters often close before they have
a chance to develop an audience. Finally, as John has often argued, in an industry so volatile, it is the small independent that gets hit hardest. Sayles's current
view of this economy suggests a filmmaker looking for more security, and he
may have found it.

Although not astronomical, the box-office success of *Lone Star* was well
timed and further cemented the relationship between Sony Pictures Classics
and John Sayles. Even while *Men with Guns* was in the editing process, Sony
picked up the distribution rights. By December 1997, the parent company,
"Big Sony," was making additional overtures to John, this time through the
new alliance of Maggie Renzi and her former co-producer, Sarah Green.

As the *Hollywood Reporter* (December 9, 1997) indicated, Green and Renzi
"have paired up and are in advanced negotiations to form a first-look production deal with Sony Pictures. Green/Renzi Productions is already in final
negotiations for its first project *The Winslow Boy*. . . . Under the deal with
Sony Pictures Entertainment, Green/Renzi will concentrate primarily but
not solely on specialized films with budgets up to $8 million." As sometimes
investor and longtime observer of his brother's career, Doug Sayles says, "This
is a ratcheting up from Sony Classics to Big Sony. Through the deal with

Maggie and Sarah, who work with John and David [Mamet], respectively, Sony can try to ensure that the Sayles and Mamet films stay within the Sony system. They'll also be looking for other products that Sony can do."

Describing the "first look" or "overhead agreement," one studio executive says, "This is a common arrangement in motion pictures and TV. In exchange for office space, overhead supplies, and reimbursements, the producers give the studio first option on their productions." That same source indicates, however, that there was "no guarantee that Maggie will be able to deliver Sayles's films." Nevertheless, it is a gateway that Columbia Pictures president Amy Paschal envisioned when she told the *Hollywood Reporter* about the Sony-financed Green/Renzi production of *Limbo* (1999). "It's extremely gratifying to bring one of the most unique and respected names in Hollywood into the Columbia Pictures family. . . . John has established a relationship with the Sony Pictures Classics team, and I look forward to broadening Sony's relationship with John through this project."

The Green/Renzi-Sony Pictures deal gives a new economic stability to the Sayles initiative and invites the kind of one-stop shopping that can provide financing and distribution of his movies. The benefits, of course, cut both ways. Columbia acquires new economic and creative flexibility provided by two experts in making low-budget movies, and Sony is not the only studio investing in the small-film future.

Maggie was optimistic about teaming with Sarah and about their arrangement with Sony. From the Green/Renzi offices in New York, she could move forward now as a producer of films for more than one director. She saw the opportunity to convince the studios and other backers that such films as *The Full Monty* (1997) can make money. She also saw herself serving as a liaison between the studios and Sayles and described that possible accord to the *Hollywood Reporter* (December 8, 1997). "In the past, John's interest as a director and Hollywood's interests have been incompatible. I am hoping that with this deal we have found a home where what he wants and what Hollywood wants are not that far apart."

For Green/Renzi Productions, its long-term docket included two bigger budget films in development, *State and Maine* and *Junketeers.* Based on a Sayles comedy script about the Hollywood foreign press corps, *Junketeers* would be produced by Renzi. The company also was developing movies by lesser-known directors, all women: *Royal Court,* written and directed by Kelly Reichardt; *Girlfight,* written and directed by Karyn Kusuma; and *Elvis Heads,* written by G. Marianne Leone and to be directed by Mary Cybulski. Two films were immediately sent into production: David Mamet's *The Winslow Boy* (1999) and Sayles's *Limbo,* each with budgets under $10 million.

In June 1998 the Green/Renzi deal with Big Sony made an immediate impact on the *Limbo* production. For the first time since *Baby It's You,* a Sayles film would have the support, if not the stamp, of a major Hollywood studio. Columbia, under the aegis of their new division, Screen Gems (formerly the title of Columbia's television movie unit), would finance and distribute the film.

Renzi would be flying solo with no Sarah Green, Peggy Rajski, Paul Miller, or John Sloss to share the load. As a consequence of their renewed membership in the Directors Guild of America, John and Maggie would be using a DGA camera crew. (Even a rebel like Haskell Wexler confessed that after his defiance of the system during the shooting of *Matewan,* he could not work nonunion again.) For *Limbo,* the first and second assistant directors and the production manager all carried DGA cards.

In Juneau, Alaska, Sayles's cast and crew were gathering to shoot a movie about a young fisherman, Joe Gastineau (David Strathairn). Traumatized by a boat accident in his past, he finds himself attracted to a singer, Donna De Angelo (Mary Elizabeth Mastrantonio), who has a daughter, Noelle (Vanessa Martinez). Their relationship begins in the fictional town of Port Henry against the larger background of growing tension between the dying fish industry and the burgeoning tourism that would turn Alaska into a giant theme park.

As Joe, Donna, and Noelle embark on a recreational boat trip with Joe's feckless brother, Bobby (Casey Siemaszko), the screen story abruptly shifts to a more intimate level. When a gang of drug dealers boards the boat and kills Bobby, the three passengers dive into the water and swim to an island with the criminals in hot pursuit. Stranded, they survive in the wilderness while facing the twin threats of the drug dealers and possible death. Their hope of rescue lies with a bush pilot, Smilin' Jack (Kris Kristofferson), with whom Joe has a bad history.

The familiar names and faces should have eased even those most apprehensive about the "new Sayles." As Joe Gastineau, Strathairn brought a Sayles-connected tradition dating back to the Williams College stage. Over the years the actor had played everything from sheriff *(Matewan)* to star pitcher *(Eight Men Out)* to courtly romancer *(Passion Fish)*. By the late 1990s, after appearances in *The River Wild* (1994) and *L.A. Confidential* (1997), Strathairn was a hot property on Broadway and in Hollywood, with nine films in 1998–99 alone. Strathairn told me of his admiration for Sayles's social ethnographic sense. "The common man is always in the foreground of an informing political backdrop."

Joining Strathairn were Kristofferson *(Lone Star)*, Leo Burmester *(Lone Star)*, Martinez *(Lone Star)*, and Siemaszko, who acted with Sayles in *My Life's in Turnaround*. Haskell Wexler headed the camera crew, which included first assistant John "J. P." Powditch and video assist Kevin Boyd, both from *Lone Star*. As Boyd observed, "There were plenty of friends of Maggie and lots of townies filling in as extras and as production assistants."

The new face on the set belonged to Mary Elizabeth Mastrantonio, for whom John had written the part of Donna. The choice of star staggered the imagination of Sayles's composer, Mason Daring. Recalling his first meeting with her in Ireland, Daring told me, "She's a fabulous actress, but who knew she could sing? John did. After John chose her, we prerecorded a number of songs in Ireland, then picked the right key for her to record them in in my studio. It just got better and better."

Early in the production, the shoot provided a challenge to Mastrantonio's talents and the crew's skill at filming them. Daring recalls an eight-minute take as one of the most amazing he's seen. "She sings the end of 'C'est la Vie,' then she makes a speech, then, by way of saying good-bye, she sings 'Better Off Without You.' Then she steps off stage, camera following, and goes over to David Strathairn. She did that master shot five times, sang great, and never blew a line. My jaw was on the floor."

In working with Sayles on eleven film scores to date, Mason has had to resolve questions of artistic integrity. The composer told me, "I'm long past where I think he's wrong. He just wants something else. It's my job to find it. This time we had more money, so it's a more ambitious score." For his part Wexler has also adapted to Sayles, but not without leaving his influence on the filmmaker—for the better, as Sayles readily admits. Of the *Limbo* shoot, Wexler says, "I have come to the point where I can say, John wants it this way, just do the best you can with what he has in mind." In Wexler's mind, even the disagreements fall into the category of creative discussions rather than politics, money, one-upmanship, advertising, publicity, and celebrity status found on other productions. In his opinion, Sayles's directing of *Limbo,* as opposed to *Matewan,* demonstrates that he is "getting the message that writing is only part of making a film."

The production of *Limbo* wrapped in late August 1998, and Columbia representatives were happy with the results. The Juneau folks also appreciated the film production and recognized the legacy of good will created among its citizens. On September 6, 1998, a *Juneau Empire* newspaper editorial thanked the John Sayles-Maggie Renzi production team: "They auctioned off their props and donated the money to Juneau-Douglas High School. They remodeled the Franklin Street location that the Juneau Theatre occupies, returning to the theater a much needed functional space with new flooring, carpeting, paint, lighting superstructure and a freshened entranceway. . . . All in all they were good neighbors who will be welcome in the Capital City anytime they decide to return."

Once again, John Sayles had used a location and told a story that the American film industry in its more than one hundred years' existence had failed to find and explore. He was now bound not for some unwinding in Hoboken or at his New York hideaway about a hundred miles north, but for the airplanes that would deliver him to the events promoting the movie. Having touched down in one airport, he met an old friend, Bruce Springsteen. Within minutes, the rock star agreed to write and perform a new song, "Lift Me Up," for the final credits of *Limbo.*

In mid-May 1999, Screen Gems screened *Limbo* as an official selection at the Cannes International Film Festival. In the *Hollywood Reporter* (May 12, 1999), Sony president John Calley referred to the exhibition at Cannes as "an honor and incredibly potent launching pad for any film." At the festival, where Spanish filmmaker Pedro Almodovar's *All About My Mother* walked off with the prize, *Limbo* received a cool reception from critics.

On June 4, 1999, *Limbo* opened in the major U.S. markets. Criticism focused on the film's lack of coherence, citing the last third of the film as weak melodrama. *L.A. Weekly* (June 4, 1999) saw a "lovely mood piece" turned into a "half-assed thriller," and *Entertainment Weekly* (June 7, 1999) called the second half a cliché, "family therapy in wild kingdom." *Newsweek* (June 14, 1999) labeled the release "a claustrophobic, stuck-on-an-island melodrama."

The most obvious target for the critics' attacks was *Limbo*'s abrupt, open-ended finale, which *Variety* (May 25, 1999) dubbed "a silly and frustrating cop-out," and *Entertainment Weekly* (June 7, 1999) described as "a cut-rate ambiguous trick ending." Although less negative, the *San Francisco Chronicle* (June 4, 1999) nevertheless judged, "It was hard not to feel cheated," then cited overheard audience responses: "'This movie sucks.'" Citing the film as "Sayles's darkest hour," the *Los Angeles Daily News* (June 4, 1999) labeled its ending "precious and frustrating."

In general, reviewers responded favorably to the film's visual style, especially in the first half. *Premiere* (July 1999) cited *Limbo* as "one of Sayles's most extraordinary, engaging, and disturbing pictures." Reviews also welcomed back Mary Elizabeth Mastrantonio after a four-year screen absence and applauded her performance, including her singing. While admitting that the two halves of the film did not always mesh, the *Los Angeles Times* (June 4, 1999) said the onscreen relationship of Mastrantonio and Strathairn was "one of the most affecting that Sayles has put on film." *Time,* in early June 1999, concurred, "They come together warily . . . with a certain subtle, last chance resolve." Conceding that the ending was "too abrupt," the *New York Times* (June 4, 1999) concluded that the "characters' humanity makes *Limbo* a compelling experience." *Entertainment Today* (June 4, 1999) added that, by ending with a question, "Sayles encourages a different kind of reaction for viewers: thinking."

Few reviewers admired the picture's problematic ending, and *Variety* accurately warned that the picture was heading toward "spotty biz." Despite Sony's all-out promotional campaign, with full-page ads in the major market dailies, *Limbo* crawled at the box office. Three weeks after its opening, having added thirty theaters the previous week, the Screen Gems release had grossed only $724,520. Given the nature of the reviews, the outlook for matching production and marketing costs was not encouraging.

Fifty-two days after its release, *Limbo* stood forty-seventh in *Hollywood Reporter*'s "Top 50 at the Boxoffice." It had total gross sales of $1.8 million. Meanwhile, in contrast, after fifty weeks, *The Winslow Boy* ranked forty-second on the *Hollywood Reporter* chart. A very low budget Green/Renzi production released by Sony Classics, the David Mamet feature had grosses of over $2 million. By December, *Limbo*—now in video, laser, and DVD formats—was looking for new audiences.

The controversy surrounding *Limbo* should put to rest the suspicion that Sayles was being seduced by the recent film industry awards, the DGA, and Sony Entertainment. Throughout the production, Sony lived up to its hands-off agreement, and clearly *Limbo* shows no sign of compromise with the studio or the audience. As John said at the 1998 John Steinbeck Award ceremony in San Jose, California, "I don't change my mind about important things."

■   ■   ■

If *Return of the Secaucus Seven* stands as an overture to Sayles's career, *Limbo* serves as a retrospective of his history as America's preeminent independent filmmaker. As usual, the production was marked by Sayles's creative control from casting to final cut. Typically as well, the filmmaker had charted new waters this time, setting his ordinary characters down in exotic Alaska. He might have selected a look-alike Canadian location, less expensive and closer to the film resources of Hollywood, but authenticity is a sacrosanct part of John's creed. During the process of transferring the film from celluloid to tape and discs, Sayles told Sony colorist John Persichetti that shooting in Alaska would employ American citizens at union wages. According to Mayor Dennis Egan (*Anchorage Daily News,* June 28, 1998), the feature also would pour about $2 million into the Juneau economy.

John's casting called on a veritable Sayles company of players, revived the career of Mary Elizabeth Mastrantonio, and used plenty of locals and assorted friends as minor characters and extras. The screenplay continued the *Lone Star* pattern of the integration of human dilemmas in the context of a community struggling with the social and economic stresses of the 1990s.

The lack of commercial interest in *Limbo* might have reminded Sayles of the disappointments that marked his first eleven features. Because of weak marketing, movies like *Matewan* and *Eight Men Out* never found an audience. In contrast, with *Lianna* and *Men with Guns,* it was Sayles's choice of topics and treatment of them that curtailed financial success. As with *The Brother from Another Planet,* sometimes his risk-taking paid off in a film with a small, but enthusiastic record of success and appreciation. Even the earnings of *The Secret of Roan Inish* and *Lone Star* together, however, could not pay the per-film salary of a Tom Hanks or a Tom Cruise. By the end of the 1990s, John recognized and accepted that neither he nor his films were marquee names.

Still, his twenty-plus years of daring, unconventional moviemaking has honored the independent legacy of his inspiration, John Cassavetes. While demanding and controversial, Sayles's motion pictures have pushed the boundaries of motion picture structure and story and, consequently, stirred thoughtful discussion among audiences. Once again, in *Limbo,* he would not compromise his vision, and therefore the two main characters neither embrace on the beach nor fly off to happier lives. That's the Hollywood plotline lie that Sayles, Martin Scorsese, Robert Altman, and other independent-minded moviemakers continually deny the audience.

Of late, the growing number of awards and accolades for his screenplays, as well as his mastery of visual storytelling, indicate the respect his development as a writer/director has earned among his peers and the critics. Sayles has responded by accepting a leadership role in the industry. His membership on boards of organizations supporting the independent film movement and his assistance to struggling young filmmakers, especially those marginalized by the industry such as women, reflect his earned status as caretaker of American independent film.

■   ■   ■

Taxed by the writing, directing, editing, and promoting of two movies in a fourteen-month period, Sayles temporarily stepped away from making his own features. Nevertheless, as he approached his fiftieth birthday, he stayed in the forefront of the independent movement. For the Green/Renzi and Independent Film Channel production of *Girlfight* he pitched in as one of the executive producers and, perhaps recalling his dad's teaching days, also played the on-camera role of the high school science teacher. Written and directed by first-timer Karyn Kusama, *Girlfight* is the coming of age story of a Brooklyn teenage girl (Michelle Rodriquez) who gets involved in boxing and finds both romance and a career (the two not always compatible). Opening at the 2000 Sundance Film Festival, the entry won the Grand Jury and Best Director prizes and rave reviews. In *Daily Variety* (February 2, 2000) Emanuel Levy called it a "strikingly accomplished feature . . . an enormously likeable film splendidly acted." The critic also attributed some of its success to the "guidance" provided by Sayles.

Still in the offing was the shooting of *Fade to Black,* a Sayles's screenplay based on Davide Ferrario's novel. Produced by the Paris-based Pandora Cinema with Oliver Parker as director, the movie sets Orson Welles in post–World War II Rome, initially directing a film at Cinecitta Studios and then plunging himself into the investigation of a series of murders on the set. For the Welles role the producers turned to actor/director Kenneth Branagh. While enjoying the respite from directing, Sayles was also penning a script for Phoenix Pictures, *The Sixth Day,* and working on a collection of short stories. "One of those," he told *Daily Variety*'s Dan Cox (May 13, 1999), "might turn into a screenplay."

Ahead lie the vagaries of an industry shifting from celluloid to digital imaging, a process that will be tested in the summer of 2000 by George Lucas in his creation of the next *Star Wars* chapter in Australia. For Sayles the advantages of the digital process will lie in cheaper cost of filming, editing, and copying movies.

John Sayles is technically a paradox. Unlike virtually every other director, he clings to the past, editing his latest feature on the old Steenbeck machine instead of on the Avid digital computer. On the other hand, as Sony colorist John Persichetti told me, "John seems open to any technology that will help him tell his stories. When we worked on the film transfer to laser and DVD, he showed up with Haskell's great footage and with a very clear idea of what he wanted. The job only took two days. Usually it's a week."

Thus, after twenty years of scrambling to make his own movies his way, Sayles is poised to continue the oldest tradition of filmmaking and what he has always strived to do: tell good stories. At the dawn of the new millennium, he and his peers (David Lynch, Spike Lee, Allison Anders, Jim Jarmusch, David Mamet, Nancy Savoca, and Kevin Smith, to name a few) are challenging the Hollywood system that reduces those narratives to motion picture pap. Through creative control, this group of moviemakers also is expanding the horizon for American film and American film independence.

Looking both backward and ahead, actor David Strathairn identifies John's unique history and posits the hope of all Sayles loyalists for his future. "The definition of a genius is a man who cannot help but speak and who is honored and respected for it. That's the privilege of being on the court with John. His canvas is so special."

Through his ever-evolving skills at visualizing his ideas and his risks at integrating the personal and the public in his films, John Sayles seems ready to make his own mark, once again, on American film as it moves into in the twenty-first century. With his past as prelude, his audience can anticipate even more challenging movie pioneering from a filmmaker whose visual skills had long ago proved to be a match for his literate scripting.

APPENDIX A

Filmography

AS DIRECTOR

Return of the Secaucus Seven
(Libra, 1979). 106 minutes, R-rated.

CREDITS

Production Company: Salsipuedes Productions. Producers: Jeffrey Nelson and William Aydelott. Director: John Sayles. Screenplay: John Sayles. Cinematography: Austin Debesche. Editor: John Sayles. Music: Mason Daring.

CAST

Bruce MacDonald (Mike Donnelly); Adam LeFevre (J. T.); Gordon Clapp (Chip Hollister); Karen Trott (Maura Tolliver); David Strathairn (Ron Desjardins); Marisa Smith (Carol); Carolyn Brooks (Meg); Nancy Mette (Lee); Brian Johnston (Norman); Ernie Bashaw (Officer); Jessica MacDonald (Stacey); Jeffrey Nelson (Man); Maggie Renzi (Kate); Maggie Cousineau (Frances); Jean Passanante (Irene Rosenblum); Mark Arnott (Jeff); John Sayles (Howie); Amy Schewel (Lacey Summers); Jack Lavalle (Booking Officer); Benjamin Zaitz (Benjamin).

Lianna
(United Artists Classics, 1983). 110 minutes, R-rated.

CREDITS

Production Company: Winwood Company. Producers: Jeffrey Nelson and Maggie Renzi. Director: John Sayles. Screenplay: John Sayles. Cinematography: Austin de Besche. Art Direction: Jeanne McDonnell. Costumes: Louise Martinez. Editor: John Sayles. Music: Mason Daring.

CAST
CAST
Linda Griffiths (Lianna); Jane Hallaren (Ruth); Jon DeVries (Dick);
Jo Henderson (Sandy); Jessica Wight MacDonald (Theda); Jesse Solomon (Spencer);
John Sayles (Jerry); Stephen Mendillo (Bob); Betsy Julia Robinson (Cindy);
Nancy Mette (Kim); Maggie Renzi (Sheila); Madelyn Coleman (Mrs. Hennessy);
Robyn Reeves (Job Applicant); Marta Renzi and D. David Porter (Dancers);
Rochelle Oliver (Betty); Nancy Elizabeth Kammer (Liz); Jean Passanante (Rose);
Maggie Task (Evelyn); Marisa Smith and Amanda Carlin (Dick's Students);
Madeline Lee (Supermarket Customer); Deborah Taylor (Receptionist).

Baby It's You
(Paramount, 1983). 105 minutes, R-rated.

CREDITS
Production Company: Paramount. A Double Play Production. Producers: Griffin
Dunne and Amy Robinson. Director: John Sayles. Screenplay: John Sayles, based on a
story by Amy Robinson. Cinematography: Michael Ballhaus. Production Designer:
Jeffrey Towsend. Costumes: Franne Lee. Editor: Sonya Polonsky. Music: Joel Dorn.

CAST
Rosanna Arquette (Jill Rosen); Vincent Spano (Sheik Capadilupo);
Joanna Merlin (Mrs. Rosen); Jack Davidson (Dr. Rosen); Nick Ferrari
(Mr. Capadilupo); Dolores Messina (Mrs. Capadilupo); High School Teachers:
Leora Dana (Miss Vernon), William Joseph Raymond (Mr. Ripeppi), Sam McMurray
(Mr. McManus); High School Girls: Liane Curtis (Jody), Claudia Sherman (Beth),
Marta Kober (Debra); College Girls: Tracy Pollan (Leslie), Rachel Dretzin (Shelly),
Susan Derendorf (Chris); Frank Vincent (Vinnie); Robin Johnson (Joann);
Gary McCleery (Rat); Matthew Modine (Steve); John Ferraro (Plasky);
Phil Brock (Biff); Merel Poloway (Miss Katz); Don Kehr (Barry); Michael Knight
(Phillip); Robert Downey Jr. (Stewart).

The Brother from Another Planet
(Cinecom, 1984). 104 minutes, PG-rated.

CREDITS
Production Company: A-Train Films. Producers: Peggy Rajski and Maggie Renzi.
Director: John Sayles. Screenplay: John Sayles. Cinematography: Ernest Dickerson.
Production Designer: Nora Chavooshian. Art Director: Stephen Lineweaver.
Costumes: Karen Perry. Editor: John Sayles. Music: Mason Daring.

CAST

Joe Morton (The Brother); Tom Wright (Sam Prescott); Caroline Aaron (Randy Sue Carter); Herbert Newsome (Little Earl); Dee Dee Bridgewater (Malverne Davis); Daryl Edwards (Fly); Leonard Jackson (Smokey); Bill Cobbs (Walter); Steve James (Odell); Edward Baran (Mr. Vance); John Sayles (Man in Black); David Strathairn (Man in Black); Maggie Renzi (Noreen); Olga Merediz (Noreen's Client); Minnie Gentry (Mrs. Brown); Ren Woods (Bernice); Reggie Rock Bythewood (Rickey); Alvin Alexis (Willis); Rosetta Le Noire (Mama); Michael Albert Mantel (Mr. Lowe); Josh Mostel (Casio Vendor).

Matewan
(Cinecom, 1987). 133 minutes, PG-13-rated.

CREDITS

Production Company: Cinecom Entertainment Group, Film Gallery, and Red Dog Films. Producers: Peggy Rajski and Maggie Renzi. Director: John Sayles. Screenplay: John Sayles. Cinematography: Haskell Wexler. Production Designer: Nora Chavooshian. Art Director: Dan Bishop. Costumes: Cynthia Flynt. Editor: Sonya Polonsky. Music: Mason Daring.

CAST

Chris Cooper (Joe Kenehan); Mary McDonnell (Elma Radnor); Will Oldham (Danny Radnor); David Strathairn (Sid Hatfield); Ken Jenkins (Sephus); Kevin Tighe (Hickey); Gordon Clapp (Griggs); James Earl Jones ("Few Clothes" Johnson); Bob Gunton (C. E. Lively); Jace Alexander (Hillard Elkins); Joe Grifasi (Fausto); Nancy Mette (Bridey Mae); Jo Henderson (Mrs. Elkins); Josh Mostel (Cabell Testerman); Gary McCleery (Ludie); Maggie Renzi (Rosaria); Tom Wright (Tom); Michael Preston (Ellix); Thomas A. Carlin (Turley); Jenni Cline (Luann); John Sayles (Hardshell Preacher); Gerald Milnes (Fiddler); Mason Daring (Picker); Jim Costa (Mandolin Player); Phil Wiggins (Harmonica Player).

Eight Men Out
(Orion, 1988). 119 minutes, PG-rated.

CREDITS

Production Company: Sanford-Pillsbury Productions; Orion Pictures Corporation; Producers: Sarah Pillsbury and Midge Sanford. Director: John Sayles. Screenplay: John Sayles, based on the book *Eight Men Out* by Eliot Asinof. Cinematography: Robert Richardson. Production Designer: Nora Chavooshian. Art Director: Dan Bishop. Costumes: Cynthia Flynt. Editor: John Tintori. Music: Mason Daring.

CAST

D. B. Sweeney ("Shoeless Joe" Jackson); David Strathairn (Eddie Cicotte);
Charlie Sheen (Hap Felsch); John Cusack (George "Buck" Weaver); Bill Irwin (Eddie
Collins); Don Harvey ("Swede" Risberg); Michael Rooker (Chick Gandil); James Read
("Lefty" Williams); Gordon Clapp (Ray Schalk); John Mahoney ("Kid" Gleason);
Clifton James (Charles Comiskey); John Anderson (Kenesaw Mountain Landis);
Michael Lerner (Arnold Rothstein); Kevin Tighe (Joseph "Sport" Sullivan);
Christopher Lloyd (Bill Burns); Richard Edson (Billy Maharg); Michael Matell
(Abe Attell); John Sayles (Ring Lardner); Studs Terkel (Hugh Fullerton); Eliot Asinof
(John Heydler); Maggie Renzi (Rose Cicotte); Tay Strathairn (Bucky); Ken Berry
(Heckler); Charles Seibert II (Reds Catcher); Mason Daring (Bugle Player).

City of Hope

(Samuel Goldwyn Company, 1991). 129 minutes, R-rated.

CREDITS

Production Company: Esperanza. Producers: Sarah Green and Maggie Renzi.
Director: John Sayles. Screenplay: John Sayles. Cinematography: Robert Richardson.
Production Designers: Dan Bishop and Dianna Freas. Art Director: Chas B. Plummer.
Costumes: John Dunn. Editor: John Sayles. Music: Mason Daring.

CAST

Vincent Spano (Nick); Barbara Williams (Angela); Joe Morton (Wynn);
Tony Lo Bianco (Joe); Anthony John Denison (Rizzo); Stephen Mendillo (Yoyo);
Chris Cooper (Riggs); Bill Raymond (Les); Charlie Yanko (Stavros);
Jace Alexander (Bobby); Todd Graf (Zip); Scott Tiler (Vinnie); John Sayles (Carl);
Frankie Faison (Levonne); Gloria Foster (Jeanette); Tom Wright (Malick);
Angela Bassett (Reesha); David Strathairn (Asteroid); Maggie Renzi (Connie);
Josh Mostel (Mad Anthony); Mason Daring (Peter).

Passion Fish

(Miramax, 1992). 136 minutes, R-rated.

CREDITS

Production Company: Atchafalaya Productions. Producers: Sarah Green and Maggie
Renzi. Director: John Sayles. Screenplay: John Sayles. Cinematography: Roger
Deakins. Production Designers: Dan Bishop and Dianna Freas. Art Director: Beth
Bernstein. Costumes: Cynthia Flynt. Editor: John Sayles. Music: Mason Daring.

CAST

Mary McDonnell (May-Alice Culhane); Alfre Woodard (Chantelle); Vondie
Curtis-Hall (Sugar Le Doux); David Strathairn (Rennie); Leo Burmester (Reeves);
John Henry Redmond (Dr. Blades); Nora Dunn (Ti-Marie); Mary Porster (Precious);
Sheila Keeley (Kim); Angela Bassett (Dawn/Rhonda); Nancy Mette (Nina);
Leonore Banks (Nurse Quick); Elaine West (Phoebe); William Mahoney (Max);
Nelle Stokes, Brett Ardoin, Daniel Dupont (Therapists); Michael Mantell (Doctor
Kline); Chuck Cain (Attendant); Shana Ledet Qualls and Paula Lafleur (Fans);
Maggie Renzi (Louise); Tom Wright (Luther).

The Secret of Roan Inish
(First Look, 1994). 102 minutes, PG-rated.

CREDITS

Production Company: Skerry Movies Corporation, Jones Entertainment Group;
Producers: Sarah Green and Maggie Renzi. Director: John Sayles; Screenplay: John
Sayles, based on the novel *The Secret of Ron Mor Skerry* by Rosalie Fry. Cinematography:
Haskell Wexler. Production Designer: Adrian Smith. Art Direction: Dennis Bosher.
Costumes: Consolata Boyle. Editor: John Sayles. Music: Mason Daring.

CAST

Jeni Courtney (Fiona Coneely); Mick Lally (Hugh); Eileen Colgan (Tess); John Lynch
(Tadhg Coneely); Richard Sheridan (Cousin Eamon); Cillian Byrne (Jamie);
Pat Howey (Priest); Dave Duffy (Jim Coneely); Declan Hannigan (Oldest Brother);
Gerard Rooney (Liam Coneely); Susan Lynch (Selkie); Michael MacCarthaigh
(Schoolmaster); Fergal McElherron (Sean Michael); Brendan Conroy (Flynn); Frankie
McCafferty (Tim); Linda Greer (Brigid Coneely); Eddie Erskine (Bar Patron).

Lone Star
(Columbia Pictures, 1996). 134 minutes, R-rated.

CREDITS

Production Company: Castle Rock Entertainment. Producers: Paul Miller
and Maggie Renzi. Director: John Sayles. Screenplay: John Sayles. Cinematography:
Stuart Dryburgh. Production Design: Dan Bishop. Art Direction: Kyler Black.
Costumes: Shay Cunliffe. Editor: John Sayles. Music: Mason Daring.

CAST

Chris Cooper (Sam Deeds); Elizabeth Peña (Pilar Cruz); Joe Morton (Delmore
Payne); Matthew McConaughey (Buddy Deeds); Kris Kristofferson (Charlie Wade);
Clifton James (Hollis Pogue); Frances McDormand (Bunny); Miriam Colon

(Mercedes Cruz); Jesse Borrego (Danny); Tony Plana (Ray); Stephen Mendillo (Cliff); LaTanya Richardson (Priscilla Worth); Stephen Lang (Mikey); Ron Canada (Otis Payne); Gabriel Casseus (Young Otis); Leo Burmester (Cody); Chandra Wilson (Athens); Eddie Robinson (Chet), Gordon Tootoosis (Wesley Birdsong); Oni Faida Lampley (Celie); Eleese Lester (Molly); Jeffrey Monahan (Young Hollis); Tay Strathairn (Young Sam).

Men with Guns [Hombres Armados]
(Sony Pictures Classics, 1998). 126 minutes, R-rated.

CREDITS
Production Company: Lexington Road Productions, Clear Blue Sky Productions in association with Independent Film Channel, Anarchists Convention. Producers: Paul Miller and Maggie Renzi. Director: John Sayles. Screenplay: John Sayles. Cinematography: Slawomir Idziak. Production Design: Felipe Fernando Del Paso. Costumes: Mayes C. Rubeo. Editor: John Sayles. Music: Mason Daring.

CAST
Federico Luppi (Dr. Fuentes); Damian Delgado (Domingo); Dan Rivera Gonzalez (Conejo); Tanai Cruz (Graciela); Damian Alcazar (Padre Oportillo); Mandy Patinkin (Andrew); Kathryn Grody (Harriet); Iquandili Lopez (Mother); Nandi Luna Ramirez (Daughter); Rafael de Quevedo (General); Carmen Madrid (Angela); Esteban Soberanes (Raul); Alejandro Springall (Carlos); Maricruz Najera (Rich Lady); Jacqueline Walters Voltaire (Rich Lady); Roberto Sosa (Bravo); Ivan Arango (Cienfuegos); Lizzie Curry Martinez (Montoya); Luis Ramirez (Hidalgo); Humberto Romero (De Soto); Gabriel Cosme (Echevarria); Horacio Trujillo (Arenas).

Limbo
(Sony Pictures Entertainment, 1999). 126 minutes, R-rated.

CREDITS
Production Company: Columbia Pictures, Green/Renzi Productions. Producer: Maggie Renzi. Director: John Sayles. Screenplay: John Sayles. Cinematography: Haskell Wexler. Production Designer: Gemma Jackson. Art Direction: Keith Neely. Costumes: Shay Cunliffe. Editor: John Sayles. Music: Mason Daring.

CAST
Mary Elizabeth Mastrantonio (Donna De Angelo); David Strathairn (Joe Gastineau); Vanessa Martinez (Noelle De Angelo); Kris Kristofferson (Smilin' Jack); Casey Siemaszko (Bobby Gastineau); Kathryn Grody (Frankie); Rita Taggart (Lou); Leo Burmester (Harmon King); Michael Laskin (Albright).

AS SCREENWRITER

Piranha
(New World, 1978). 92 minutes, R-rated.

CREDITS

Production Company: New World. Producers: Jon Davison and Chako van Leuwen.
Director: Joe Dante. Screenplay: John Sayles. Cinematography: Jamie Anderson.
Production Designer: William Sandell. Art Director: Kerry Mellin.
Editors: Mark Goldblatt, Joe Dante. Music: Pino Donaggio.

CAST

Bradford Dillman (Paul Grogran); Heather Menzies (Maggie McKeown);
Kevin McCarthy (Dr. Robert Joak); Keenan Wynn (Jack);
Barbara Steele (Dr. Mengers); Richard Miller (Buck Gardner).

The Lady in Red [Retitled *Guns, Sin and Bathtub Gin*]
(New World, 1979). 93 minutes, R-rated.

CREDITS

Production Company: New World. Producers: Julie Corman and Roger Corman.
Director: Lewis Teague. Screenplay: John Sayles. Cinematography: Daniel Lacambre.
Production Designer: Jack McAnelly. Art Director: Philip Thomas.
Costumes: Pat Tonnema. Editor: Lewis Teague. Music: James Horner.

CAST

Pamela Sue Martin (Polly Franklin); Robert Conrad (John Dillinger); Louise Fletcher
(Anna Sage); Christopher Lloyd (Frognose); Laurie Heineman (Rose Shimkus);
Robert Hogan (Jake Lingle); Glenn Withrow (Eddie); Richard Miller (Patek).

Alligator
(Group 1, 1980). 94 minutes, R-rated.

CREDITS

Production Company: Group 1. Producers: Brandon Chase and Robert S. Bremson.
Director: Lewis Teague. Screenplay: John Sayles. Cinematography: Joseph Mangine.
Production Designer: Michael Erlere. Music: Craig Hundley.

CAST

Robert Forster (David Madison); Michael Vincente Gazzo (Police Chief Clark);
Dean Jagger (Slade); Perry Lang (Kelly); Henry Silva (Colonel Brock); Jack Carter
(Mayor); Bart Braverman (Kemp); Corky Ford (Chi Chi); Royce D. Applegate
(Callan); Sidney Lassick (Gutchel); Robin B. Riker (Marion).

Battle Beyond the Stars
(New World, 1980). 105 minutes, PG-rated.

CREDITS

Production Company: New World. Producer: Ed Carlin.
Director: Jimmy T. Murakami. Screenplay: John Sayles. Cinematography: Daniel
Lacambre. Production Designer: Sharon Compton. Art Directors: Charles William
Breen and James Cameron. Costumes: Dorinda Rice Wood. Editors: Allan Holzman
and Robert J. Kizer. Music: James Horner.

CAST

Richard Thomas (Shad); Robert Vaughan (Gelt); George Peppard (Cowboy);
John Saxon (Sandor); Darlanne Fluegel (Sadcor); Sam Jaffe (Dr. Hephaestus);
Morgan Woodward (Cayman); Jeff Corey (Zed); Julia Duffy (Mol);
Sybil Danning (St. Exmin).

A Perfect Match
(CBS-TV, 1980). 120 minutes, not rated.

CREDITS

Production Company: Lorimar Productions, Andre Guttfreund.
Director: Mel Damski. Teleplay: John Sayles, based on a story by Andre Guttfreund
and Mel Damski. Cinematography: Ric Waite. Art Director: Tom. H. John.
Editor: John Farrell. Music: Billy Goldenberg.

CAST

Linda Kelsey (Miranda McLloyd); Michael Brandon (Steve Triandos); Lisa Lucas
(Julie Larson); Charles Durning (Bill Larson); Colleen Dewhurst (Meg Larson);
Clyde Kusatsu (Dr. Tommy Chang); Bonnie Bartlett (Judge Greenberg);
Hildy Brooks (Esther).

The Howling

(Avco Embassy, 1981). 91 minutes, R-rated.

CREDITS

Production Company: Avco Embassy. Producers: Michael Finnell and Jack Conrad. Director: Joe Dante. Screenplay: John Sayles, based on the book by Gary Brander. Cinematography: John Hora. Production Designer: Steven G. Legler. Art Director: Robert A. Burns. Costumes: Jack Buehler. Editor: Joe Dante. Music: John Hora.

CAST

Dee Wallace (Karen White); Patrick Macnee (Dr. George Waggner); Dennis Dugan (Chris); Christopher Stone (R. William "Bill" Neill); Belinda Balaski (Terry Fisher); Kevin McCarthy (Fred Francis); Slim Pickens (Sam Newfield); Richard Miller (Bookstore Owner); John Carradine (Erle Kenton). *Uncredited:* Roger Corman (Man on the Phone); John Sayles (Morgue Attendant); Forrest J. Ackerman (Bookstore Customer).

The Challenge [a.k.a. Equals and Sword of Ninja]

(Embassy, 1982). 112 minutes, R-rated.

CREDITS

Production Company: CBS Theatrical Films Group. Producers: Ron Beckman and Robert Rosen. Director: John Frankenheimer. Screenplay: Richard Maxwell, Marc Norman, and John Sayles. Cinematography: Kozo Okazaki. Production Designer: Yoshiyuki Ishida. Editors: Jack Wheeler and John W. Wheeler. Music: Jerry Goldsmith.

CAST

Donna Kei Benz (Akido); Scott Glenn (Rick); Toshiro Mifune (Yoshida); Atsuo Nakamura (Hideo); Calvin Young (Ando); Yoshio Inaba (Instructor); Calvin Jung (Ando); Clyde Kusatsu (Go); Seiji Miyaguchi (Old Man); Sab Shimono (Toshio); Mijko Taka (Yoshida's Wife).

Enormous Changes at the Last Minute [a.k.a. Enormous Changes and Trumps]

(ABC Films, 1983). 115 minutes, PG-13-rated.

CREDITS

Production Company: Ordinary Lives Inc. Producer: Mirra Bank. Directors: Mirra Bank, Ellen Hovde, and Muffie Meyer. Screenplay: Grace Paley, Susan Rice, and

John Sayles, based on stories by Grace Paley. Cinematography: Tom McDonough. Art Directors: Sandy Lewis and Roberta Neiman. Costumes: Kay Preston Stine. Editors: Mirra Bank, Ellen Hovde, and Muffie Meyer. Music: Peter Link.

CAST

Ellen Barkin (Virginia); David Strathairn (Jerry); Ron McLarty (John); Sudie Bond (Mrs. Rafferty); Lynn Milgrim (Faith); Jeffrey DeMunn (Ricardo); Zvees Schooler (Pa); Eda Reiss Merin (Ma); Fay Bernardi (Mrs. Hegel-Shtein); Maria Tucci (Alexandra); Kevin Bacon (Dennis); John Wardwell (Doc); Lou Criscuolo (George).

The Clan of the Cave Bear
(Warner Bros., 1986). 98 minutes, R-rated.

CREDITS

Production Company: Jonesfilm, Guber-Peters Company, Jozak Company, Decade Productions. Producer: Gerald I. Isenberg. Director: Michael Chapman. Screenplay: John Sayles, based on the novel by Jean Auel. Cinematography: Jan de Bont. Production Designer: Tony Masters. Art Directors: Guy Comtois and Richard Wilcox. Costumes: Kelly Kimball. Music: Alan Silvestri.

CAST

Daryl Hannah (Ayla); Pamela Reed (Creb); Thomas G. Waites (Broud); John Doolittle (Brun); Curtis Armstrong (Goov); Martin Doyle (Grod); Adel C. Hammoud (Vorn); Tony Martanaro (Zoug); Mike Muscat (Dorv); John Wardlow (Droog); Paul Carafotes (Brug); Janne Mortil (Orva); Lycia Naff (Uba); Rory L. Crowley (Durc); Colin Doyle (Young Boy).

Unnatural Causes
(NBC-TV, 1986). 100 minutes, not rated.

CREDITS

Production Company: A Blue Andre Production in Association with ITC Productions. Producers: Blue Andre and Robert Myman. Director: Lamont Johnson. Teleplay: John Sayles, based on a story by Martin M. Goldstein, Stephen Dora, and Robert Jacobs. Cinematography: Larry Pizer. Production Designer: Anne Prithard. Costumes: Tom Dawson. Editor: Paul LaMastra.

CAST

John Ritter (Frank Coleman); Alfre Woodard (Maude DeVictor); John Vargas ("Nando" Sanchez); John Sayles (Lloyd); Gwen E. Davis (Ethel Owens).

Wild Thing
(Atlantic, 1987). 92 minutes, PG-rated.

CREDITS
Production Company: Atlantic Entertainment/Fine Line. Producers: David Calloway, Nicholas Clermont, Thomas Coleman, and Pieter Kroonburg. Director: Max Reid. Screenplay: John Sayles. Cinematography: Rene Verzier. Production Designer: Jocelyn Joli. Costumes: Paul-Andre Guerin. Editor: Battle Davis. Music: George C. Clinton.

CAST
Robert Knepper (Wild Thing); Kathleen Quinlan (Jane); Robert Davi (Chopper); Betty Buckley (Leah); Clark Johnson (Winston); Sean Hewitt (Father Quinn); Maury Chaykin (Trask); Guillaume LeMay-Thivierge (Wild Thing at ten years old); Robert Bedarski (Wild Thing at three years old).

Breaking In
(Samuel Goldwyn Company, 1989). 91 minutes, R-rated.

CREDITS
Production Company: Breaking In Productions, Samuel Goldwyn Company. Producer: Harry Gittes. Director: Bill Forsyth. Screenplay: John Sayles. Cinematography: Michael Coulter. Production Designer: Adrienne Atkinson. Editor: Michael Ellis. Music: Denise McCormick.

CAST
Burt Reynolds (Ernie); Casey Siemaszko (Mike); Sheila Kelley (Carrie); Lorraine Toussaint (Delphine); Albert Salmi (Johnny Scot); Harry Carey Jr. (Shoes); Maury Chaykin (Tucci); Stephen Tobolowsky (District Attorney); Richard Key Jones (Lou); Tom Lasswell (Bud); Walter Shane (Boss); John Baldwin (Sam the Apostle).

Shannon's Deal
(NBC-TV, 1989). 95 minutes, not rated.

CREDITS
Production Company: Stan Rogow Productions. Producer: Stan Rogow. Director: Lewis Teague. Teleplay: John Sayles. Cinematography: Andrew Dinenfass. Production Designer: John Vallone. Costumes: Jodie Lynne Tillen. Editor: Neil Travis. Music: Wynton Marsalis.

CAST

Jamey Sheridan (Jack Shannon); Elizabeth Peña (Lucy Acosta); Richard Edson (Wilmer); Jenny Lewis (Neala Shannon); Alberta Watson (Terri); Martin Ferrero (Lou Gandolph); Miguel Ferrer (Todd Spurrier); Claudia Christian (Molly Tempke).

Shannon's Deal

(NBC-TV, 1990). 60-minute series installments, not rated.
"Words to Music." Director: Allan Arkush. Teleplay: John Sayles.
"Custody." Director: Joel Oliansky. Teleplay: John Sayles.

Men of War

(Buena Vista, 1994). 102 minutes, R-rated.

CREDITS

Production Company: MDP Worldwide, Pomerance Corporation, Grandview Avenue Pictures. Producers: Arthur Goldblatt and Andrew Pfeffer. Director: Perry Lang. Screenplay: John Sayles, Ethan Reiff, and Cyrus Voris, based on a story by Stan Rogow. Cinematography: Ron Schmidt. Production Designers: James William Newport and Steve Spence. Costumes: Sean Gunflach. Editor: Jeffrey Reiner. Music: Gerald Gouriet.

CAST

Dolph Lundgren (Nick Gunnar); Charlotte Lewis (Loki); B. D. Wong (Po); Anthony John Denison (Jimmy G.); Tim Guinee (Ocker); Don Harvey (Nolan); Perry Lang (Lyle).

UNCREDITED SCREENWRITING CONTRIBUTIONS

Love Field

(1991). Director: Jonathan Kaplan.

The Quick and the Dead

(1995). Director: Sam Raimi.

Apollo 13

(1995). Director: Ron Howard.

Mimic

(1997). Director: Guillermo Del Toro.

Passing Glory

(TV Movie, 1999). Director: Steve James.

SCREENPLAYS WRITTEN BUT NOT YET PRODUCED

Night Skies

(1980).

Blood of the Lamb

(1981).

Terror of Loch Ness

(1982).

A Yellow Raft in Blue Water

(1990).

USS Indianapolis

(1991); for Jonathan Demme.

The Fifth Child

(1996); for Maggie Renzi and Paul Miller.

Tom Mix Died for Your Sins
(1996); for Sydney Pollack.

Brother Termite
(pending); for James Cameron.

Gold of Exodus: The Discovery of the True Mount Sinai
(pending); for Castle Rock.

Black Magic
(pending); for Pandora Company.

AS CREATIVE CONSULTANT

Shannon's Deal
(TV movie, 1989).

SPECIAL ASSISTANCE

True Love
(1989). Director: Nancy Savoca.

Grace of My Heart
(1996). Director: Allison Anders.

AS EXECUTIVE PRODUCER

Girlfight
(2000). Director, Karyn Kusama.

APPENDIX B

Videography

TELEVISION: DIRECTING

Mountain View
(1989). With Marta Renzi.

MUSIC VIDEOS

"Born in the U.S.A."
(1985). Bruce Springsteen and the E Street Band.

"Glory Days"
(1985). Bruce Springsteen and the E Street Band.

"I'm on Fire"
(1985). Bruce Springsteen and the E Street Band.

CREATIVE CONSULTANT

Shannon's Deal
(TV series, 1989–91).

UNPRODUCED TELEVISION WORKS

The Brother from Another Planet
(pilot); for television program.

Killing Mr. Watson
Adaptation for TNT cable.

APPENDIX C

Acting Credits

FILM AND TELEVISION

Return of the Secaucus Seven
(1980); Howie.

The Howling
(1981); Morgue Attendant (uncredited).

Lianna
(1983); Jerry.

The Brother from Another Planet
(1984); Man in Black.

Unnatural Causes
(TV 1986); Lloyd.

Hard Choices
(1986); Don.

Something Wild
(1986); Motorcycle Cop.

Matewan
(1987); Hardshell Preacher.

Eight Men Out
(1988); Ring Lardner.

Untamaguru
(1989); Military High Commissioner.

La Fine della Notte
(1989); Unbilled bit.

Little Vegas
(1990); Mike.

City of Hope
(1991); Carl.

Naked Hollywood
(TV series, 1981); Interviewee.

Passion Fish
(1992); Doctor in Soap Opera (uncredited).

Straight Talk
(TV, 1992); Guy Girardi.

Malcolm X
(1992); FBI Agent.

Mathnet: The Case of the Unnatural
(TV special, 1992); Roy "Lefty" Cobbs.

My Life's in Turnaround
(1993); Marginal Producer.

Matinee
(1993); Bob.

Baseball
(TV series, 1994–95); "Third Inning: The Faith of Fifty Million People"; Interviewee.

Gridlock'd
(1997); Cop No. 1.

Big Guns Talk: The Story of the Western
(TV special, 1997); Interviewee.

Making of Men with Guns
(1998); Interviewee.

Girlfight
(1999); Science teacher.

STAGE

The Glass Menagerie;
Tom Wingfield. Williamstown Theatre Festival, August 1985.

SOURCE NOTES

SOURCES FOR CHAPTER OPENING QUOTES

1. Cassavetes, John, in Carney, Ray. *The Films of John Cassavetes*. Cambridge, England: University of Cambridge Press, 1994.

2. Sayles, John, in Ratner, Megan. "Borderlines." *Filmmaker*, Summer 1996: 32.

3. Sayles, Doug. Personal interview. May 22, 1998.

4. Sayles, John, in Dreifus, Claudia. "Interview with John Sayles." *The Progressive*, November 1991: 30.

5. Mulvaney, Larry. Personal interview. May 21, 1998.

6. Sayles, John, in Harmetz, Aljean. "Heady Journey of a Director and His *Secaucus Seven*." *New York Times*, March 6, 1981: C: 9.

7. Unsigned review of *Pride of the Bimbos*. *Time*, July 7, 1975.

8. Lifeguard in *Piranha*. 1978.

9. Sayles, John, in Foner, Eric. "A Conversation Between Eric Foner and John Sayles." *Past Imperfect: History According to the Movies*. Edited by Mark C. Carnes. New York: Henry Holt, 1995.

10. Tighe, Kevin. Personal letter. September 6, 1998.

11. Sayles, John, in Asinof, Eliot. "Independent DGA Filmmakers." *DGA Film Special Issue*, December 1997 / January 1998: 40.

12. Dickerson, Ernest. Phone conversation. September 25, 1998.

13. O'Connor, John. "From John Sayles: A Flawed Hero for the 90's." *New York Times*, June 4, 1989: II: 27.

14. Jones, James Earl. Phone conversation. April 7, 1998.

15. Terkel, Studs. Phone conversation. January 29, 1998.

16. Doel, Frances. Phone conversation. August 6, 1998.

17. Redmond, John Henry. Phone conversation. September 2, 1998.

18. John Furia Jr. Career Achievement Award 1997 Program. Writers Guild Foundation. Writers Guild Theatre, Los Angeles, California, February 13, 1998.

19. Kristofferson, Kris. Phone conversation. March 4, 1999.

20. Savoca, Nancy. Phone conversation. March 3, 1999.

21. Wexler, Haskell. Phone conversation. January 11, 1999.

SOURCES FOR CHAPTERS

CHAPTER 1

THE INDEPENDENT FILMMAKER AND HIS PRODUCTION MODEL

Dante, Joe. Phone conversation. November 23, 1998.

Doel, Frances. Phone conversation. August 6, 1998.

Pierson, John. *Spike, Mike, Slackers & Dykes.* New York: Hyperion, 1995.

Schwarzbaum, Lisa. "Independents' Day." *Entertainment Weekly Special Issue,* November/December 1997: 60.

CHAPTER 2

THE MAKING OF *RETURN OF THE SECAUCUS SEVEN:* THE SCRIPT

Chute, David. "John Sayles: Designated Writer." *Film Comment,* May/June 1981: 54–59.

Doel, Frances. Phone conversation. August 6, 1998.

Gleiberman, Owen. "The New Hollywood: Inside the World of Independent Films." *Entertainment Weekly Special Issue,* November/December 1997: 88.

"Guns for Sayles." *Venice,* April 1998: 41–43.

Harmetz, Aljean. "Heady Journey. . . . " *New York Times,* March 16, 1981: C: 9.

Johnston, Trevor. "Sayles Talk." *Sight and Sound,* September 1993: 26.

Katz, Steven D. "Interview with John Sayles." *Cinematic Motion: Film Directing: A Workshop for Staging Scenes.* Los Angeles: Michael Wiese Productions, 1992: 11–19.

Lawson, Steve. "John Sayles: A Man for All Media." *New York Times Magazine,* April 17, 1983: 108.

Ryan, Jack. *Ordinary People: The Cinema of John Sayles.* Ann Arbor, Mich.: UMI Research Press, 1994.

Sayles, John. Harold Lloyd Masters Seminar at the American Film Institute. Los Angeles, California, December 10, 1985.

———. *Sayles on Sayles.* Edited by Gavin Smith. Boston: Faber and Faber, 1998.

———. *Thinking in Pictures: The Making of the Movie* Matewan. Boston Houghton Mifflin, 1987.

Schwarzbaum, Lisa, "Independents' Day," *Entertainment Weekly Special Issue,* November/December 1997: 60.

Span, Paul. "The Independent Obsession." *Washington Post,* October 15, 1987: C: 1.

Strathairn, David. Phone conversation. May 26, 1999.

CHAPTER 3

THE MAKING OF *RETURN OF THE SECAUCUS SEVEN*

THE PRODUCTION

Asinof, Eliot. "Independent DGA Filmmakers." *DGA Film Special Issue,* December 1997/January 1998: 40.

Bernard, Tom. Phone conversation. March 5, 1999.

Chute, David. "John Sayles: Designated Writer." *Film Comment,* May/June 1981: 54–59.

Daring, Mason. Personal interview. Marblehead, Massachusetts. June 2, 1998.

Ebert, Roger. "Review of *Return of the Secaucus Seven.*" *Philadelphia Evening Bulletin,* February 28, 1981.

Harmetz, Aljean. "Financial Security Aids Sayles in Making Movies." *New York Times,* October 25, 1983: 3: 25.

Johnston, Trevor. "Sayles Talk." *Sight and Sound,* September 1993: 26.

Jost, Jon. "The End of the Indies: Death of the Sayles Men." *Film Comment,* January/February 1989: 42.

Lawson, Steve. "John Sayles: A Man for All Media." *New York Times Magazine,* April 17, 1983: 108.

Persichetti, John (film colorist). Personal interview. Sony Pictures Studios, Culver City, California. May 25, 1999.

Pierson, John. *Spike, Mike, Slackers & Dykes.* New York: Hyperion, 1995.

Rainier, Peter. "The Young and the Gifted." *Vogue,* September 1981: 383.

Ratner, Megan. "Borderlines." *Filmmaker,* Summer 1996: 32.

Rosen, David, with Peter Hamilton. *Off-Hollywood: The Making and Marketing of Independent Films.* New York: Grove Weidenfeld, 1987.

Sayles, Doug. Personal interview. Albany, New York. May 22, 1998.

Sayles, John. "Cassavetes Sources. . . . " *New York Times,* May 12, 1991.

Schwarzbaum, Lisa. "Independents' Day." *Entertainment Weekly Special Issue,* November/December 1997: 60.

Skorman, Richard. *Off-Hollywood Movies: A Film Lover's Guide.* New York: Harmony, 1989.

Thomson, David. *Overexposures: The Crisis in American Filmmaking.* New York: William Morrow, 1981.

CHAPTER 4

THE SAYLES FAMILY OF SCHENECTADY, NEW YORK

Coburn, Randy Sue. "This Generation Isn't Lost. . . . " *Esquire,* November 1982: 68.

Daring, Mason. Personal interview. Marblehead, Massachusetts. June 2, 1998.

"Guns for Sayles." *Venice,* April 1998: 41–43.

Lawson, Steve. "John Sayles: A Man for All Media." *New York Times Magazine,* April 17, 1983: 108.

Maddaus, Elsie M. (archivist). Schenectady County Historical Society, letter and clippings. July 29, 1997.

Otis, Caroline (Hall). Phone conversation. October 10, 1998.

Sayles, Donald. Personal interview. Schenectady, New York. May 20–21, 1998. Phone conversations and letters, 1998–1999.

Sayles, Doug. Personal interview. Albany, New York. May 22, 1998.

Sayles, John. "The Making of a Writer." *New York Times Book Review,* September 6, 1981: 3.

———. *Writers Dreaming.* Edited by Naomi Epel. New York: Vintage, 1993.

Sayles, Mary. Personal interview. Schenectady, New York. May 20–21, 1998.

CHAPTER 5

NUMBER 80, JOHN SAYLES, 1967 ALL-COUNTY FOOTBALL

Aldi, Al (high school classmate and teammate). Personal interview. Schenectady, New York. May 20, 1998.

Lawson, Steve. "John Sayles: A Man for All Media." *New York Times Magazine,* April 17, 1983: 108.

Lida, David. "John Sayles: Militant Moviemaker." *W,* June 15–22, 1987: 17.

Mara, Philip (boyhood friend). Personal interview. Schenectady, New York. May 21, 1998.

Mulvaney, Larry (football coach). Personal interview. Schenectady, New York. May 21, 1998.

O'Connor, Adelle (teacher). Phone conversation. May 21, 1998.

Sayles, Donald. Personal interview. Schenectady, New York. May 20–21, 1998. Phone conversations and letters, 1998–99.

Sayles, Doug. Personal interview. Albany, New York. May 22, 1998.

Sayles, John. "Hoop." *The Anarchist's Convention and Other Stories.* New York: Little, Brown, 1979.

———. *Sayles on Sayles.* Edited by Gavin Smith. Boston: Faber and Faber, 1998.

Sayles, Mary. Personal interview. Schenectady, New York. May 20–21, 1998.

CHAPTER 6

THE ODD DUCK OF THE GREEN ROOM

Beezard, Tom (alumni director, Williams College). Personal interview. Williamstown, Massachusetts, January 5, 1999. E-mail correspondence.

Criden, Andrew (psychology professor). Phone conversation. May 24, 1998.

Davis, Thulani. "Blue Collar Auteur." *American Film,* June 1991: 19–22.

Dreifus, Claudia. "Interview with John Sayles." *The Progressive,* November 1991: 30.

Fonteneau-McCann, Lynne K. (archivist, Williams College). Letter. October 14, 1997.

Freedman, Samuel G. "John Sayles' Labor of Love." *Rolling Stone,* October 8, 1987: 27.

Jacobs, Ron. "*Of Mice and Men* Opens. . . . " *Williams Record,* March 5, 1971: 2.

Johnston, Trevor. "Sayles Talk." *Sight and Sound,* September 1993: 26.

Kerr, Paul. "John Sayles Imaging Women." (British) *Monthly Film Bulletin,* January 1984: 28.

Mara, Philip (boyhood friend). Personal interview. Schenectady, New York. May 21, 1998.

Otis, Caroline (Hall). Phone conversation. October 10, 1998.

Renzi, Ralph. Personal interview. Williamstown, Massachusetts. May 22, 1998. Phone conversations and letters.

Rioaben, Charles. "Review of *My Piece of the Pie.*" *Williams (Mass.) Record,* October 21, 1971.

Sayles, Donald. Personal interview. Schenectady, New York. May 20–21, 1998. Phone conversations and letters, 1998–99.

Sayles, Doug. Personal interview. Albany, New York. May 22, 1998.

Sayles, John. Harold Lloyd Master, Seminar at the American Film Institute. Los Angeles, California, December 10, 1985.

———. "Making of a Writer. . . . " *New York Times Book Review,* September 6, 1981: 3.

———. "This Place." *Gulielmensian 1972.* Williamstown, Massachusetts: Williams College, 1972.

———. *Writers Dreaming.* Edited by Naomi Epel. New York: Vintage, 1993: 219–28.

Sayles, Mary. Personal interview. Schenectady, New York. May 20–21, 1998.

Strathairn, David. Phone conversation. May 26, 1999.

Vecsey, George. "John Sayles Steps Up to Bat." *New York Times,* August 28, 1988: H: 20.

CHAPTER 7
THE REAL WORLD AND THE WRITER

Coburn, Randy Sue. "This Generation Isn't Lost. . . . " *Esquire,* November 1982: 68.

Dreifus, Claudia. "Interview with John Sayles." *The Progressive,* November 1991: 30.

Katz, Susan. "A Conversation with John Sayles." *The Journal,* July 1996: 31.

Lawson, Steve. "John Sayles: A Man for All Media." *New York Times Magazine,* April 17, 1983: 108.

Levitt, Shelly. "John Sayles." *People,* March 8, 1993: 86.

McClellan, Joseph. "Review of *The Pride of the Bimbos.*" *Washington Post,* August 24, 1975: WBK1.

McConville, Edward. "Review of *Union Dues.*" *The Nation,* October 22, 1977: 225.

Mewshaw, Michael. "Review of *Union Dues.*" *New York Times,* August 4, 1977: VII: 15.

Renzi, Ralph. Personal interview. Williamstown, Massachusetts. May 22, 1998. Phone conversations and letters.

"Review of *Pride of the Bimbos.*" Unsigned. *Time,* July 7, 1975: 61.

Sayles, Doug. Personal interview. Albany, New York. May 22, 1998.

Sayles, John. "The Making of a Writer. . . . " *New York Times Book Review,* September 6, 1981: 3.

———. *Sayles on Sayles.* Edited by Gavin Smith. Boston: Faber and Faber, 1998.

———. *Writers Dreaming.* Edited by Naomi Epel. New York: Vintage, 1993.

Still, Alexander. "Review of 'I-Nebraska.'" *The Nation,* April 7, 1979: 376.

Strathairn, David. Phone conversation. May 26, 1999.

CHAPTER 8
WRITER FOR HIRE: THE ROGER CORMAN YEARS

Corman, Roger. Phone conversation. July 22, 1998.

Dante, Joe. Phone conversation. November 23, 1998.

Dillman, Bradford. Personal letter. March 30, 1998.

Doel, Frances. Phone conversation. August 6, 1998.

Dreifus, Claudia. "Interview with John Sayles." *The Progressive,* November 1991: 30.

Hillier, Jim. *The New Hollywood.* London, England: Studio Vista, 1992.

Katz, Susan. "A Conversation with John Sayles." *The Journal,* July 1996: 31.

Otis, Caroline (Hall). Phone conversation. October 10, 1998.

Pollack, D. "Review of *Piranha.*" *Variety,* August 9, 1978.

"*Piranha* Remake." *Hollywood Reporter,* December 7, 1997.

Sayles, John. Harold Lloyd Masters Seminar at the American Film Institute. Los Angeles, California, December 10, 1985.

Stein, Ruthie. "Sticking to Their Guns." *San Francisco Chronicle,* March 8, 1998: 34–35.

CHAPTER 9
WRITER FOR HIRE: THEATER, FILM, TELEVISION, AND PRINT

Bernstein, Abbie. "Director/Writer John Sayles. . . . " *Drama-Logue,* June 9–15, 1993.

Chute, David. "John Sayles: Designated Writer." *Film Comment,* May/June 1981: 54–59.

Coburn, Randy Sue. "This Generation Isn't Lost. . . . " *Esquire,* November 1982: 68.

Corliss, Richard. "Review of *The Howling.*" *Time,* April 20, 1981: 83.

Corman, Roger. Phone conversation. July 22, 1998.

Dante, Joe. Phone conversation. November 23, 1998.

Denby, David. "Review of *The Howling.*" *New York,* February 15, 1983: 48.

Dreifus, Claudia. "Interview with John Sayles." *The Progressive,* November 1991: 30.

Hillier, Jim. *The New Hollywood.* London, England: Studio Vista. 1992.

Jenkins, Steve. "Review of *Alligator.*" (British) *Monthly Film Bulletin,* March 1982: 39.

Johnston, Trevor. "Sayles Talk." *Sight and Sound,* September 1993: 26.

Kawain, Bruce. "*The Funhouse* and *The Howling.*" *American Horrors: Essays on the Modern American Horror Film.*" Edited by Gregory A. Waller. Urbana, IL: University of Illinois Press, 1987.

Lawson, Steve. "John Sayles: A Man for. . . . " *New York Times Magazine,* April 17, 1983: 108.

Long, Marion. "Interview with John Sayles." *Omni,* June 1983: 44.

Martin, Pamela Sue. Personal letter. May 12, 1998.

Minsky, Terri. "Sayles and Bargains." *Premiere,* September 1991: 38–40.

Molyneaux, Libby. "Interview with John Sayles." *UCLA Bruin,* November 5, 1981.

Osbourne, David. "From Hoboken to Hollywood—And Back." *American Film,* October 1982: 30.

Seegers, F. "Review of *Battle Beyond the Stars.*" *Variety,* July 30, 1980.

McCarthy, T. "Review of *The Lady in Red.*" *Variety,* August 1, 1979.

Rich, Frank. "Review of *Turnbuckle* and *New Hope for the Dead.*" *New York Times,* July 8, 1981: C: 25.

Sayles, John. Harold Lloyd Masters Seminar at the American Film Institute. Los Angeles, California, December 10, 1985.

———. "At the Republican Convention." *New Republic,* August 2, 1980: 20–25.

Sterrett, David. "Review of *Alligator.*" *Christian Science Monitor,* June 25, 1981: 18.

Winsten, Archer. "Review of *Alligator.*" *New York Post,* June 5, 1981: 43.

CHAPTER 10

LIANNA AND THE RISE OF MAGGIE RENZI

Bernard, Tom. Phone conversation. March 5, 1999.

Bernstein, Abbie. "Director/Writer John Sayles. . . . " *Drama-Logue,* June 9–15, 1993.

Biskind, Peter. "The Sweet Hell of Success." *Premiere,* October 1997: 85–100.

Canby, Vincent. "Review of *Lianna.*" *New York Times,* January 19, 198: III: 22.

Chute, David. "John Sayles: Designated Writer." *Film Comment,* May/June 1981: 54–59.

Corliss, Richard. "Review of *Lianna*." *Time,* March 14, 1983: 90.

Donahue, Suzanne Mary. *American Film Distribution:The Changing Marketplace.* Ann Arbor, MI: UMI Research Press, 1987.

Harmetz, Aljean. "Heady Journey. . . . " *New York Times,* March 1981: C: 9.

Holmund, Christine. "When Is a Lesbian. . . . " *Camera Obscura, A Journal of Feminism and Film Theory 25/26,* 1991: 145–78.

Kaplan, Nelly. *Shot/Countershot: Film Tradition and Women's Cinema.* Eited by Lucy Fischer. Princeton, N.J.: Princeton University Press, 1989.

Kerr, Paul. "John Sayles Imaging Women." (British) *Monthly Film Bulletin,* January 1984: 600.

Lawson, Steve. "John Sayles: A Man for All Media." *New York Times Magazine,* April 17, 1983: 108.

Maltin, Leonard. *Movie & Video Guide 1999.* New York: Signet, 1998.

Marney, Angela. "*Lianna:* A Movie. . . . " *Off Our Backs,* April 1983: 18.

Osbourne, David. "From Hoboken to Hollywood—And Back." *American Film,* October 1982: 30.

Otis, Caroline (Hall). Phone conversation. October 10, 1998.

Palley, Marcia. "Women in Love." *Film Comment,* March/April 1986: 35–39.

Parish, James Robert. *Gays and Lesbians in Mainstream Cinema.* Jefferson, N.C.: McFarland, 1993: 44.

Reed, Rex. "Review of *Lianna*." *New York Post,* January 19, 1983.

Renzi, Ralph. Personal interview. Williamstown, Massachusetts. May 22, 1998. Phone conversations and letters.

Rickey, Carrie. "Review of *Lianna*." *Village Voice,* January 25, 1983: 28, 50.

Russo, Vito. *The Celluloid Closet.* New York: Borgo Press, 1991.

Sayles, Donald. Personal interview. Schenectady, New York. May 20–21, 1998. Phone conversations and letters, 1998–99.

Sayles, John. *Sayles on Sayles.* Eited by Gavin Smith. Boston: Faber and Faber, 1998.

Sayles, Mary. Personal interview. Schenectady, New York. May 20–21.

Seidenberg, Robert. "In Production: *Matewan*." *Theater Crafts,* April 1987: 45–48.

Skorman, Richard. *Off-Hollywood Movies:A Film Lover's Guide.* New York: Harmony, 1989.

Stacey, Jackie. "If You Don't Play. . . . " *Immortal Invisible: Lesbians and the Moving Image.* London, England: Routledge, 1995.

Sterritt, David. "Review of *Lianna*." *Christian Science Monitor,* May 12, 1983: 16

Stone, Judy. "John Sayles." *Eye on the World: Conversations with International Filmmakers.* New York: Silman James, 1997.

Van Gelder, Lindsey. "Director/Screenwriter John Sayles. . . . " *Ms.,* June 1983: 31–36.

CHAPTER 11

BABY IT'S YOU AND THE BATTLE WITH PARAMOUNT

Armstrong, Curtis. Phone conversation. April 13, 1998.

Auty, Chris. "Review of *Baby It's You.*" (British) *Monthly Film Bulletin,* November 1984: 330.

Benson, Sheila. "Review of *The Clan of the Cave Bear.*" *Los Angeles Times,* January 24, 1986: 1.

Bernard, Tom. Phone conversation. March 5, 1999.

Chanko, Kenneth. "John Sayles." *Films in Review,* February 1983: 94–98.

Denby, David. "Review of *The Clan of the Cave Bear.*" *New York,* February 10, 1986: 63.

Hoffman, Jan. "Review of *The Clan of the Cave Bear.*" *Village Voice,* February 4, 1986: 60.

"Interview with John Sayles." *Video Review,* November 1982.

Kopkind, A. "Review of *Enormous Changes.*" *The Nation,* April 13, 1985: 44.

Kroll, Jack. "Review of *The Clan of the Cave Bear.*" *Newsweek,* January 27, 1986: 86.

Lawson, Steve. "John Sayles: A Man for All Media." *New York Times Magazine,* April 17, 1983: 108.

Maltin, Leonard. *Movie & Video Guide 1999.* New York: Signet, 1998.

Maslin, Janet. "Review of *Baby It's You.*" *New York Times,* April 11, 1983: III: 6.

McGhee, Dorothy. "Solidarity Forever." *American Film,* September 1987: 42.

Osbourne, David. "From Hoboken to Hollywood—And Back." *American Film,* October 1982: 30.

"Review of *Baby It's You.*" *Variety,* March 9, 1983: 18.

Robertson, Nam. "MacArthur Award Winners." *New York Times,* July 17, 1988: II: 1.

Rosen, David, with Peter Hamilton. *Off-Hollywood: The Making and Marketing of Independent Films.* New York: Grove Weidenfeld, 1987.

Shone, Tom. "A Singular Voice." *London Times,* October 13, 1996.

Stein, Harry. "How John Sayles Learned. . . . " *Premiere,* July 1999: 90–110.

CHAPTER 12

THE BROTHER FROM ANOTHER PLANET:

BACK TO GUERRILLA FILMMAKING

Auferdheide, Pat. "Sayles in Harlem." *Film Comment,* March/April 1984: 4.

Bernard, Tom. Phone conversation. March 5, 1999.

Dickerson, Ernest. Phone conversation. September 25, 1998.

George, Nelson. *Blackface: Reflections on African-Americans and The Movies.* New York: HarperCollins, 1994.

Guerrero, Ed. *Framing Blackness: The African-American Image in Film*. Philadelphia: Temple University Press, 1993.

Jones, James Earl. Phone conversation. April 7, 1998.

McGhee, Dorothy. "Solidarity Forever." *American Film*, September 1987: 42.

Reed, Rex. "Review of *Brother*." *New York Post*, September 14, 1984: 24.

"Review of *Brother*." *Variety*, May 23, 1984: 13–15.

Ryan, Jack. *John Sayles, Filmmaker*. Jefferson, N.C.: McFarland, 1998.

Ryan, Michael, and Douglas Kellner. *Camera Politica: The Politics and Ideology of Contemporary Hollywood Film*. Bloomington: Indiana University Press, 1988.

Salamon, Julie. "Sayles Pitch. . . . " *Wall Street Journal*, May 11, 1984: 28.

Sayles, John. Harold Lloyd Master Seminar at the American Film Institute. Los Angeles, California, December 10, 1985.

———. *Writers Dreaming*. Edited by Naomi Epel. New York: Vintage, 1993.

Skorman, Richard. *Off-Hollywood Movies: A Film Lover's Guide*. New York: Harmony, 1989.

"Talk of the Town: *Brother*." *The New Yorker*, January 2, 1984: 20-22.

Vecsey, George. "Interview with John Sayles." *New York Times*, August 23, 1987: H: 20.

Wexler, Haskell. Phone conversation. January 11, 1999.

CHAPTER 13

WHAT'S A GENIUS TO DO?

Cliff, Molly. "Review of *The Glass Menagerie*." *Berkshire (Mass.) Eagle*, August 21, 1985.

Collins, Monica. "Review of *Unnatural Causes*." *USA Today*, November 11, 1986.

Ebert, Roger. "Review of *Hard Choices*." *Chicago Sun-Times*, September 26, 1986.

Geeslin, Ned. "I'm on Fire." *Time*, April 15, 1985: 15.

Henry, William A., III. "Williamstown Caps Season. . . . " *Time*, September 2, 1985: 72.

Hoberman, J. *Vulgar Modernism: Writing on Movies and other Media*. Philadelphia, PA: Temple University Press, 1991.

Hulse, Thomas. "Review of *The Glass Menagerie*." *Berkshire (Mass.) Eagle*, August 21, 1985.

Johnson, Lamont. Phone conversation. May 6, 1998.

Levine, Jonathan. "Theater Season." *Berkshire (Mass.) Eagle*, August 21, 1988.

Marsh, David. *Glory Days*. New York: Pantheon, 1987.

Renzi, Ralph. Personal interview. Williamstown, Massachusetts. May 22, 1998. Phone conversations and letters.

Rotundi, Cesar. *Films in Review*, January 1985: 48.

Ryan, Jack. *John Sayles, Filmmaker*. Jefferson, N.C.: McFarland, 1998.

Seidenberg, Robert. "In Production: *Matewan*." *Theater Crafts*, April 1987: 45–48.

Shales, Thomas. "Review of *Unnatural Causes.*" *Washington Post,* November 11, 1986: D: 1.

Tighe, Kevin. Personal letter. September 6, 1998.

Van Gelder, Lawrence. "At the Movies: John Sayles' Double Life." *New York Times,* May 30, 1986: C: 8.

Wilmington, Michael. "Review of *Hard Choices.*" *Los Angeles Times Calendar,* August 1, 1986: 6.

CHAPTER 14

MATEWAN: THE SAYLES PRODUCTION COMPANY

AND ITS FIRST CELEBRITIES

Bishop, Dan. Phone conversation. October 5, 1998.

Daring, Mason. Personal interview. Marblehead, Massachusetts. June 2, 1998.

Freedman, Samuel G. "Review of *Matewan.*" *Rolling Stone,* October 8, 1987: 27–28.

Harmetz, Aljean. "Independent Films. . . . " *New York Times,* April 6, 1987: C: 11.

Jones, James Earl. Phone conversation. April 7, 1998.

Kauffmann, Stanley. "Review of *Matewan.*" *New Republic,* September 7, 1987: 24.

Lida, David. "John Sayles: Militant Moviemaker." *W,* June 15, 1987: 17.

Maltin, Leonard. *Movie & Video Guide 1999.* New York: Signet, 1998.

Margaranois, Maria. "Review of *Matewan.*" *The Nation,* October 17, 1987: 427.

McGhee, Dorothy. "Solidarity Forever." *American Film,* September 1987: 42.

O'Brien, Tim. "Review of *Matewan.*" *Commonweal,* November 6, 1987: 626.

Renzi, Ralph. Personal interview. Williamstown, Massachusetts. May 22, 1998. Phone conversations and letters.

Ryan, Jack. *John Sayles, Filmmaker.* Jefferson, N.C.: McFarland, 1998.

Sayles, John. Harold Lloyd Masters Seminar at the American Film Institute. Los Angeles, California, December 10, 1985.

———. *Thinking in Pictures: The Making of the Movie* Matewan. Boston: Houghton Mifflin, 1987.

Seidenberg, Robert. "In Production: *Matewan.*" *Theater Crafts,* April 1987: 45–48.

Sheehan, Henry. "Review of *Men with Guns.*" *Orange County (Calif.) Register,* March 13, 1998.

———. "Union Busting." *Reader,* September 4, 1987: 1f.

Span, Paul. "The Independent Obsession. . . . " *Washington Post,* October 15, 1987: C: 1.

Tighe, Kevin. Personal letter. September 6, 1998.

Wexler, Haskell. Phone conversation. January 11, 1999.

CHAPTER 15

EIGHT MEN OUT: THE PLAYERS AND THEIR PASTIME

Angell, Roger. "No, But I Saw the Game." *New Yorker,* July 31, 1989: 41–56.

Asinof, Eliot. "Independent DGA Filmmakers."*DGA Film Special Issue,* December 1997/January 1998: 40.

Bishop, Dan. Phone conversation. October 5, 1998.

Daring, Mason. Personal interview. Marblehead, Massachusetts. June 2, 1998.

Kozak, Jim. "The Sayles Pitch." *Box Office,* September 1988: 7–8.

Erickson, Hal. *Baseball in the Movies:The Comprehensive Reference, 1915–1991.* Jefferson, N.C.: McFarland, 1992: 117-28.

Foner, Eric. "A Conversation between Eric Foner and John Sayles." *Past Imperfect: History According to the Movies.* Edited by Mark C. Carnes. NewYork: Henry Holt, 1995.

Lerner, Michael. Personal interview. Beverly Hills, California. March 4, 1998.

Maslin, Janet. "A Nation Disillusioned." *New York Times,* September 2, 1988: III: 3.

Read, James. Phone conversation. May 8, 1998.

Roberts, Jerry. "Pitching Indie Ethic." *Variety,* July 20, 1994: 22.

Sayles, Doug. Personal interview. Albany, NewYork. May 22, 1998.

Sayles, John. Harold Lloyd Masters Seminar at the American Film Institute. Los Angeles, California, May 29, 1996.

Schickel, Richard. "Review of *Eight Men Out.*" *Time,* September 15, 1988: 63.

Sheed, Wilfred. "Why Can't the Movies. . . . " *New York Times,* May 14, 1989: II: 1.

Siebert, Charles. "It's the 1919 World Series. . . . " *Esquire,* August 1988: 129–37.

Terkel, Studs. Phone conversation. January 29, 1998.

Tighe, Kevin. Personal letter. September 6, 1998.

Vecsey, George. "John Sayles Steps Up. . . . " *New York Times,* August 28, 1988: H: 1.

Will, George. "Touching a National Nerve." *Berkshire (Mass.) Eagle,* October 6, 1999: A: 11.

Wulf, Steve. "Review of *Eight Men Out.*" *Sports Illustrated,* September 12, 1988: 18.

CHAPTER 16

SHANNON'S DEAL, LOS GUSANOS, AND *CITY OF HOPE*: THE SAYLES DISCIPLES AND COMMUNITY ISSUES

Bishop, Dan. Phone conversation. October 5, 1998.

Boyd, Kevin. Phone conversation. October 21, 1998.

Brown, Georgia. "Review of *City of Hope*." *Village Voice*, October 22, 1991: 64.

Cady, Patrick. Phone conversation. August 8, 1998.

Cantor, Jay. "Review of *Los Gusanos*." *New York Times Book Review*, July 16, 1991: VII: 7.

Dante, Joe. Phone conversation. November 23, 1998.

Denby, David. "Review of *City of Hope*." *New York*, October 28, 1991: 56.

DiMatteo, Robert. "Philadelphia Lawyer." *Film Comment*, July 1990: 2–3.

Firmat, Gustavo Perez. "Memories of a Lost Island." *Washington Post*, May 26, 1991: WBK1.

Foner, Eric. "A Conversation between Eric Foner and John Sayles." *Past Imperfect: History According to the Movies*. Edited by Mark C. Carnes. New York: Henry Holt, 1995.

Freedman, Samuel G. "How John Sayles. . . . " *New York Times*, April 15, 1990: H: 33.

Freeman, "Interview with John Sayles." *Pulse*, March 1993: 73.

Gazzale, Robert. Phone conversation. March 10, 1999.

Goldstein, Patrick. "Spring Sayles on TV." *Interview*, May 5, 1990: 23.

"Guns for Sayles." *Venice*, April 1998: 41–43.

Haitman, Diana. "Making a Big 'Deal'. . . . " *Los Angeles Times*, April 12, 1990: F: 1.

Henson, Robby. Phone conversation. April 13, 1998.

hooks, bell. *Reel to Real: Race, Sex, and Class at the Movies*. New York: Routledge, 1996.

Lee, Robert. "Review of *Los Gusanos*." *American Book Review*, August/September 1992: 22.

Lopate, Philip. "With Pen in Hand." *New York Times*, August 10, 1992: II: 7.

Minsky, Terri. "Sayles and Bargains." *Premiere*, September 1991: 38–40.

Newman, Kim. "Review of *City of Hope*." *Sight and Sound*, December 1991: 37.

O'Connor, John. "From John Sayles: A Flawed Hero for the '90's." *New York Times*, June 4, 1989: H: 27.

Pierson, John. *Spike, Mike, Slackers & Dykes*. New York: Hyperion, 1995.

"Review of *City of Hope*." *Hollywood Reporter*, January 25, 1991: 10.

"Review of *City of Hope*." *Variety*, January 25, 1991: 2.

Rosenthal, Stuart. "Bill Forsyth Plots. . . . " *New York Times*, September 18, 1988: H: 22.

St. John, Edward B. "Review of *Los Gusanos*." *Library Journal*, April 15, 1991: 128.

Savoca, Nancy. Phone conversation. March 3, 1999.

Sayles, John. *Sayles on Sayles*. Edited by Gavin Smith. Boston: Faber and Faber, 1998.

Shales, Tom. "Great Deal on NBC." *Washington Post*, May 16, 1990: D: 1.

Sterritt, David. "Review of *City of Hope*." *Christian Science Monitor*, November 19, 1991: 10.

Turan, Kenneth. "Review of *City of Hope*." *Los Angeles Times Calendar*, October 25, 1991: 1.

Zurawick, David. "Review of *Shannon's Deal*." *Baltimore Sun*, 1991.

CHAPTER 17

PASSION FISH: SOME CRITICAL CONVERSIONS

Cady, Patrick. Phone conversation. August 8, 1998.

Charity, Tom. "Sayles Pitch." *Time Out* (London), August 25, 1993.

Johnston, Trevor. "Sayles Talk." *Sight and Sound,* September 1993: 26.

Levitt, Shelly. "John Sayles." *People,* March 8, 1993: 86.

Redmond, John Henry. Phone conversation. September 2, 1998.

Renzi, Ralph. Personal interview. Williamstown, Massachusetts. May 22, 1998. Phone conversations and letters.

Sayles, Mary. Personal interview. Schenectady, New York. May 20–21, 1998.

United States Court of Appeals for the Fourth Circuit. No. 90-1147 (CA 93-704-A). *Virginia L. Towler, Plaintiff Appellant vs. John Sayles et al., Defendant Appellees.* Filed March 20, 1996.

West, Elaine. Phone conversation. August 5, 1998.

CHAPTER 18

THE SECRET OF ROAN INISH: A GIFT TO MAGGIE RENZI

Dante, Joe. Phone conversation. November 23, 1998.

Daring, Mason. Personal interview. Marblehead, Massachusetts. June 2, 1998.

Frogley, Mike, and Matt Symonds. "Interview with John Sayles." *Sprocket,* matdel.eng.cam.ac.uk/sprocket/interviews/sayles.html

Kemp, Philip. "Review of *Roan Inish.*" *Sight and Sound,* August 1996: 63.

Gamerman, Amy. "Review of *Roan Inish.*" *Wall Street Journal,* March 2, 1995: 12.

Henson, Robby. Phone conversation. April 13, 1998.

Jackson, Kevin. "How to Beat the System." *The Independent* (London), October 6, 1996.

Levy, Shawn. "The Secret of *Roan Inish's* Success." *Sunday Oregonian,* July 7, 1995.

Miller, Paul. Phone conversation. March 19, 1999.

Moser, Margaret. "*Lone Star* Producer Maggie Renzi." *Austin* (Texas) *Chronicle,* June 28, 1996: 34–35.

"Review of *Roan Inish.*" *Entertainment Weekly,* February 10, 1995.

"Review of *Roan Inish.*" *Variety,* May 9, 1994.

Sayles, John. Harold Lloyd Masters Seminar at the American Film Institute. Los Angeles, California, May 29, 1996.

———. Interview with Leonard Maltin. Writers Guild Foundation Awards. Writers Guild Theatre. Los Angeles, California, February 13, 1998.

———. *Sayles on Sayles.* Edited by Gavin Smith. Boston: Faber and Faber, 1998.

Skerry Movies Corporation. "*Secret of Roan Inish* Production Notes." October 27, 1993: 1–30.

Turan, Kenneth. "Review of *Roan Inish.*" *Los Angeles Times Calendar,* February 3, 1995: 1.

Wexler, Haskell. Phone conversation. January 11, 1999.

Young, Josh. "Mr. Rewriter Returns." *Esquire,* June 1996: 36.

CHAPTER 19

LONE STAR: A BIG SCORE, A SECOND START

Alexander, Max. "Sayles-manship." *Variety,* June 17, 1996.

Boyd, Kevin. Phone conversation. October 21, 1998.

Daring, Mason. Personal interview. Marblehead, Massachusetts. June 2, 1998.

Dempsey, John. "*Lone Star* on Cable." *Variety,* January 27, 1997: 3.

Fitzgerald, Nate. Phone conversation. October 10, 1998.

Frogley, Mike, and Matt Symonds. "Interview with John Sayles." Sprocket, matdel.eng.cam.ac.uk/sprocket/interviews/sayles.html

Henson, Robby. Phone conversation. April 13, 1998.

Hornaday, Ann. "At Many a Multiplex." *New York Times,* August 4, 1996: II: 18.

Johnston, Trevor. "Sayles Talk." *Sight and Sound,* September 1993: 26.

Katz, Susan. "A Conversation with John Sayles." *The Journal,* July 1996: 31.

Kristofferson, Kris. Phone conversation. March 4, 1999.

Lamoreaux, Michelle. "Independent Streak." *Entertainment Weekly,* June 14, 1996: 6.

LaSalle, Mick. "Review of *Lone Star.*" *San Francisco Chronicle,* June 21, 1996: D: 3.

Longsdorf, Amy. "Review of *Lone Star.*" *Allentown (Pa.) Call,* August 8, 1996.

Maslin, Janet. "Review of *Lone Star.*" *New York Times,* June 21, 1996: B: 1.

Miller, Paul. Phone conversation. March 19, 1999.

Moser, Margaret. "*Lone Star* Producer Maggie Renzi." *Austin (Texas) Chronicle,* June 28, 1996: 34–35.

Otis, Caroline (Hall). Phone conversation. October 10, 1998.

Parks, Louis B. "Law and Borders." *Houston (Texas) Chronicle,* June 30, 1996.

Rea, Steve. "Interview with John Sayles." *Philadelphia Inquirer,* July 7, 1996: G: 7.

Spines, Christine. "Interview with John Sayles." *Premiere,* July 1996: 40–51.

Ratner, Megan. "Borderlines." *Filmmaker,* Summer 1996: 32.

Sayles, John. Harold Lloyd Masters Seminar at the American Film Institute. Los Angeles, California, May 29, 1996.

Shones, Tom. "A Singular Voice." *Sunday Times* (London), October 13, 1996.

Stein, Harry. "How John Sayles Learned. . . . " *Premiere,* July 1999: 90–110.

Tucker, Ken. "Review of *Lone Star.*" *Entertainment Weekly,* June 21, 1996.

Turan, Kenneth. "Review of *Lone Star.*" *Los Angeles Times,* June 21, 1996: F: 1.

CHAPTER 20

MEN WITH GUNS: FINANCING THE SAYLES FILM

Bernard, Tom. Phone conversation. March 5, 1999.

Caro, Mark. "Director Makes. . . . " *Chicago Tribune,* April 27, 1998: E: 8.

DeNardo, James. Personal interview. Los Angeles, California. February 2, 1999.

Ebert, Roger. "Review of *Men with Guns.*" *Chicago Sun-Times,* March 27, 1998.

Furia, John Jr.. Career Achievement Award 1997 Program. Writers Guild Foundation. Writers Guild Theatre. Los Angeles, California, February 13, 1998.

Hernandez, Eugene. "IFC Puts Money. . . . " March 6, 1998: Indiewire.com/film/biz/biz_07306_IFCdeal.html

Independent Film Channel Productions. "The Making of *Men with Guns.*" 1998.

Maslin, Janet. "Review of *Men with Guns.*" *New York Times,* March 6, 1998: E: 29.

Miller, Paul. Phone conversation. March 19, 1999.

Pierson, John. *Spike, Mike, Slackers & Dykes.* New York: Hyperion, 1995.

Sayles, Donald. Personal interview. Schenectady, New York. May 20–21, 1998. taped conversations and letters, 1998–99.

Sayles, Doug. Personal interview. Albany, New York. May 22, 1998.

Shillington, Susan (Director of Steinbeck Center). E-mail. May 14, 1998.

Simon, Joel. "John Sayles, Long a Director at the Edge Crosses a Border." *New York Times,* March 9, 1997: II: 15.

Stein, Ruthie. "Sticking to Their Guns." *San Francisco Chronicle,* March 8, 1998: 34–35.

Sterngold, James. "At the Movies: Sayles' New Parable." *New York Times,* February 20, 1998: C: 8.

"Screen Writers Guild Award." *Variety,* February 17, 1998.

Whipp, Glenn. "Review of *Men with Guns.*" *Los Angeles Daily News Weekend* section, March 13, 1998: 9.

Wilmington, Michael. "Review of *Men With Guns.*" *Chicago Tribune,* March 27, 1998.

CHAPTER 21

LIMBO AND THE NEW DEAL

Boyd, Kevin. Phone conversation. October 21, 1998.

Daring, Mason. Personal interview. Marblehead, Massachusetts. June 2, 1998.

Dunkley, Cathy. "The Boxoffice." *Hollywood Reporter,* July 27-August 2, 1999: 71.

Giles, Jeff. "Review of *Limbo.*" *Newsweek,* June 14, 1999: 74.

Gleiberman, Owen. "Review of *Limbo.*" *Entertainment Weekly,* June 4, 1999: 59.

Grove, Martin. "Calley Not Left in *Limbo.*" *Hollywood Reporter,* May 12, 1999: 8.

Guthman, Edward. "Review of *Limbo.*" *San Francisco Chronicle,* June 4, 1999.

Holden, Stephen. "Review of *Limbo.*" *New York Times,* June 4, 1999: E: 14.

"It's a Wrap." Editorial. *Juneau Empire,* September 6, 1998: D: 2.

Kenny, Glenn. "Review of *Limbo.*" *Premiere,* June 1999: 28.

Kit, Zorianna. "Branagh Weighs Welles Role. . . . " *Hollywood Reporter,* December 13, 1999: 1.

Lemmons, Stephen. "Review of *Limbo.*" *Entertainment Today,* June 4, 1999: 8.

McCarthy, Todd. "Review of *Limbo.*" *Variety,* May 25, 1999: 16.

Persichetti, John (film colorist). Personal interview at Sony Pictures Studios, Culver City, California. May 25, 1999.

Sayles, Doug. Personal interview. Albany, New York. May 22, 1998.

Schickel, Richard. "Review of *Limbo.*" *Time,* June 7, 1999: 76.

Stein, Harry. "How Sayles Learned. . . . " *Premiere,* July 1999: 90–110.

Steuer, Joseph. "Green, Renzi Look to SPC. . . . " *Hollywood Reporter,* December 8, 1997: X: 10.

Strathairn, David. Phone conversation. May 26, 1999.

Taylor, Ella. "Review of *Limbo.*" *Los Angeles Weekly,* June 4, 1999: 37.

Turan, Kenneth. "Review of *Limbo.*" *Los Angeles Times,* June 4, 1999: F: 6.

Walsh, Rebecca Ascher, and Jeff Jensen. "Un-American Cannes Activities." *Entertainment Weekly,* June 4, 1999: 50–57.

Weinrab, Bernard, and Geraldine Fabrikant. "The Revenge of the Bean Counters." *New York Times,* June 13, 1999: 3: 1.

Wexler, Haskell. Phone conversation. January 11, 1999.

Whipp, Glenn. "Review of *Limbo.*" *Los Angeles Daily News Weekend* section, June 4, 1999: 10.

BIBLIOGRAPHY

PRIMARY SOURCES

The following chronological list of writings, lyrics, and lectures
have all been written by John Sayles.

THEATER: SCRIPTWRITING AND DIRECTING

New Hope for the Dead. Off-off Broadway, 1981.

Turnbuckle. Off-off Broadway, 1981.

FICTION: NOVELS AND SHORT STORY COLLECTIONS

Pride of the Bimbos. New York: Little, Brown, 1975. New York: Little, Brown, 1977.

The Anarchists' Convention and Other Stories. New York: Little, Brown, 1979.

Los Gusanos. New York: HarperCollins, 1991.

FICTION: SHORT STORIES

"I-80 Nebraska, m.490-m.205." *Atlantic Monthly,* May 1975.

"Breed." *Atlantic Monthly,* July 1976: 52–63.

"Hoops." *Atlantic Monthly,* March 1977: 37–44.

"Golden State." *Atlantic Monthly,* June 1977: 70–81.

Pride of the Bimbos (excerpt). *Fielder's Choice.* Edited by: Jerome Holtzman.
     New York: Harvest, 1979.

"Dillinger in Hollywood." *Triquarterly,* Spring 1980.

"Tan." *Soldiers and Civilians: Americans at War and at Home.* Edited by Tom Jenks. New
     York: Bantam, 1986.

"Treasure." *Esquire,* March 1988: 168–80.

"The Halfway Diner." *Atlantic Monthly,* June 1987: 59–68.

"Peeling." *Atlantic Monthly,* September 1993: 69–74.

"Keeping Time." *Rolling Stone,* December 1993: 48–52, 82–84.

SCREENPLAY

Men with Guns and *Lone Star.* New York: Faber and Faber, 1998.

LYRICS

"Homeboy" and "Promised Land" for *The Brother from Another Planet,* 1984.

"I Be Blue" for *Eight Men Out,* 1988.

"Calle Loca" for *City of Hope,* 1991.

"Guide Us to Thy Side" with Clark Walker for *The Winslow Boy,* 1999.

NONFICTION: BOOKS

Thinking in Pictures: The Making of the Movie Matewan. Boston: Houghton Mifflin 1987.

Sayles on Sayles. Edited by Gavin Smith. New York: Faber and Faber, 1998.

ARTICLES AND REVIEWS

"At the Republican Convention." *New Republic,* August 1980: 20–25.

"The Making of a Writer; I Never Think Positively." *New York Times Book Review,* September 6, 1981: 7: 3.

"Goldman, Biro, and Nyuk-Nyuk-Nyuk." Review of *Adventures in the Screen Trade* by William Goldman. *Film Comment,* May/June 1983: 72–73.

"Pregame Jitters: Shirts and Skins." *Esquire,* June 1986: 55–57.

Savage, Lon K. Forward to *Thunder in the Mountains: The West Virginia Mine Wars, 1920–21.* Pittsburgh, Pa.: University of Pittsburgh Press, 1990.

"Cassavetes's Sources Seemed to Be Our Own Doubting Lives." *New York Times,* May 12, 1991: II-17.

"Director's Cut: Punchy Delivery." *The Independent,* November 29, 1991.

Writers Dreaming. Edited by Naomi Epel. New York: Vintage, 1993.

"The Big Picture: The Twenty Best Political Films." *Mother Jones* Interactive, May/June 1996: Online Internet. Available: bsd.mojones.com

"Chicago Guy: Nelson Algren." *Conjunctions: Tributes: American Writers on American Writers.* Edited by Martine Bellen, Lee Smith, and Bradford Morrow. Annandale-on-Hudson, N.Y.: Bard College, Fall 1997.

"Inside *Eight Men Out.*" *Sport,* July 1998.

LECTURES AND SEMINARS

Harold Lloyd Masters Seminar. American Film Institute. Los Angeles, California, December 10, 1985.

Harold Lloyd Masters Seminar. American Film Institute. Los Angeles, California, May 29, 1996.

On Stage Interview: John Sayles and Leonard Maltin. A Tribute to John Sayles. Writers Guild Foundation. Los Angeles, California, February 13, 1998.

On Stage Interview. Martha Heasley Cox Center for Steinbeck Studies. San Jose, California, February 14, 1998.

INTERVIEWS

The following list includes those who generously helped me with information
about John Sayles and about matters pertinent to the topic.
The date given indicates the occasion of the first interview, many of which
were followed by further interviews on later dates.

Albert Aldi (classmate)	In-person/e-mail	May 20, 1998
Curtis Armstrong (actor)	Phone	April 13, 1998
Leonore Bank (actor)	Letter	July 29, 1998
Thomas Bernard (studio president)	Phone	March 5, 1999
Daniel Bishop (art director)	Phone	October 5, 1998
Thomas Bleezard (alumni director)	In-person/e-mail	October 23, 1998
Kevin Boyd (video assistant)	Phone	October 21, 1998
Patrick Cady (production assistant)	Phone	August 8, 1998
John Carpenter (actor)	Letter	April 4, 1998
Roger Corman (studio owner)	Phone	July 22, 1998
Andrew Crider (professor)	Phone	May 22, 1998
Joe Dante (director)	Phone	November 23, 1998
Mason Daring (composer)	In-person/phone	June 2, 1998
Jon Davison (producer)	Phone	November 11, 1998
James DeNardo (financier)	In-person/e-mail	February 2, 1999
James DeRosa (director)	In-person/e-mail	December 15, 1997
Ernest Dickerson (director)	Phone	September 25, 1998
Bradford Dillman (actor)	Letter	March 30, 1998
Daniel DiNicola (film critic)	Phone	June 1998
Frances Doel (script supervisor)	Phone	August 6, 1998
Nate Fitzgerald (production assist.)	Phone/e-mail	October 10, 1998
Lynne K. Fonteneau-McCann (archivist)	Phone/letters	October 14, 1997
John Frankenheimer (director)	Letter	April 13, 1998
Robert Gazzale (festival director)	Phone	March 10, 1999
Jody Gillen (public relations)	Phone/letter	March 5, 1998
Beverly Gray (author)	Phone/e-mail	July 23, 1998
Robby Henson (director)	Phone	April 13, 1998
Lamont Johnson (director)	Phone	May 6, 1998
James Earl Jones (actor)	Phone	April 7, 1998
Elwood Keiser (studio head)	In-person	February 2, 1999
Kris Kristofferson (actor)	Phone	March 4, 1999
Michael Lerner (actor)	In-person/phone	March 4, 1998

Philip Mara (friend)	In-person	May 21, 1998
Pamela Sue Martin (actor)	E-mail	May 12, 1998
Kevin McCarthy (actor)	E-mail	April 13, 1998
Paul Miller (producer)	Phone	March 19, 1999
Larry Mulvaney (coach)	In-person	May 21, 1998
Joseph Nardelli (producer/director)	In-person/phone	October 10, 1998
Adelaide O'Connor (teacher)	Phone	May 15, 1998
Jerry Orbach (actor)	Phone	April 1998
Caroline (Hall) Otis (friend)	Phone	October 19, 1998
John Persichetti (film colorist)	In-person	May 25, 1999
John Pierson (author-agent)	Phone	February 19, 1999
Diana Pokorney (producer)	Letter	January 20, 1999
Jo Proctor (news director)	E-mail	October 21, 1988
James Read (actor)	Phone/e-mails	May 8, 1998
John Henry Redmond (actor)	Phone	September 2, 1998
Helen Renzi (friend)	In-person	May 22, 1998
Ralph Renzi (friend)	In-person/letters	May 22, 1998
Nancy Savoca (director)	Phone	March 3, 1999
Donald Sayles (father)	In-person/phone, letters	May 20, 1998
Doug Sayles (brother)	In-person/e-mail	May 22, 1998
Mary Sayles (mother)	In-person	May 20, 1998
David Strathairn (actor)	Phone	May 26, 1999
Kevin Tighe (actor)	Letters/e-mail	September 6, 1998
Studs Terkel (author/actor)	Phone	January 29, 1998
Robert Vaughn (actor)	Phone	April 26, 1998
Elaine West (actor)	Phones/e-mail	August 5, 1998
Haskell Wexler (cinematographer)	Phone	January 11, 1999
Bill Wine (critic)	In-person	June 25, 1999
Riley Woodford (reporter)	Phone/letters	July 21, 1998

SECONDARY SOURCES

BOOKS AND PERIODICALS

Albanes, Alex. "Review of *Lone Star*." *Box Office*, May 1996.

Allen, Carol. "The Self-Made Lifetime in His Own Legends." *Times,* (London) July 8, 1996.

Angell, Roger. "No, But I Saw the Game." *New Yorker,* July 31, 1989: 41–56.

Anonymous. "Dialogue on Film: John Sayles." *American Film,* May 1986: 13–15.

Ansen, David. "Review of *Baby It's You.*" In *Produced and Abandoned: The Best Films You've Never Seen.* Edited by Michael Sragow. San Francisco: Mercury House, 1990.

Arnold, William. "Success in Sayles." *Albany Times Union,* July 5, 1996: C: 1.

Asinof, Eliot. *Bleeding Between the Lines.* New York: Holt, Rinehart and Winston, 1979.

————. *Eight Men Out.* New York: Holt, Rinehart, and Winston, 1963.

————. "John Sayles." *DGA Magazine,* December 1997–January 1998: 40–43, 89.

————. *1919 America's Loss of Innocence.* New York: Donald I. Fine, 1990.

Aufderheide. Patricia. "Coal Wars: On Location with John Sayles." *Mother Jones,* August/September 1981: 24–29, 44–45.

————. "Sayles in Harlem." *Film Comment,* March/April 1984: 4.

Auster, Al, and Leonard Quart. *The Cineaste Interviews.* Chicago: Lake View, 1983.

Auty, Chris. "Review of *Baby It's You.*" (British) *Monthly Film Bulletin,* November 1984: 330.

Badley, Linda. *Film, Horror and the Body Fantastic.* Westport, Conn.: Greenwood Press, 1995.

Barnes, Harper. "Review of *Lone Star.*" *St. Louis Post Dispatch,* July 5, 1996: D: 1, 7.

Bernstein, Abbie. "Director/Writer John Sayles Not a 'Typical' Filmmaker." *Hollywood Drama-Logue,* June 9–15, 1993: 1.

Biskind, Peter. "The Sweet Hell of Success." *Premiere,* October 1997: 85–100.

Black, Kent. "Profile of John Sayles." *Los Angeles Times Calendar,* February 5, 1995.

Borden, Lizzie. "Grass-Roots Filmmaking." In *Making Movies.* Edited by John Russo. New York: Fireside, 1989.

Brown, Georgia. "Review of *Lone Star.*" *Village Voice,* June 25, 1996: 65.

————. "Review of *The Secret of Roan Inish.*" *Village Voice,* February 2, 1995: 51.

Bourjaily, Vance. "Review of *The Anarchists' Convention.*" *New York Times,* April 1, 1979: 15, 33.

Burman, John. "Director Power '98." *Hollywood Reporter,* October 20, 1998: 15–22.

Campbell, Bob. "Award Marks Director as Heir to Steinbeck's Social Conscience." *Newark Star Ledger,* February 8, 1998.

Campbell, Virginia. "High Noon in the Holler." *Movieline,* September 11, 1987: 17–18.

Canby, Vincent. "Film/1991." *New York Times,* December 29, 1991: E: 9.

————. "Review of *Matewan.*" *New York Times,* August 28, 1987: C: 3.

————. "Review of *Return of the Secaucus Seven.*" *New York Times,* September 14, 1980: 68

————. "Rejoice It's Independents' Day." *New York Times,* April 24, 1982: B: 1.

Cantor, Jay. "The Opera Is Gone, The Blood Is Red." Review of *Los Gusanos. New York Times Book Review,* July 16, 1991:7.

Carnes, Mark C., ed. "A Conversation between Eric Foner and John Sayles." *PastImperfect: History According to the Movies.* New York: Henry Holt, 1995.

Carney, Ray. *The Films of John Cassavetes: Pragmatism, Modernism and the Movies.* Cambridge, England: Cambridge University Press, 1994.

Caro, Mark. "Director Makes His Own Kind of Movies." *Chicago Tribune,* April 27, 1998: E: 8.

―――. "Director Sayles Reveals His Independent Mind." *Long Beach Press Telegram,* April 5, 1998.

Castle Rock Entertainment. "*Lone Star* Production Notes." Beverly Hills, California, 1996.

Chanko, Kenneth. "John Sayles." *Films in Review,* February 1983: 94–98.

―――. "The Secret of John Sayles." *Boston Globe,* February 19, 1995: B: 31.

Charity, Tom. "Sayles Pitch." *Time Out* (London), August 25–September 1, 1993.

Christenson, Terry. *Reel Politics: American Political Movies from Birth of a Nation to Platoon,* New York: Basil Blackwell, 1987.

Chute, David. "John Sayles: Designated Writer." *Film Comment,* May/June 1981: 54–59.

Clarke, Neale R. "Review of *Matewan.*" *Beckley (W.Va.) Register/Herald,* October 7, 1986.

Coburn, Randy Sue. "This Generation Isn't Lost; It's Living in Hoboken." *Esquire,* November 1982: 68–76.

Composer, Coyote. "Review of '*Battle Beyond the Stars:* The Music of James Horner.'" Accessnv.cpm/doggman.

Corliss, Richard. "Review of *Passion Fish.*" *Time,* January 25, 1993: 69.

Corrigan, Timothy. *A Cinema Without Walls: Movies and Culture After Vietnam.* New Brunswick, N.J.: Rutgers University Press, 1991.

Crosette, Barbara. "79th Street Boat Basin Gets Theater-in-the-Rotunda." *New York Times,* August 3, 1981: C: 3.

Daring, Mason. *The Brother from Another Planet.* With Joe Morton, Rex Woods, Efrain Selgado, Frank London, Lee "Scratch" Perry, Dee Dee Bridgewater, Martin Broody, Jeffrey Southworth, Mason Daring, John Sayles. Daring Records CD 1007, 1984.

―――. *Lone Star.* With Duke Levine, Tim Jackson, Larry Ludecke, Mike Turk, Evan Harlen, Freddie Fender, Ivory Joe Hunter. Daring Records CD 3023, 1996.

―――. *Matewan.* With Hazel Dickens, John Curtis, John Hammond, Gerry Milnes, Phil Wiggins, Kent Lilly. Daring Records CD 1011, 1994.

―――. *Men with Guns.* With El General, Jeannie Stahl, Lito Barrientos, El Chane, Les Miserables Brass Band, Toto la Momposina. Rykodisc CD 10437, 1998.

―――. *Passion Fish.* With Duke Levine, John Delafoss and the Eunice Playboys, Larry Luddecke, the Balfa Brothers, Willis Purdhomme and the Zydeco Express,

Loup Garoux, Le Trio Cadien, James MacDonell, Stuart Schulman. Daring
      Records CD 3008, 1993.

————. *The Secret of Roan Inish*. With Marie Breatnach, Cormac Breatnach, Gerard
      Foley, Mark Roberts, Billy Novick, Sandai Astauski, Ronan Browne, the
      Hawthorne String Quartet. Daring Records CD 3015, 1995.

Davis, Thulani. "Blue Collar Auteur." *American Film,* June 1991: 19–22.

————. "Color Bar." *American Film,* April 1988: 37.

Demyanko, Alex. "One Man Out." *Village View* (Los Angeles), November 1–7, 1991:
      22–23, 31–35.

Denby, David. "Review of *Passion Fish*." *New York*. February 15, 1993: 60.

DeWitt, Karen. "Incest as a Selling Point." *New York Times,* March 30, 1997: E: 6.

DiCaprio, Lisa. "Review of *Lianna*." *Jump Cut,* February 1984: 45.

DiMatteo, Robert. "Philadelphia Lawyer." *Film Comment,* July 1990: 2–3.

Donahue, Suzanne Mary. *American Film Distribution: The Changing Marketplace*. Ann
      Arbor, Mich.: UMI Research Press, 1987.

Dreifus, Claudia. "Interview with John Sayles." *The Progressive,* November 1991: 30.

Dunkley, Cathy. "Pandora Behind *Fade to Black*." *Hollywood Reporter,* June 7, 1999: 35.

Dwyer, Michael. "Review of *Lone Star*." *Irish Times,* November 11, 1996.

Ebert, Roger. "Review of *Passion Fish*." *Chicago Daily News,* January 31, 1993.

————. "Review of *Return of the Secaucus Seven*." *Philadelphia Bulletin,* February 28,
      1981.

————. "Taking a Closer look at Independence." *Off-Hollywood Report,*
      November–December 1988: 8.

Ellis, Carol Schwartz. "With Eyes Uplifted: Space Aliens as Sky Gods." In *Screening the
      Sacred: Religion, Myth, and Ideology in Popular American Films*. Edited by Joel W.
      Martin and Conrad E. Ostwalt Jr. Boulder, Colo.: Westview, 1995.

Elrick, Ted. "Interview with Maggie Renzi of *Men with Guns*." *DGA Magazine,*
      December 1997/January 1998: 43.

Erickson, Hal. *Baseball in the Movies: The Comprehensive Reference 1915–1991*.
      Jefferson, N.C.: McFarland, 1992:117-28.

Feld, Bruce. "John Sayles." *Drama-Logue,* October 31–November 6, 1991: 5.

Feldman, Gayle. "Review of *Los Gusanos*." *Publisher's Weekly,* December 14, 1990: 29.

Felperin, Leslie. "John Sayles Walking Alone." *Sight and Sound,* September 1996: 22–24.

Ferncase, Richard K. *Outside Features: American Independent Films of the 1980s*. Westport,
      Conn.: Greenwood Press, 1996.

Fine, Marshall. "The 'Secret' of Sayles's Success." *USA Today,* April 4, 1995.

Firmat, Gustavo Perez. "Memories of the Lost Island." Review of *Los Gusanos*.
      Washington Post, May 26, 1991: WBK1.

Fischer, Lucy, ed. *Shot/Countershot: Film Tradition and Women's Cinema*. Princeton, NJ:
      Princeton University Press, 1989.

Freedman, Samuel G. "How John Sayles Shuffled 'Shannon's Deal.'" *New York Times,*
    April 15, 1990: H: 33.

————. "John Sayles's 'Labor of Love.'" *Rolling Stone,* October 8, 1987: 27–28.

French, Philip. "Who Shot the Sheriff?" *The Observer,* October 13, 1996.

Frogely, Mike, and Matt Symonds. "Interview with John Sayles about *Lone Star.*"
    Matdel.eng.cam.ac.uk/sprocket/interviews/Sayles.html

Furia, John, Jr. *Career Achievement Award, 1997 Program.* Los Angeles, Calif.: Writers
    Guild Foundation, 1998.

Gallagher, John. *Film Directors on Directing.* Westport, Conn.: Greenwood Press, 1989.

Gallo, Bill. "Just Another Final Frontier." *New Times Los Angeles,* June 3, 1990: 40.

Gamerman, Amy. "Review of *The Secret of Roan Inish.*" *Wall Street Journal,* March 2,
    1995: 12.

Geier, Thom. "Sayles, IFC Pick *Girlfight* Project." *Hollywood Reporter,* June 22–28,
    1999: 64.

Gingold, Michael. "History of the Horror: The 1980." In *Fangoria's Best Horror Films.*
    Edited by Anthony Pimpone. Avenel, N.J.: Crescent, 1994.

Ginsberg, Merle. "Independents' Day." *W,* February 1998.

Gleiberman, Owen. "Auteurmatic Pilot." Review of *Limbo. Entertainment Weekly,* June
    4, 1999: 59.

Gleberman, Owen, and Lisa Schwarzbaum. "The Indie 50 Essential Movies."
    Entertainment Weekly Special Edition: The New Hollywood: Inside the World of
    Independent Films, November/December 1997: 88.

Goldstein, Patrick. "Sayles on TV." *Interview,* March 1990: 42.

————. "Spring Sayles on TV." *Interview,* May 5, 1990: 23.

Gordinier, Jeff. "Dimension 13: The Directors." *Entertainment Weekly* Special Edition:
    "The New Hollywood: Inside the World of Independent Films,"
    November/December 1997: 64.

Gordon. Andrew. "*Star Wars:* A Myth for Our Time." In *Screening the Sacred: Religion,*
    Myth, and Ideology in Popular American Films. Edited by Joel W. Martin and Conrad
    Ostwalt Jr. Boulder, Colo.: Westview, 1995.

Graham, Renee. "Filming What Happens in the World." *Boston Globe,* March 8, 1998:
    N: 11.

————. "Review of *Men with Guns.*" *Boston Globe,* March 22, 1998: N: 11.

Gravestock, Steve. "Lone Director: John Sayles Discusses the Making of *Lone Star.*"
    www. Idmagazine.com/arts/3artcle/sayles.html

Greenberg, Jamie. "Cinecom Seals Distribution Deal for '*Brother from Another Planet.*'"
    Variety, July 10, 1984: 10.

Grenier, Richard. *Capturing the Culture: Film, Art, and Politics.* Washington, D.C.: Ethics
    and Public Policy Center, 1990.

Grove, Martin A. "Hollywood Report: Calley Not Left on Limb with Sayles Screen
    Gem." *Hollywood Reporter,* May 12, 1999: 8.

Guerrero, Ed. *Framing Blackness: The African American Image in Film.* Philadelphia: Temple University Press, 1993.

"Guns for Sayles." Interview with John Sayles. *Venice,* April 1998: 41–43.

Haithman, Diane. "Review of *Shannon's Deal.*" *New York Times,* April 12, 1990: F: 11.

Handelman, David. "The Brother from Another Planet." *Rolling Stone,* May 21, 1987: 59–64.

Harmetz, Aljean. "Financial Security Aids Sayles in Making Films." *New York Times,* October 25, 1983. Arts and Entertainment: 25.

————. "Heady Journey of a Director and his *'Secaucus Seven.'"* *New York Times,* March 6, 1981: C: 9.

————. "Independent Films Making It Big." *New York Times,* April 6, 1987: C: 11.

Hartl, John. "Review of *The Secret of Roan Inish.*" *Seattle Times,* February 16, 1995.

Hatfield, Bill. "The Case of the Unnatural." The Semi-Official *Mathnet* Episode Site." www.saturn.holowww.com/w004000.htm

Henry, William A., III. "Williamstown Caps Its Season with a Splendid Glass Menagerie." *Time,* September 2, 1985: 72.

Hensley, Tim. "Trapped in Time, Tiny Railroad Town Goes Hollywood." *CSX News,* November 1986.

Hernandez, Eugene. "IFC Puts Its Money Where Its Name Is." Indiewire.com/film/biz 970306_/Fcdeal. html

Hillier, Jim. *The New Hollywood.* London: Studio Vista, 1992.

Hinson, Hal. "Review of *Lone Star.*" *Washington Post,* July 12, 1996: F: 6.

Hoberman, J. *Vulgar Modernism: Writing on Movies and Other Media.* Philadelphia: Temple University Press, 1991.

Hogan, David J. *Dark Romance: Sexuality in the Horror Film.* Jefferson, N.C.: McFarland, 1986.

Holden, Stephen. "Bucking the System, but Still Part of the Buzz." *New York Times,* March 5, 1995: H: 13.

————. "Real Men and Endangered Species in Film." *New York Times,* July 7, 1996: H: 9.

————. "Review of *The Secret of Roan Inish.*" *New York Times,* February 3, 1995.

————. "Review of *Limbo.*" *New York Times,* June 4, 1999.

Holmund, Christine. "When Is a Lesbian Not a Lesbian?" *Camera Obscura: A Journal of Feminism and Film Theory,* 1991: 145–78.

hooks, bell. *Reel to Real: Race, Sex, and Class at the Movies.* New York: Routledge, 1996.

Horn, John. "John Sayles Pitches for Creativity." *Berkshire (Mass.) Eagle,* September 22, 1988: C: 1.

Hornaday, Ann. "At Many a Multiplex, Lots of Screens but Little Choice." *New York Times,* August 4, 1996: II: 18.

Horner, Carol. " . . . to the '60s Spirit." *Philadelphia Inquirer,* March 26, 1981: D: 1.

"It's a Wrap." Editorial. *Juneau Empire,* September 6, 1998: D: 2.

Jackson, Kevin. "How to Beat the System." *The Independent* (London), October 6, 1996.

———. "Return of a Man Called Sayles." *The Independent* (London), October 13, 1996.

Jacobs, A. S. "The Lingo." *Entertainment Weekly* Special Edition: "The New Hollywood: Inside the World of Independent Films," November/December 1997: 23.

Jacobson, Harlan. "Interview with John Sayles." *Interview,* April 1993.

James, Caryn. "*Passion Fish* Nourishes the Grown-Ups." *New York Times,* January 1, 1993: H: 11.

Jenkins, Steve. "Review of *Eight Men Out.*" (British) *Monthly Film Bulletin,* July 1989: 204–5.

"John Sayles: Biography." *People,* March 8, 1993: 86.

Johnston, Trevor. "Sayles Talk: An Interview with John Sayles." *Sight and Sound,* September 1993: 26–29.

Jost, Jon. "End of the Indies: Death of the Sayles Men." *Film Comment,* January/February 1989: 42–45.

Kaplan, Nelly. *Shot/Countershot: Film Tradition and Women's Cinema.* Edited by Lucy Fischer. Princeton, N.J.: Princeton University Press, 1989.

Karon, Paul. "Sayles Joins Aperture Pic Grant Board." *Variety,* August 21, 1997: 4.

Katcher, Leo. *Big Bank Roll.* New York: Harper, 1955.

Katz, Steven D. "Interview with John Sayles." *Cinematic Motion: Film Directing: A Workshop for Staging Scenes.* Los Angeles, Calif.: Michael Wiese Productions, 1992: 11–19.

Katz, Susan Bullington. "A Conversation with John Sayles." *The Journal,* July 1996: 30–34, 42–43.

Kaufman, Anthony. "Lone Gun: A Conversation with John Sayles." Indiewire.com/film/interviews/int_sayles_john_980306.html

Kauffman, Stanley. "Review of *Matewan.*" *New Republic,* September 7, 1987: 24.

Kawin, Bruce. "*The Funhouse* and *The Howling.*" In *American Horrors: Essays on the Modern American Horror Film.* Edited by Gregory A. Waller. Urbana: University of Illinois Press, 1987.

Kemp, Philip. "Review of *The Secret of Roan Inish.*" *Sight and Sound,* August 1996: 63.

———. "John Sayles." *St. James Film Directors Encyclopedia.* Detroit: Visible Ink 1998.

Kempley, Rita. "Review of *City of Hope* (videotape)." *Washington Post,* November 5, 1992: D: 7.

Kenny, Glenn. "Review of *Limbo.*" *Premiere,* July 1999: 28.

Kerr, Paul. "John Sayles Imaging Women." (British) *Monthly Film Bulletin,* January 1984: 28.

Kirkland, Bruce. "Review of *Men with Guns.*" *Toronto Star,* March 27, 1998: 65.

Klady, Leonard. "Same Old Song and Dance: the 22nd Annual Grosses Gloss." *Film Comment,* March/April 1997: 50–54.

Kozak, Jim. "The Sayles Pitch." *Box Office,* September 1988: 7–8.

Lamoreaux, Michelle. "Independent Streak." *Entertainment Today,* June 14–20, 1996: 6.

Lardner, Ring, Jr. "Foul Ball: John Sayles's *Eight Men Out*—or How My Father Watched the White Sox Throw the 1919 World Series." *American Film,* July/August 1988: 45.

La Salle, Mike, and Ruthie Stein. "Beyond the Blockbuster: Summer Movie Guide." *San Francisco Chronicle,* May 16, 1999: 38–39.

Lask, Thomas. "Sayles Winning Way in Short Stories." *New York Times,* September 13, 1979: III: 12.

Lawrence, Randall G. "Matewan: A Story of Working Class Formation." *Radical Historians Newsletter,* February 1988: 1, 4.

Lawson, Carol. "Broadway." *New York Times,* June 26, 1982: C: 2.

Lawson, Steve. "John Sayles: A Man for All Media." *New York Times Magazine,* April 17, 1983: 108.

Lee, Felicia. "At Home with Joe Morton." *New York Times,* May 18, 1995: C: 1.

Lemons, Stephen. "Review of *Limbo.*" *Entertainment Today,* June 4–10, 1999: 8.

———. "Sailing into *Limbo.*" *Entertainment Today,* June 4, 1999: 8.

Levitt, Shelly. "John Sayles." *People,* March 8, 1993: 86.

Levy, Shawn. "The Secret of *Roan Inish*'s Success." *The Oregonian,* July 9, 1995.

Lida, David. "John Sayles: Militant Moviemaker." *W,* June 15–22, 1987: 17.

Long, Marion. "Interview with John Sayles," *Omni,* June 1987: 44.

"Long View Part II: John Sayles." *Off-Hollywood Report,* April 1988: 6–8.

Lopate, Philip. "With Pen in Hand, They Direct Movies." *New York Times,* August 10, 1992: II: 7.

Maltin, Leonard. "Interview with John Sayles." Writers Guild Tribute to John Sayles. Writers Guild Theatre, Los Angeles, California, February 13, 1998.

Marney, Angela. "*Lianna:* A Move Toward Better Things." *Off Our Backs,* April 1983: 18.

Marsh, Dave. *Glory Days.* New York: Pantheon, 1987.

Martin, Douglas. "Playing the Odd Sayles Role." *New York Times,* January 24, 1993: H: 16.

Maslin, Janet. "How to Market a Film Full of Misery: Smile!" *New York Times,* February 5, 1993: C: 23.

———. "A Nation Disillusioned." Review of *Eight Men Out. New York Times,* September 2, 1988: C: 3.

———. "Review of *Men with Guns.*" *New York Times,* March 6, 1998 E: 29.

———. "Review of *Passion Fish.*" *New York Times,* December 14, 1992: C: 16.

———. "Sleepy Texas Town with an Epic Story." Review of *Lone Star. New York Times,* June 21, 1996: B: 1.

McCarthy, Rex. "Vivid Portrayal of West Virginia Coal Wars." *Frontline,* October 26, 1987: 1.

McCormick, Patrick. "A Sayles Pitch." *U.S. Catholic,* March 1, 1997: 38–41.

McDonald, Scott. *A Critical Cinema 2: Interviews with Independent Filmmakers*. Berkeley, CA: University of California Press, 1992.

McEwan, Nicole. "Man with a Movie Camera." In *At the Ritz Filmbill* (Ritz Theatres, Philadelphia), March/April 1998: 15–23.

McGhee, Dorothy. "Solidarity Forever: In an Era of Union Busting, John Sayles's *Matewan* Celebrates the Miners' Struggle of the Twenties." *American Film*, September 1987: 42.

McGuigan, Cathleen. "Splitting a Double-Header." Review of *Eight Men Out*. *Newsweek*, September 12, 1988: 74.

Minsky, Terri. "Sayles and Bargains." *Premiere*, September 1991: 38–40.

Miramax. *Passion Fish* Press Kit. New York, 1992.

Mitchell, Sean. "Bard of the Low Budget." *Los Angeles Times*, October 20, 1991: 8–44.

Molyneaux, Libby. "Interview with John Sayles." *UCLA Bruin*, November 5, 1980.

NB. "Icon and Everyman: Interview with John Sayles." www.readcat.nybooks.com/sayles1.html

Nechak, Paula. "Reflections of a Renaissance Man." *Moviemaker*, July/August 1996: 25.

Nelson, George. *Blackface: Reflections on African-Americans and the Movies*. New York: HarperCollins, 1994.

Newman, Kim. *Nightmare Movies: A Critical Guide to Contemporary Horror Films*. New York: Harmony Books, 1988.

O'Brien, Tom. "Review of *Matewan*." *Commonweal*, November 6, 1987: 626.

O'Connor, John J. "From John Sayles, A Flawed Hero for the '90s." *New York Times*, June 4, 1989: 4: 27.

Oppenheimer, Jean. "The Secrets of John Sayles." *Village View* (Los Angeles), February 3–9, 1995: 13.

Orion Pictures. *Eight Men Out* Press Kit. New York, 1988.

Osbourne, David. "John Sayles: From Hoboken to Hollywood— and Back." *American Film*, October 1983: 30.

Packer, George. "Decency and Muck." *Dissent*, Summer 1997: 105–9.

Painter, Jamie. "Actor's Director." *Back Stage West*, July 10, 1999: 12.

Parish, James Robert. *Gays and Lesbians in Mainstream Cinema*. Jefferson, N.C.: McFarland, 1993.

Parks, Louis B. "Law and Borders." Review of *Lone Star*. *Houston Chronicle*, June 30, 1996.

———. "*Men with Guns*: A Foreign Film." *Houston Chronicle*, April 5, 1998.

Patton, Cindy. "A Nice Lesbian Like You." In *Immortal Invisible: Lesbians and the Moving Image*. Edited by Tamsin Wilton. London: Routledge, 1995.

Pennella, Erica J. "Final Frontier." *Philadelphia Weekly*, June 2, 1999: 35.

Pierson, John. *Spike, Mike, Slackers & Dykes*. New York: Hyperion, 1995.

Pooley, Eric. "The First Score." *New York*, April 24, 1984.

Rainier, Peter. "The Young and the Gifted." *Vogue*, September 1981: 383.

Ratner, Megan. "Borderlines." *Filmmaker*, Summer 1996: 32–35.

Rauzi, Rolen. "The Indie Icon." *Los Angeles Times Calendar*, March 1, 1998: 7.

Rhudy, Vaughan. "Taking the Risk." *Beckley (W.V.) Register Herald*, October 1, 1986: B: 1.

Rich, Frank. "Theater: A Pair of One-Actors by John Sayles." *New York Times*, July 8, 1981: C: 25.

Rich, Kim. "Reeling in a Movie Job." *Anchorage Daily News*, June 28, 1998: C: 4.

Rioaben, Charles. "*My Piece of the Pie* Opens Tonight." *Williams (Mass.) Record*, October 21, 1971.

Roberts, Jerry. "Pitching Indie Ethic." Interview with John Sayles. *Variety*, July 20, 1994: 16–22.

———. "True Indie: The Films of John Sayles." www. Cinemania.msn come / videorewind/ article / 13

Roberts, Sam. "Real Politics in a Celluloid City." *New York Times*, October 13, 1991: H: 13.

Roman, Monica. "Cable Net Bows Indie Pro'n Unit." *Variety*, March 5, 1997: 1.

Roman, Monica, and Dan Cox. "Sayles, Sloss Part Ways." *Variety*, January 4, 1997.

Romano, Lois. "The Message of John Sayles: Down-to-Earth Director with a Penchant for Independence." *Washington Post*, October 20, 1991: G: 1.

Rosen, David, with Peter Hamilton. *Off-Hollywood: The Making and Marketing of Independent Films*. New York: Grove Weidenfeld, 1987.

Ross, Steven J. *Working-Class Hollywood*. Princeton, N.J.: Princeton University Press, 1998.

Rothstein, Carolyn Green. *Now I'll Tell*. New York: Vanguard, 1934.

Russo, John. *Making Movies: The Inside Guide to Film Production*. New York: Dell, 1989.

Ryan, Jack. *John Sayles, Filmmaker*. Jefferson, N.C.: McFarland, 1998.

———. *Ordinary People: The Cinema of John Sayles*. Ann Arbor, Mich.: UMI Dissertation Services, 1994.

Ryan, Michael, and Douglas Kellner. *Camera Politica: The Politics and Ideology of Contemporary Hollywood Film*. Bloomington: Indiana University Press, 1988.

Salamon, Julie. "Sayles Pitch: Hustling a Film at Cannes." *Wall Street Journal*, May 11, 1984: 28.

Samuel Goldwyn Co. *City of Hope* Production Notes. Los Angeles, California, 1991.

Sarris, Andrew. "*Baby It's You*: An Honest Man Becomes a True Filmmaker." *Film Comment*, May/June 1993: 28–30.

Savage, Lon. *Thunder in the Mountains: The West Virginia Mine Wars, 1920–1921*. Foreword by John Sayles. Pittsburgh: University of Pittsburgh Press, 1990.

Schlesinger, T. "Putting People Together: An Interview with John Sayles." *Film Quarterly*, Summer 1981: 2–8.

Schwarzbaum, Lisa. "Independents' Day." *Entertainment Weekly* Special Edition: The New Hollywood: Inside the World of Independent Films, November/December 1997: 10.

Schickel, Richard. "Paradise Regained." *Time,* June 7, 1999: 76.

————. "Review of *Eight Men Out." Time,* September 12, 1988: 18.

"The Secret of Sayles's Seals." *Toronto Star,* December 2, 1995.

Seidenberg, Robert. "*Matewan." Theater Crafts,* April 1987: 45–48.

————. "Review of *Shannon's Deal." American Film,* March 1990: 61.

————. "Sayles Talk." *Horizon,* September 1987: 12–14.

Shales, Tom. "Great 'Deal' on NBC." *Washington Post,* May 16, 1990: D: 1.

Shapiro, Erin. "Small Films Help a Lawyer Make It Big." *Wall Street Journal,* March 31, 1995: B: 12.

Sharkey, Nancy. "Don't Wait for the Movie." Review of *Los Gusanos. New York Times Book Review,* July 16, 1991: 7.

Sheed, Wilfred. "Why Can't the Movies Play Ball?" *New York Times,* May 14, 1989: II-1.

Sheehan, Henry. "Review of *Men with Guns." Orange County (Calif.) Register,* March 13, 1998: F: 9.

Shone, Tom. "A Singular Voice." *Times* (London), October 13, 1996.

Siebert, Charles. "It's the 1919 World Series. And Catching for the Reds Is Yours Truly." *Esquire,* August 1988: 129-37.

Simanthon, Keith. "Big Budget Movies Pay for Sayles's Small Films." *Seattle Times,* March 22, 1998.

Simon, Joel. "John Sayles, Long a Director at the Edge Crosses a Border." *New York Times,* March 9, 1997: C: 14, 20.

Simpson, Janice C. "Neck Deep in the Culture." *Time,* August 5, 1991: 64.

Skolnick, Dylan. "John Sayles." *Films in Review,* c. 1996: 268.

Skorman, Richard. *Off-Hollywood Movies: A Film Lover's Guide.* New York: Harmony, 1989.

Snyder, Michael. "Man with Guts." www.salon1999.com/ent/int/1998/03/13int.html

Span, Paul. "The Independent Obsession of John Sayles." *Washington Post,* October 15, 1987: C: 1.

Spines, Christine. "Interview with John Sayles." *Premiere,* July 1996: 40–51.

Sragow, Michael. "Review of *Men with Guns." Dallas Observer,* March 26, 1998: 29.

Stacey, Jackie. "If You Don't Play, You Can't Win: *Desert Hearts* and the Lesbian Romance Film." In *Immortal Invisible: Lesbians and the Moving Image.* Edited by Tamsin Wilton. London: Routledge, 1995.

Stein, Harry. "How John Sayles Learned to Stop Worrying and Love the Studio." *Premiere,* July 1999: 90–110.

Stein, Ruthie. "Sticking to Their Guns." *San Francisco Chronicle,* March 8, 1998: 34–35.

———. "The Woman Beside Filmmaker John Sayles." *San Francisco Chronicle,* April 1, 1998.

Sterrett, David. "Review of *Lianna." Christian Science Monitor,* May 12, 1987: 16.

Steur, Joseph. "Green, Renzi Look to SPE for Mamet, Sayles." *Hollywood Reporter,* December 12, 1997.

Stone, Alan A. "The Prophet of Hope." *Boston Review,* October/November 1996: 20.

Stone, Judy. "John Sayles." *Eye on the World: Conversations with International Filmmakers.* New York: Silman James, 1997.

Straayer, Chris. *Deviant Eyes, Deviant Bodies: Sexual Orientation in Film and Video.* New York: Columbia, 1996.

"Talk of the Town: *Brother." The New Yorker,* January 2, 1984: 20–22.

Tallmer, Jerry. "Review of *Lone Star." Bergen County* (N.J.) *Record,* June 21, 1996.

Tartara, Paul. "Review of *Men with Guns.*" www.cnn.com/showbiz/9804/01/men.with.guns.review/

Taubin, Amy. "Independence Way." *Village Voice,* June 25, 1996: 70.

Terkel, Studs. *Working.* New York: New Press, 1974.

Thomas, Kevin. "*Secaucus Seven:* Low Budget, High Rating." *Los Angeles Times,* November 5, 1980: D: 1.

Thompson, Cliff. "The Brother from Another Race: Black Characters in the Films of John Sayles." *Cineaste.* Special Issue: Race in Contemporary American Cinema, Part 7, December 1996: 32–33.

Thomson, David. *Overexposures: The Crisis in American Filmmaking.* New York: William Morrow, 1981.

Travers, Peter. "Review of *Brother from Another Planet.*" *Time,* September 17, 1984: 12.

Tunison, Michael. "Men with Cameras: Interview with John Sayles." *Entertainment Today,* March 6–12, 1998.

———. "Review of *Limbo.*" *Entertainment Today,* June 4, 1999: 16–18.

———. "Review of *Men with Guns.*" *Entertainment Today,* March 13–19, 1998.

Turan, Kenneth. "John Sayles Masters the Possibilities." *GQ,* October 1987: 179.

———. "Review of *Limbo.*" *Los Angeles Times,* June 4, 1999: F: 6.

———. "Review of *Lone Star.*" *Los Angeles Times,* June 21, 1996: F: 12.

Ulin, David. "Interview with John Sayles." *Bomb,* Spring 1998: 50–53

———. "Print vs. Film vs. Cynicism." *Los Angeles Reader,* October 25, 1991.

Ungar, Sanford. "Immigrants' Tales, in Subtle Shades of Gray." *New York Times,* June 23, 1996: H: 15.

Van Gelder, Lindsey. "Director, Screenwriter John Sayles: At Home on Our Turf." *Ms.,* June 1983: 31–36.

Vaucher, Andrea. "Final Frontier." *Hollywood Reporter,* June 8–14, 1999: 18–20.

Vecsey, George. "John Sayles Mines the Coal Wars." *New York Times,* August 23, 1987: II: 1.

———. "John Sayles Steps Up to Bat." *New York Times,* August 28, 1988: H: 1, 20.

————. "Review of *Matewan*." *New York Times,* August 28, 1987: III: 3.

Vineberg, Steve. *No Surprises Please: Movies in the Reagan Decade.* New York: Macmillan, 1993.

Von Busack, Richard. "Film: Of Movies and Men." *San Jose Mercury:* Metro Section, February 12–18, 1998.

Weinraub, Bernard, and Geraldine Fabrikant. "The Revenge of the Bean Counters." *New York Times,* June 13, 1999: 3: 1.

West, Dennis, and Joan M. West. "Borders and Boundaries: An Interview with John Sayles." *Cineaste,* December 1996: 14–17.

————. "Review of *Lone Star*." *Cineaste,* December 1996: 34–36.

Whipp, Glenn. "A Lone Star in His Own Right." *Los Angeles Daily News: L.A. Life,* March 12, 1998: 3–6.

Will, George. "Touching a National Nerve." *Berkshire (Mass.) Eagle,* October 6, 1999: A: 11.

Willis, Sharon. *High Contrast: Race and Gender in Contemporary Hollywood Film.* Durham, N.C.: Duke University Press, 1997.

Wilton, Tamsin, ed. *Immortal Invisible: Lesbians and the Moving Image.* London: Routledge, 1995.

Wolf, William. "New Faces of 1980." *New York,* April 28, 1980: 62.

Woodford, Riley. "Extras Needed for Sayles Movie." *Juneau Empire,* May 26, 1999.

Woolard, John. "Blue-Collar Auteur." *Long Beach (Calif.) Press Telegram,* October 25, 1991: W: 16.

Writers Guild Foundation. Career Achievement Award, 1997 Program. Los Angeles, California, 1998.

Wulf, Steve. "Review of *Eight Men Out*." *Sports Illustrated,* September 12, 1988: 18.

Wuntch, Philip. "Review of *The Secret of Roan Inish*." *Dallas Morning News,* March 18, 1995.

Yardley, Jonathan. "The Eclipse of Editing." *Washington Post,* August 6, 1990.

Young, Josh. "Mr. Rewriter Returns." *Esquire,* June 1996: 36.

Zaniello, Tom. *Working Stiffs, Union Maids, Reds and Riffraff: An Organized Guide to Films about Labor.* Ithaca, N.Y.: Cornell University Press, 1996.

Zucker, Carole. "Interview with John Sayles." *Figures of Light: Actors and Directors Illuminate the Art of Film Acting.* New York: Plenum Press, 1995.

OFFICIAL SAYLES WEB SITE
Site of the "John Sayles Border Stop Newsletter": Rskelley@usc.edu

INDEX

Aaron, Caroline, 129
Albany (New York), 72–73
Aldi, Al, 53–57
Alexander, Jane, 170, 192
Algren, Nelson, 77, 166
Alligator, 90, 93, 96–97, 197–98
Amalgamated Butcher Workers and Meat Packers of North America, 74
American Film Institute, 18, 25, 82, 100, 116, 120, 126, 131, 134, 149, 168–69, 211, 217, 220, 230, 247
Anarchists' Convention, The, 26, 73, 98, 101, 144
Anarchist Convention (office), 183
"Anarchists' Convention, The" (short story), 73
Anders, Allison, 14, 258
Aperture Pictures, 233
Apollo 13, 217–18
Armstrong, Curtis, 122–23
Arquette, Rosanna, 115, 163
Arrow, The, 51
Asinof, Eliot, 80, 166–67, 169, 177–78
Atlanta (Georgia), 3
Atlantic Monthly Press, 75–77
Atlantic Monthly, 75
Altman, Robert, 13, 19, 25, 192, 257
Auel, Jean, 123
Avco Pictures, 94
Aydelott Associates of Boston, 32

Baby It's You, 58, 63, 104, 113–25, 139, 163, 232, 252
Bacon, Kevin, 122
Ballhaus, Michael, 118
Barker, Michael, 109, 230
Baseball Hall of Fame, 173
Battle Beyond the Stars, 18, 92–93, 232
Bedlam, 210
Bergman, Ingmar, 35, 63, 242
Bernard, Tom, 38, 109, 113, 230, 239
Berry, Ken, 172
Big Chill, The, 21, 36
Bishop, Dan, 148–51, 173, 192–93, 227
Blood of the Lamb, 99–100
"Born in the U.S.A." (music video), 140
Boston (Massachusetts), 74–78
Boyd, Kevin, 184, 253

Breaking In, 182
Brother from Another Planet, The, 51, 124–37, 148, 152, 154, 161, 183, 227, 232, 257–58
Brother Termite, 93, 232
Burmester, Leo, 204, 253
Burnt Hills School, 44

Cady, Patrick, 184, 203
Cagney, James, 172
Cameron, James, 18, 81, 87, 93, 232–33, 247
Cannes International Film Festival, 135, 155, 161, 231, 255
Cap and Bells, 63–65, 68, 74
Cassavetes, John, 11, 14–15, 19, 32, 257
Castle Rock Entertainment, 220–21, 232
Challenge, The. See *Sword of Ninja, The*
Chavooshian, Nora, 148–49, 151
Cincinnati (Ohio), 167, 169, 192
Cinecom International, 136, 148, 155
City of Hope, 74, 181, 184, 190–95, 201, 204, 207, 221, 227
Clan of the Cave Bear, The, 122
Clapp, Gordon, 21, 25, 27, 63–64, 102, 152, 170
Clemente, Roberto, 55
Cobbs, Bill, 130
Comiskey, Charles, 166–67, 174
Cooper, Chris, 147, 152, 184, 192, 225–26, 228–29, 231
Coppola, Francis Ford, 18–19, 23, 67, 81
Corman, Roger, 12, 15, 17–18, 22–23, 25, 79–93, 95, 98, 103
Curtis-Hall, Vondie, 204, 233
Cusack, John, 170–71

Dante, Joe, 16, 25, 82, 85–87, 94–96, 98, 125, 193, 198, 217
Daring, Mason, 26, 33, 35, 112, 136, 154–55, 176, 192–93, 213–15, 227, 229–30, 253–54
Davis, Kurt, 129
Davison, Jon, 82
Deakins, Roger, 201
Demme, Jonathan, 18, 37, 81, 183, 207
DeNardo, James, 238–43
DePalma, Brian, 19, 140
Dewhurst, Colleen, 100, 142
Dickens, Hazel, 154
Dickerson, Ernest, 125–26, 131–36

Dillman, Bradford, 84, 86
Directors Guild of America, 25, 126, 256
Doel, Frances, 12, 18, 22–23, 81, 84, 86, 181
Dryburgh, Stewart, 227
Dunne, Griffin, 103, 114–15

"Earth Dead Ahead," 51
Eastern Slope Playhouse, 20–21, 65
Ebenwyck, 54–55
Edwards, Darryl, 129
Eight Men Out, 50, 104, 111, 165–79, 181, 192, 196–98, 221, 230, 253, 257, 264
Enormous Changes at the Last Minute, 121

Fade to Black, 258
Ferrara, Abel, 14, 19
Fifth Child, The, 232
Film Society at Lincoln Center, 34
Fina della Notte, La, 185
Finley, Randy, 34–35
Fitzgerald, Nate, 227–28
Flynt, Cynthia, 148
Forsyth, Bill, 182
Frankenheimer, John, 100
Furia, John, 209, 246

General Electric, 42, 52, 57
Girlfight, 252, 258
Glass Menagerie, The, 138–39
"Glory Days" (music video), 141
Gold of Exodus, The, 232
"Golden State," 67
Gonda, Lou, 236
Green, Sarah, 210, 212, 250, 258
Green/Renzi Productions, 250–52, 256, 258
Gridlock'd, 233
Guns, Sins and Bathtub Gin. See *Lady in Red, The*

Hackman, Gene, 233
"Halfway Diner, The," 144, 179
Hard Choices, 142
Henson, Robby, 184, 215, 226
High School Teachers of Foreign Languages Award, 246–47
Hoboken (New Jersey), 107, 116, 128, 141, 184, 190, 215
Howard, Ron, 18, 81, 217
Howe School, 44
Howling, The, 90, 93–98

"I-80 Nebraska, m.490–m.205," 67, 75–76
"I'm on Fire" (music video), 140
Indianapolis (Indiana), 172–77
Internal Revenue Service, 105

Jackson, Leonard, 129
Jarmusch, Jim, 14, 19, 37, 195
Jaws, 82–83, 87
John Cassavetes Award, 195
John Steinbeck Award, 246, 256
Johnson, Lamont, 138, 142–43
Jones, James Earl, 135, 145, 152–53, 203
Junketeers, 251–52
Justice, Larry, 130

Kristofferson, Kris, 184, 219, 225–26, 228–31, 246, 253
Kurosawa, Akira, 92, 163
Kusuma, Karyn, 252, 258–59

Ladd, Alan, Jr., 99
Lady in Red, The, 18, 90–91
LaFevre, Adam, 21, 24, 27–28, 102
Lang, Perry, 197–98
Lee, Spike, 14, 19, 22, 37, 194, 236, 258
Lerner, Michael, 175–76
Lianna, 102–13, 115, 117, 126, 154, 182, 257
Libra Films, 34–35, 101
Limbo, 141, 163–64, 184, 249–56
Linton High School, 40, 51, 56
Little Vegas, 198
Lloyd, Christopher, 170, 176
Lone Star, 67, 152, 156, 184, 218–32, 235, 237, 250, 257
Los Angeles Film Critics Best Screenplay Award, 37
Los Gusanos, 181, 188–90
Lucas, George, 13, 82, 92
Lynch, David, 14, 19, 37, 258

MacArthur Foundation Award, 124
Mahoney, John, 170, 176
Malcolm X, 198
Mamet, David, 251, 256, 258
Mara, (Dr.) Philip, 49–51, 53
Marcus, Paul, 126, 173–74
Martin, Pamela Sue, 91–92
Mastrantonio, Mary Elizabeth, 163, 252–53, 255, 257
Matewan, 57, 67, 74, 78, 104, 123–25, 136, 144–57, 165, 168, 170, 175, 177, 181, 198, 202–203, 213, 221, 226, 252–53, 257
"Mathnet," 197
Matinee, 198
McCarthy, Kevin, 84, 87, 95
McConaughey, Matthew, 225–26, 229, 231
McDonnell, Mary, 152, 200, 202, 206
McDormand, Frances, 213, 224, 226
McGinnis, Matthew (great grandfather), 41
Men of War, 198
Men with Guns, 157, 219, 235–45, 249–50, 257
Miller, Paul, 212–13, 219, 225, 227, 236–40, 252
Mimic, 233

Miramax Films, 201, 206
Mont Pleasant High School, 5, 40–42, 44, 48, 52, 54–55, 114, 171, 201, 206
Morton, Joe, 128–37, 192. 194, 224, 227–28
"Mountainview," 182
Mulvaney, Larry, 49, 56
Mummy, The, 217
My Life's in Turnaround, 198
My Piece of Pie, 65, 68

National Book Award, 77
National Book Critics Circle Award, 77
National Film Registry, 37
Nelson, Jeffrey, 20–21, 105
New Directors/New Films, 34
New Hope for the Dead, 64, 101–102
New World Pictures, 12, 17–18, 22, 25, 79–88, 90–94, 103
Next Wave Films, 233
Night Skies, 99, 105
Northville (New York), 40, 44, 66

Of Mice and Men, 64–65
O'Henry Award for Best Short Stories, 75
Oh, Carolina, 232
Oldham, Will, 147, 151
Oneida Junior High School, 50, 52
Orion Classics, 168–69, 110, 178, 230
Oscar nomination: Best Screenplay, 206, 232
Otis, Caroline (Hall), 46, 63–64, 74, 80, 228–29

Paramount Pictures, 104, 113, 116–24
Passante, Jean, 33
Passion Fish, 73, 152, 199–207, 213–14, 221, 232, 253
Patton, Jody, 239
Pena, Elizabeth, 187, 224, 226, 229, 231
Perfect Match, A, 100, 142
Persichetti, John, 33, 257–58
Pharaoh's Army, 184, 215, 226
Pierson, John, 15, 236
Pillsbury, Sara, 167–69, 176,
Piranha, 18, 25, 79–81, 84–87, 89–90, 95
Pittsburgh Pirates, 39, 55, 166
Polonsky, Sonya, 118
Powditch, John, 227, 253
Pride of the Bimbos, 50, 71, 76, 166

Quick and the Dead, The, 233

Rajski, Peggy, 106, 126, 131, 134–36, 148, 183, 252
Read, James, 171–72, 174
Red Dog Films, 148
Redmond, John (Henry), 197, 202–203
Reiner, Rob, 220
Renzi, Helen, 107, 232

Renzi, Maggie, 17, 21, 26, 33–34, 63, 74, 79–80, 93–94, 101–106, 108, 110, 112, 121, 123, 126, 130–36, 148–49, 154, 157, 160–61, 170, 179, 181, 183–84, 190–92, 196, 198–99, 202–203, 206, 209–12, 215, 218–20, 226, 228–29, 232, 236–37, 241, 244, 246, 250–54
Renzi, Marta, 107, 139, 182
Renzi, Ralph, 63–64, 74, 107, 137, 151, 160, 203
Republican National Convention, 89, 101
Return of the Secaucus Seven, 15–38, 50, 63–64, 79, 89, 93–94, 96, 98, 101–106, 108–109, 111–13, 115, 154, 156, 205, 233, 256
Richardson, Robert, 172–73, 192, 201
Robinson, Amy, 103, 113–15
Robinson, Stu, 246
Robinson, Weinstraub, Gross, and Associates, 18, 80
Roman Catholic, 43, 45, 60–61, 107, 210
Rousch, Fred (maternal grandfather), 41, 188

Safe Place, A, 210
Samuels, Charles Thomas, 63
San Diego International Film Festival, 247
Sanford, Midge, 167–69, 176
Santa Barbara (California), 17, 34, 93
Santitos, 233
Savoca, 14, 183, 235, 258
Sayles, Mae McGinnis (paternal grandmother), 41
Sayles on Sayles, 54–55
Sayles, Andrew (nephew), 42, 162
Sayles, Burton (uncle), 41
Sayles, Donald (father), 39, 51, 53–4, 57–58, 60, 66, 74–76, 107, 162
Sayles, Doug (brother), 31, 34, 45–51, 53, 55, 57, 60, 66, 68–69, 75, 158, 162, 174, 188, 209, 236–43, 250
Sayles, Henry (grandfather), 41
Sayles, John
    Acting, 27, 57–58, 64–65. *See* appendices and main entries
    Awards, 36–37, 56, 58, 75, 77, 124, 185, 194–95, 206, 232, 244, 246–47
    Birth, 43
    Childhood, 43–48, 158
    College, 59–69, 160
    Creative consultant, 185–87
    Different cultures, 57–58, 61, 73, 77, 98, 106, 108, 110–11, 115, 125–36, 145–47, 154–56, 188–90, 193–96, 198–200, 210, 216, 222–27, 229, 236, 240–44
    Directing consultant, 183
    Early education, 44–48, 50–51
    First film, 17–31
    Heritage, 41–43
    High school, 51–58, 158
    Hitchhiking, 29, 66–67, 73, 145

Lyrics. *See* appendices (bibliography) and main entries
Music videos, 140–41. *See also* Springsteen, Bruce
New filmmakers, supporting of, 14, 121, 183, 233
Novels and books. *See* appendices (bibliography) and main entries
Photos, 158–64
Physical impairments, 46–48, 62, 71
Relationship, 74, 221–22. *See* Renzi, Maggie
Religion, 43, 45, 60–61, 107, 210
Screenplays. *See* appendices and main entries
Scripts for television. *See* appendices and main entries
Scripts for the stage. *See* appendices and main entries
Short stories and articles. *See* appendices and main entries
Spanish writing, 188–90, 241–42
Sports, 45, 49–50, 52–58, 66, 101–102, 165–79, 197
Sayles, Mary Rousch (mother), 45, 60, 64–65, 107
Schenectady (New York), 39–58, 65–66, 114, 171
Schlensker, Henry. *See* Sayles, Henry
Scorsese, Martin, 13, 15, 18–19, 81, 104, 118, 142, 201, 210, 228, 236, 257
Screen Actors Guild, 23, 105, 152
Screen Gems, 252, 255, 257–58
Screen Writers Guild, 36, 81, 217–18, 232
Screen Writers Guild Awards, 36, 245–46
Seattle Film Festival, 215
Secret of Roan Inish, The, 199, 207, 209–17, 219, 221, 232, 236, 257
Seidelman, Susan, 19, 37
sex, lies and videotape, 13, 191, 233
Shannon's Deal, 181, 185–87, 221, 226
Shapiro, Barbara, 128, 151–52
Sheen, Charlie, 170–71
Siebert, Charles, 166, 172–73, 177
Siemaszko, Casey, 182, 252
Sloss, John, 201, 239, 252
Smith, Kevin, 14, 22, 258
Soderberg, Steven, 13, 19, 191, 233
Something Wild, 142
Sony Pictures Classics, 215, 230, 239, 244, 250–51, 256
Sony Pictures Entertainment, 250
Spano, Vincent, 115, 163, 192
Spielberg, Steven, 13, 19, 77, 82, 99, 138–41, 148, 182, 210, 217, 246, 254
Stack, Robert, 37
Steambath, 65
Steele, Barbara, 84
Steinbeck, John, 64, 77, 246
Straight Talk, 198
Strathairn, David, 20–21, 25, 27, 63, 102, 122, 130, 137, 152, 170, 175, 192, 204, 252–53, 255, 259
Sumner Avenue, 42, 48–49, 66

Sundance Film Festival, 14, 183, 194, 233
Suskind, David, 166–67
Sweeney, D. B., 169
Sword of Ninja, The, 101

Taylor, Gil, 129
Teague, Lewis, 91, 96, 186
Terkel, Studs, 165, 176–77
Terror of Loch Ness, The, 99
Thinking in Pictures: The Making of the Movie Matewan, 24, 145, 157
"This Place," 68
Thomas, Richard, 92–93
Thurmond (West Virginia), 150–51
Tighe, Kevin, 103, 141, 152, 170, 175
Time of Your Life, The, 65
Tokyo International Film Festival Award, 194
Tom Mix Died for Your Sins, 232
Towler, Virginia, 206–207
"Treasure," 179
TriStar Pictures, 99
True Love, 14, 183
Turnbuckle, 101–102

Union Dues, 22, 67, 77–78, 80, 145
United Artists Classics, 38, 109–10, 113, 230
Unnatural Causes, 142–43, 185, 202
Untamaguru, 185
Untouchables, The, 37, 47

Vaughan, Robert, 60–61, 71, 77, 84–85, 92, 142–43, 193
Virginia Film Festival Award, 185
Virginia Towler Law Suit, 206–207

Warner Bros., 99, 123
West, Doris Sayles (aunt), 41–44
West, Elaine, 203, 206
West, Everett (uncle), 42, 44
Wexler, Haskell, 128, 149–51, 155–56, 201, 211, 213, 216, 241, 245–46, 249, 252–54
Wild Thing, 157
Williams College, 20–21, 58–72, 74, 114, 203, 253, Williams College Black Alumni Association Award, 58, 232
Williamstown Theatre Festival, 63–64, 138–39
Wise, Robert, 246–47
Woodard, Alfre, 143, 200, 202
Woodward, Joanne, 102, 138–39
Wynn, Keenan, 84, 87

Yellow Raft in Blue Waters, 187
Yntema, Peggy, 75

ABOUT THE AUTHOR

PROFESSOR AND CHAIR of the Communication Department at La Salle University, Philadelphia, Gerard Molyneaux earned a bachelor's degree from that institution, then followed it with a master's degree in English from the University of Notre Dame, and a doctorate in communication from the University of Wisconsin-Madison. In 1983 he authored *Charlie Chaplin's City Lights* (Garland Press). For the Greenwood Press bio-bibliography series, he wrote *James Stewart* (1992) and *Gregory Peck* (1995). His essay "Charlie Chaplin's *Modern Times* and the American Culture of the 1930's" appears in *Charlie Chaplin and Modern Times* (Mouton de Gruyter, 1991), and his essay "DeSica's *Bicycle Thieves* and the Attack on the Classical Hollywood Film" was published in *Intertextuality in Literature and Film* (University Press of Florida, 1994). Twice a National Endowment Fellow (Princeton and CUNY–Manhattan), he has lectured on film and mass media in Florida, Canada, and France. He also has acted as a consultant for college communication programs and two corporations, and served on the evaluation teams of the Middle States Association of Colleges and High Schools. As a Brother of the Christian Schools, a Catholic religious order, he has addressed their international and regional assemblies in Barcelona, Spain (1997), and Chicago, Illinois (1998). He also appeared in the Charlie Chaplin installment of E! Entertainment Television's *Mysteries and Scandals* series, first broadcast in May 1998.